# CASSEROLE TREASURY

By Lousene Rousseau Brunner

*Author of* CASSEROLE MAGIC

Harper & Row, Publishers,
for
The Cookery Book Club

*To my husband* EDMUND DE SCHWEINITZ BRUNNER
*Who has cheerfully played the role of guinea pig*
*for all my recipe testing*

# CONTENTS

# GUIDE TO AMERICAN MEASURES

# FOR ENGLISH COOKS

Throughout this book you'll find the recipes are given in standard American measures.

The main point of difference to remember is that the standard half-pint American measuring cup used in all these recipes equals 8 fluid ounces and not 10 fluid ounces. To get the very best results from your cooking and baking, it is helpful to change American measures into British measures accurately. Below you will find a table of equivalents.

|  | American | English |
|---|---|---|
| 1 cup of breadcrumbs (fresh) | $1\frac{1}{2}$ oz | 3 oz |
| 1 cup of flour (or powdered grains) | 4 oz | 5 oz |
| 1 cup of sugar | 7 oz | 8 oz |
| 1 cup of icing sugar | $4\frac{1}{2}$ oz | 5 oz |
| 1 cup of butter or other fats | 8 oz | 8 oz |
| 1 cup of raisins, etc. | 5 oz | 6 oz |
| 1 cup of grated cheese | 4 oz | 4 oz |
| 1 cup of syrup, etc. | 12 oz | 14 oz |

| | |
|---|---|
| 1 English pint | 20 fluid oz |
| 1 American pint | 16 fluid oz |
| 1 American cup | 8 fluid oz |
| 1 American tablespoon | $\frac{1}{2}$ fluid oz |
| 3 American teaspoons | $\frac{1}{2}$ fluid oz |
| 1 English teaspoon | $\frac{2}{3}$ to 1 fluid oz |
| 1 English tablespoon | 4 teaspoons |

*The American measuring tablespoon holds $\frac{1}{4}$ oz flour

# FOREWORD

The continuing success of my first collection of casserole recipes, *Casserole Magic,* published some eleven years ago, has encouraged me to prepare a second cookbook of this type.

*Casserole Treasury* is an all-new collection of more than four hundred more of the many hundreds of casserole recipes which could be assembled. They have come from many countries, from great chefs and from peasant kitchens. Their ingredients run the gamut from truffles and pâtés to cabbage and beer.

New features in *Casserole Treasury* are a section on soups and chowders and one on desserts that lend themselves to casserole preparation and service. Many dishes are included that call for flaming, either early in their preparation or at the table. Wines and liqueurs lend their magic to many of the casseroles, as do herbs, especially fresh herbs, now featured in so many gardens. Many delightful buffet casseroles are included.

Many of these recipes make use of so-called "convenience foods," especially frozen vegetables and canned soups. In a few recipes mixes are suggested. But it has been no part of my intention to play up short cuts in cooking at the expense of that careful and painstaking preparation which is the essence of good cooking. One of the principal advantages of casserole cookery is that it usually makes it possible to do all the drudgery part of cooking early in the day, thus making the preparation of the evening meal a relatively painless process.

As in *Casserole Magic,* I have tried to make directions explicit enough for even the most inexperienced cook to follow. Cooking times, oven temperatures, and number of servings are clearly stated. However, these will depend to some extent upon the material of the casserole (clay, glass, stainless steel, copper, porcelain-coated cast iron, etc.), its size and shape, and the depth of the food in it.

It is my hope that *Casserole Treasury* will bring new eating pleasure to many American homes.

*Lousene Rousseau Brunner*

*Wilton, Connecticut*

# NOTES ON THE RECIPES

1. A useful ingredient in practically all casserole dishes except desserts is monosodium glutamate (MSG), better known by such trade names as Accent. It is not listed here because it would appear in almost every recipe. I use it as I use salt and pepper. A little experimentation will provide a guide to quantities to use—it can go from a shake to a teaspoonful.

2. Oven temperatures indicated always mean that the oven should be *preheated* to that temperature.

3. Many of these casseroles can be cooked on top of the stove as easily as in the oven. However, this will mean a somewhat shorter cooking time and more careful watching to prevent overcooking and scorching. Obviously, soufflés and custards must always be baked in the oven.

4. Where casseroles do not have their own close-fitting lids, lids can be readily improvised with heavy-duty foil.

5. If you do much casserole cooking, keep certain basic supplies on hand. Frozen chopped onions and green peppers, for example, save time with no sacrifice of flavor whatever. Chicken Stock Base, a relatively new product, keeps indefinitely on the shelf and produces in an instant a most satisfactory chicken stock—an ingredient frequently called for. Grated Parmesan cheese is called for repeatedly, and keeps well in the refrigerator. Canned condensed cream of mushroom soup

and cream of celery soup are often called for. Freeze-Dry Mushrooms, a new product, makes it possible to have the equivalent of fresh mushrooms always available. Slivered and sliced almonds are called for repeatedly, and keep well in the refrigerator. If you do not grow your own herbs, keep small jars of dried herbs on hand, replacing them every few months. Packaged cornflake crumbs are often more flavorful than bread crumbs and keep perfectly.

# SOUPS

# BORSCH

1 pound chuck
2 quarts water
2½ pounds beets, peeled and
    grated coarsely
2 carrots, scraped and
    cut in julienne strips
1 large onion, cut in fine strips
1 large tomato or 2 medium,
    skinned and chopped

1 tablespoon butter or margarine
1 cup finely shredded cabbage
1 small bay leaf
2 tablespoons vinegar
1 tablespoon sugar
1 teaspoon salt
½ teaspoon fresh-ground pepper
    Sour cream

This is probably the best known of all Russian dishes, and certainly one of the best liked. There are innumerable recipes for it, all including beets, cabbage, and sour cream. This is an excellent way of making it.

1. Cover the meat with 2 quarts of water, salted, and cook, covered, over low heat, for at least 2 hours. Skim the top several times to remove the scum and fat. Remove the meat and strain the stock.

2. In a heavy casserole put the carrots, onion, tomato, and all but 1 cup of the beets, which will be used later.

3. Add enough stock just to cover, and the butter. Cover and simmer about 20 minutes.

4. Add the cabbage, bay leaf, 1 tablespoon of the vinegar, sugar, salt, pepper, and all but 1 cup of the remaining stock. Mix well, cover, and simmer 20 minutes more.

5. Add the reserved cup of stock to the cup of grated beets held out at the beginning, with the remaining tablespoon of vinegar. Bring to a boil, simmer a few minutes, and strain the red liquid into the soup pot to give it the proper red color. Put a large dollop of sour cream on top of each serving. Makes 8 large plates or 10 smaller bowls.

## BOUILLABAISSE (for 12)

1 pound each 4 kinds of fish
2 pounds each sea bass and
  whiting
1 dozen crabs
2 lobsters 1½ pounds each, alive
2 quarts mussels or clams
  Salt and pepper
¾ cup olive oil

3 large onions, chopped
1 clove garlic
¼ cup minced parsley
¼ cup chopped celery tops
3 tomatoes, peeled, seeded, and
  slightly mashed
1½ teaspoons crumbled saffron
  Dry white wine

A TRUE French bouillabaisse calls for varieties of fish not available in the United States, but you can make a good substitute with what we have available—and many kinds of fish can be used.

1. Cut all the fish into 2-inch chunks, sprinkle with salt and fresh-ground pepper, and let stand while the rest is being prepared.

2. Cut the crabs in two, clean, dust with salt, and add to the fish.

3. The lobsters *must* be alive. With a sharp cleaver or hatchet cut them up in 2-inch hunks. Wash the pieces in water to which a little lemon juice or vinegar has been added. Add to the fish.

4. The mussels or clams can either be shelled or they can have just the top half of the shell removed—the latter method is the usual one. Set these aside separately.

5. Make this "soup" in a large Dutch oven or porcelain-coated casserole. Heat the olive oil in it and add the onions, garlic, parsley, celery, and tomatoes.

6. Cook this 4-5 minutes, stirring constantly, and then stir in the saffron. Add all the fish and seafood except the mussels or clams. Cover, but just barely, with half water and half dry white wine. Bring to a gentle boil and keep boiling for 8-10 minutes. Add the mussels or clams and boil 5 minutes longer.

If you have made this in an iron Dutch oven, transfer to a large casserole for serving. Serve in big soup plates in which you first place two or 3 thick pieces of slightly dry French bread. Do not remove lobster, crab, or clam shells when you serve. You can't be dainty in eating bouillabaisse. Serves 12.

*Serve with warm garlic bread and follow it with a tossed salad.*

# CORN CHOWDER

1-pound can cream-style corn or
  fresh corn cut off the cob
3 slices bacon cut in strips
1 medium onion sliced
1 cup diced or thinly sliced potato
  Salt and pepper to taste
1 tablespoon sugar

3 cups boiling water
1 large can evaporated milk or
  2 cups rich milk scalded
2 egg yolks stirred with a fork
1 tablespoon butter
  Chopped parsley or chives

1. Make this chowder in a large casserole. Fry the bacon in it until it is *almost* crisp. Add the onion and potato and sauté lightly—do not brown.

2. Stir in the corn and seasonings. Add the boiling water, cover, and bake about 45 minutes in a 350° oven, or cook on top of the stove over the least possible heat for 30-35 minutes, stirring occasionally. Add the milk and continue to cook until it is very hot.

3. When you are about ready to serve stir a little of the hot mixture into the egg yolks and stir all back together. Add the butter, dust the top with parsley or chives, and serve at once. Serves 4-5 as a main course, or 8 as a first course.

*As a main course, serve with the chowder warm garlic bread or Brown-'n-Serve French bread or salty rolls, and a green salad with vegetables added.*


# CRABMEAT CHOWDER BOSTON STYLE

½ pound fresh, frozen, or canned
  crabmeat
1 can condensed cream of mushroom soup
1 can condensed cream of celery
  soup
1½ cups top milk

1 cup cooked potatoes diced
  quite small
2 tablespoons minced or grated
  onion
1 cup cooked peas
1 tablespoon lemon juice
  Salt and pepper
2 tablespoons minced parsley

THIS is really a meal in itself, and needs nothing but hot rolls or garlic bread and a green salad to make a hearty lunch.

Flake the crabmeat carefully, being sure to remove all the membranes, but leaving much of it in lumps. Combine all of the ingredients except parsley in a heatproof tureen or large casserole, cover, and heat 20-25 minutes in a 325° oven. Stir well and sprinkle with parsley before serving. Or make in a heavy casserole on top of the stove, but stir occasionally to keep it from lumping. Serves 4 generously.

## CREAMED CRAB SOUP

2 cups fresh cooked, frozen, or
   canned crabmeat
3 tablespoons butter
   Grated rind of 1 lemon
1 tablespoon flour
1 teaspoon Worcestershire sauce
   Pinch mace (optional)
2 chopped hard-cooked eggs

3 mushrooms chopped
3 stalks celery chopped
1 scallion or shallot minced
4 cups milk scalded
1 cup cream scalded
   Salt and pepper to taste
½ cup dry sherry

THIS crab soup, made from all fresh ingredients, is especially good. Like the others, it is hearty enough for a main dish. Note, though, how differently it is made.

1. Mash 2 tablespoons butter, lemon rind, flour, Worcestershire sauce, mace, and eggs to a paste. Mix with the crabmeat (which has been carefully picked over.)

2. Heat the remaining tablespoon butter in a large casserole on top of the stove and lightly sauté the mushrooms, celery, and scallion (green onion) or shallot. Stir in the scalded milk and cream and the crabmeat mixture. Season to taste, cover, and heat to just under boiling in a 300° oven—about 20-25 minutes. Stir two or three times while it is heating.

3. Add the sherry just before serving. Serves 6 large plates or 8 cups.

*If this is the main luncheon course, serve with a large green tossed salad and sesame seed rolls.*

# CRABMEAT AND CORN CHOWDER

1 cup crabmeat flaked, fresh, frozen, or canned
2½ cups fresh grated corn or canned cream-style corn
2 thin slices onion, or 1 tablespoon minced or grated
2½ cups rich milk scalded
2½ cups thin white sauce
Salt and pepper to taste
Grating of nutmeg
2 egg yolks slightly beaten
1 tablespoon butter

THIS is a smooth, velvety chowder. The crab-corn combination is intriguing.

1. Put the corn, onion, and milk in the top of a double boiler and cook over hot water for 20-25 minutes. Force through a sieve or a food mill into a casserole, or give it about 20 seconds in a blender.

2. Make the white sauce with 3½ tablespoons butter or margarine, 3 tablespoons flour, and 2½ cups milk. Season to taste with the salt, pepper, and nutmeg. Stir into the corn mixture in the casserole, cover, and bake in a 300° oven 20 minutes or until heated almost to boiling.

3. Uncover and stir in the crabmeat. Add a little of the soup to the egg yolks and stir them quickly into the soup. Heat a few minutes, add the butter, and serve at once. Or the whole chowder can be made on top of the stove, though it has to be watched more carefully. Serves 6 large plates or 8 bowls or small plates.

*If you make this your main luncheon course, serve with pilot crackers crisped in the oven and buttered, and a vegetable salad.*

# CURRIED CHICKEN SOUP

2 cups cooked chicken cut up coarsely
¼ cup butter or margarine
1 medium onion minced
1 tart apple peeled and chopped
3 cups chicken broth
¼ teaspoon dried thyme or 1 teaspoon fresh, chopped
1 tablespoon curry powder or to taste
Salt and pepper to taste
¼ cup raisins
¼ cup salted peanuts coarsely chopped
1 cup cooked hot rice

A CURRIED soup is rather unusual, and this is an exceptionally good one. Like all the soups in this section it is hearty enough for the main course of a luncheon or Sunday supper.

Put the butter in a heavy casserole and heat on top of the stove. Simmer the onion and apple in it lightly, but do not brown. Add remaining ingredients except peanuts and rice, cover, and bake half an hour in a 350° oven.

When ready to serve stir in the peanuts and check the seasoning. Put ¼ cup of rice in each soup plate and ladle the soup over. Serves 4.

## FRENCH PEASANT SOUP

2 tablespoons butter or margarine
2 medium carrots chopped rather
  coarsely
1 small white turnip peeled and
  chopped
2 leeks (white part only) chopped
2 small onions chopped
1 cup chopped cabbage
1 stalk celery chopped

¼ teaspoon sugar
  Salt and pepper
1 quart chicken broth,
  consommé, or water
1 medium potato chopped
½ cup green peas
½ cup cut green beans
  French bread

1. Heat the butter in a heavy casserole and add the carrots, turnip, leeks, onions, cabbage, and celery. Sprinkle with sugar, salt and pepper to taste. Cook about 10 minutes, over medium heat, stirring often.
2. Cover the skillet, turn the heat down as far as possible, and simmer half an hour, stirring frequently.
3. Add half the liquid. Increase the heat a little, and when it is boiling stir in the potato, peas, and beans.
4. Turn the heat down again and simmer another half hour. Add the remainder of the stock and continue to simmer another half hour.
5. When you are ready to serve, toast enough half-inch slices of French bread to cover the soup. Butter the toast, lay on top of the soup, and put the whole casserole under the broiler for 2-3 minutes, or until the toast is sizzling. Serves 6.

# HEARTY TURKEY SOUP

1 cup diced cooked turkey
3 cups turkey broth (or chicken broth)
¼ cup butter or margarine
2 tablespoons chopped onion
1 teaspoon curry powder
1 cup diced potatoes
½ cup diced carrots
½ cup celery sliced diagonally

Salt and pepper to taste
½ package frozen Frenched string beans
1 teaspoon minced fresh orégano or ½ teaspoon dried
1 tablespoon minced parsley
14½-ounce can evaporated milk or 1⅔ cups light cream
2 tablespoons flour

THIS is one of the most delectable soups you can imagine—far better than the usual after-the-turkey soup. It is one of the heartiest soups I know, and needs nothing but garlic bread or buttered pilot crackers, crisped in the oven, to accompany it, with a tossed green salad to follow.

1. Melt the butter in a good-sized casserole on top of the stove and cook the onion until it is just transparent. Stir in the curry powder and cook a minute or two longer.

2. Stir in the potatoes, carrots, celery, broth, seasoning to taste, and bring to a boil. Transfer to a slow oven, 300°, and bake 10 to 15 minutes. Or cook entirely on top of the stove, with low heat.

3. Stir in the green beans, turkey, orégano, and parsley and continue baking about 15 minutes, or until the vegetables are barely tender, but still a little crisp.

4. Combine milk and flour and stir in gently until well blended. The soup should be slightly thickened. Check seasoning. Serves 4 hungry people amply or 6 if more food is to follow.


# LENTIL SOUP

1 cup dried lentils
1 pound veal shank
½ cup chopped onion
2 teaspoons salt
½ teaspoon pepper

1¾ quarts boiling water
3 tablespoons lemon juice
1 teaspoon Worcestershire sauce
⅓ cup chopped parsley

LENTIL soup can be so delicious that it seems a pity more people are not familiar with it.

1. In a large casserole put the veal shank, the lentils, onion, salt, pepper, and water. Cover and put in a 275° oven for about 1½-1¾ hours, stirring occasionally.

2. Remove the veal shank from the casserole, cut off the meat, and cut it up. Return it to the casserole with the lemon juice, Worcestershire sauce, and parsley. Continue to bake 10 minutes more. Serves 8 in cups or 6 in large plates.

*It is nice to serve this soup, like many others, with a large spoonful of sour cream on top, dusted with paprika.*

## HOTCHPOT CHOWDER

2 cups corn cut off the cob or whole kernel corn canned or frozen
2 cups celery chopped
½ green pepper cut in strips
1 onion sliced thin
1 cup chopped tomatoes, canned or fresh
1 tablespoon salt

⅛ teaspoon pepper
1 cup cold water
¼ cup butter or margarine
3 tablespoons flour
¼ teaspoon paprika
3½ cups milk scalded
½ cup grated sharp Cheddar cheese
1 pimiento sliced thin

THIS is a very old recipe for a most unusual kind of creamed vegetable soup. Like the other soups in this section it is practically a meal in itself.

1. Start the casserole on top of the stove. Put in it the corn, celery, green pepper, onion, tomatoes, salt and pepper, and water. Bring it just to a boil, turn down the heat, cover, and simmer for 15 minutes.

2. Knead the butter, flour, and paprika together and stir into the hot milk. Then stir this mixture into the casserole, cover, and bake in a slow oven, 300°, 15 to 20 minutes. Add the cheese and pimiento just before serving, continuing to bake just until the cheese is melted. Serves 6 generously.

*Serve with a big bowl of buttered croutons or buttered pilot crackers crisped in the oven. Follow with a green salad.*

# LAMB AND LENTIL SOUP LUNCHEON

1 pound ground lamb shoulder
1 pound lentils
2½ quarts cold water
2 tablespoons salt
½ teaspoon fresh-ground pepper
½ cup butter
2½ cups chopped tomatoes, fresh
  or canned
1 large onion minced

2 tablespoons fresh chopped dill
  or 2 teaspoons dried
3 medium cloves garlic mashed
1 bay leaf
1½ teaspoons salt
1 egg beaten slightly
Flour
1 tablespoon salad oil
½ cup elbow macaroni

THIS looks like a lot of ingredients, but actually the dish is a simple one, and all except the last step can be done early in the morning.
1. Wash the lentils well and put in a large casserole with the water, the 2 tablespoons salt, ¼ teaspoon of the pepper, butter, tomatoes, onion, dill, garlic, and bay leaf. Stir well, cover, and put in a slow oven, 275°, for 1¾-2 hours.
2. While this is cooking combine the ground lamb with the 1½ teaspoons salt, the remaining ¼ teaspoon pepper, and the egg. Shape into 24 small balls and roll in flour. Heat the salad oil in a heavy skillet and brown the lamb balls well on all sides.
3. If you have cooked the casserole early, heat it about 20 minutes before you are ready to serve, and stir in the lamb balls and the macaroni. Continue to bake, checking seasoning before serving. Serves 8 in large plates or bowls, about 12 in cups.


# NEW ENGLAND FISH CHOWDER

1 pound fresh or frozen fish fillets,
  preferably cod or haddock, or a
  larger chunk with bone in
2 quarter-inch slices salt pork diced
  small
3 medium onions sliced

3 medium potatoes diced
2 cups water
2 cups top milk
1 teaspoon Worcestershire sauce
  Salt and pepper

FOR generations this has been a New England classic. However, now that frozen fish is available anywhere, the rest of the country can enjoy this delicacy. Make the chowder in a heavy casserole on top of the stove, or make it in a Dutch oven and transfer it to a casserole to serve at the table.

1. Put the salt pork in the casserole and cook until crisp. Skim out the pieces and reserve. Add the onions and cook gently until transparent but not browned at all. Add the potatoes and cook 3-4 minutes.

2. At the same time, put the fish into a saucepan with the water, bring to a boil, lower the heat, and simmer 10-15 minutes, or until the fish will flake with a fork. A chunk of fish will, of course, take considerably longer than fillets.

3. Add the fish and water to the casserole (lifting out the bone, if any) and simmer until the potatoes are soft—5-10 minutes.

4. Stir in milk and season to taste with Worcestershire sauce, salt, and pepper. Scatter salt pork on top. Serves 4 in large plates.

## FRENCH ONION SOUP

1 pound onions sliced thin
4 tablespoons butter or margarine
4 cans condensed beef consommé
  Salt and pepper

¼ cup grated Parmesan cheese
4 slices French bread toasted on
  one side

ONION soup is a universal favorite, but the canned variety can't compete with a good home-made onion soup, and it is simple to make.

1. Heat 3 tablespoons of the butter in a large casserole on top of the stove and sauté the onions until they are soft and barely beginning to brown.

2. Add the undiluted consommé and salt and pepper to taste. Go slow with the salt until you taste it. Cover and bake in a 350° oven 30 minutes. Check in about 15 minutes, and if the soup is too bland—not "beefy" enough—add a little concentrate of beef, such as Maggi, Bovril, or the like.

3. Spread the hot toast (on the untoasted side) with the remaining butter and gently lay on top of the casserole. Cover with cheese and brown under the broiler. Serve with a bowl of extra cheese. Serves 6 in large plates or 8 in cups or bowls.

# PETITE MARMITE

1 hen cut up
2 veal bones
6 pints water
   Pinch thyme
1 small bay leaf
3 medium onions
2 cloves
   Salt and pepper

3 carrots
1 stalk celery
2 leeks (white part only)
1 small white turnip
1 cup chopped cabbage
   Grated cheese
   Croutons

THIS is a classic of French cookery, such a staple of French homes that the wonderful French soup pot is usually called a marmite. If you do not have a marmite, make the soup in a Dutch oven or a large heavy casserole. The porcelain-lined iron ones are perfect for such soups.

1. Put in the pot the chicken pieces, veal bones, water, thyme, bay leaf, one of the onions stuck with the two cloves, and salt and pepper to taste. Bring the water to a boil, turn the heat down to the merest simmer, cover, and cook for anywhere from 4-12 hours. (The latter is the French way.)

2. Remove the chicken pieces, cool the soup, strain it, and skim off as much fat as you can. Skin and bone the chicken.

3. Chop all the vegetables quite fine. Add to the soup with good-sized hunks of the chicken. Simmer until the vegetables are tender, correcting the seasoning.

4. Serve from the casserole into individual bowls, topping each one with a little cheese and crisp croutons. Serves 10.

# ROMAN BEAN SOUP

½ pound pink or pinto beans
1 carrot minced
1 medium onion minced
1 stalk celery minced
2 tablespoons salad oil
2 cloves garlic mashed
2 tablespoons chopped parsley

1 cup peeled, seeded, and chopped
   tomatoes, or 1 small can
   Salt and pepper to taste
¼ teaspoon rosemary
1 cup hot rice
   Grated Parmesan or Romano
   cheese

1. Soak the beans overnight in water to cover well. In the morning drain them, put in a good-sized heavy casserole, cover generously with fresh water, add the carrot, onion, and celery, and bake, covered, in a very slow oven, 275°, about 2½ hours, or until the beans are medium soft. This can be done on top of the stove instead, over the lowest possible heat, using an asbestos plate if necessary. Stir occasionally. If it seems rather thick thin out with water.
2. In a heavy skillet heat the oil and sauté in it the garlic, parsley, and tomatoes, until the tomatoes are soft.
3. Add this mixture to the casserole as soon as the beans are ready, and season to taste with salt and pepper and rosemary.
4. Simmer the soup 30 minutes longer. Remove about a cup of beans and set aside. Strain the rest and put the solid part through a food mill, or add a little of the liquid and blend 30-40 seconds. Put it all together again in the casserole, add the reserved beans and the rice, check seasoning and reheat. Serve with a bowl of cheese. Serves 4.

## VEGETABLE CHOWDER

6 large potatoes diced small
5-6 medium onions chopped
4 stalks celery cut in ½-inch pieces
½ green pepper chopped
1 cup chopped salted peanuts
1 can condensed tomato soup
1 can cream-style corn
1 can green pea soup
2 soup cans milk

1 package frozen cut green beans partly thawed
½ teaspoon dried basil or 1½ teaspoons fresh, chopped
1 teaspoon minced parsley
½ teaspoon dried marjoram or 1½ teaspoons fresh, chopped
Salt to taste

THIS is a wonderful solution for a simple but hearty meal, especially since it can be put together in the morning and requires no attention in cooking.

If you combine the ingredients hours in advance, hold out the salted peanuts until you put the soup on to cook. Otherwise, mix everything together in a large heavy casserole and simmer about 30 minutes, or until the potatoes and celery are tender. Serves 12.

*Serve with warm garlic bread or hot corn muffins and a tossed salad.*

# PEASANT VEGETABLE SOUP

2 potatoes sliced
2 tablespoons salad oil or
  margarine
2 leeks well cleaned and sliced
  (white part only)
2 onions sliced
2 carrots sliced
2 tomatoes sliced

1 white turnip sliced
1 clove
1 sprig parsley
  Salt and pepper to taste
2 pints consommé or chicken broth
  plus 1 pint water, or 3 pints water
½ cup sour cream
1 egg yolk slightly beaten

THIS is an old family recipe, and it makes a soup so different from the usual vegetable soup as to be a most welcome change. Make it on top of the stove in a heavy casserole that can go directly to the table.
1. Heat the oil in the casserole and lightly sauté all the sliced vegetables until they are almost but not quite tender.
2. Add the clove, parsley, salt and pepper, and the liquid, a pint at a time. Simmer 45 minutes to an hour over the lowest possible heat, stirring occasionally.
3. Strain the soup and put the thick part through a food mill or a ricer, force it through a coarse sieve, or purée it in a blender.
4. Combine again with the liquid, reheat, and stir in the sour cream and egg yolk, well mixed, just before serving. Serves 6 generously.

*Serve with hot corn muffins and a salad of green beans, cucumber sliced without peeling, and mixed greens.*

# MEATS

# BEEF

## BAKED ALASKA MEAT LOAF

2 pounds lean chuck ground
2 eggs slightly beaten
2 scant teaspoons salt
⅛ teaspoon pepper
1½ cups soft bread crumbs
¼ cup minced onion
½ teaspoon dried orégano or 1½
teaspoons fresh, chopped

½ teaspoon dried sweet basil or
1½ teaspoons fresh, chopped
2 tablespoons minced parsley
3½ cups fresh mashed potato
(instant will do)
2 egg yolks
Paprika
Parmesan cheese (optional)

THIS is a sort of cross between a regular meat loaf and a shepherd's pie, but to my mind better than either and more appealing to the eye.
1. Blend well in a mixing bowl the meat, eggs, salt and pepper, crumbs, onion, and herbs. Pack firmly into a round ovenproof bowl and bake 1 hour and 20 minutes at 400°.
2. Drain off the liquid which will accumulate and invert the bowl on a wire rack to drain completely. Pat the loaf dry with paper towels and slide it onto a shallow casserole or a Pyrex pie plate somewhat larger than the loaf.
3. In the meantime prepare the mashed potatoes. Beat them until they are fluffy and beat in the egg yolks. (As indicated above, you can use your favorite instant mashed—an 8-serving box.)
4. Frost the meat loaf thickly with the potatoes. Sprinkle with paprika and grated Parmesan cheese (if you use it) and set the loaf back in the oven 25-30 minutes, or until the surface is golden. Serves 6 amply.

*Serve with green peas mixed with tiny white onions.*

# BEEF AND BURGUNDY CASSEROLE

3 pounds lean chuck or round steak
   cut in 2-inch cubes
4 tablespoons butter or margarine
2 tablespoons bacon fat
3 tablespoons flour
2 teaspoons salt
½ teaspoon fresh-ground pepper
1 bay leaf
½ teaspoon dried sweet basil or
   1½ teaspoons fresh, chopped
1 clove garlic minced or mashed

½ teaspoon dried orégano or 1½
   teaspoons fresh, chopped
1 pound tiny white onions peeled
   and parboiled or 1-pound can
1 large or 2 small cans baby
   carrots
1 cup Burgundy or other dry red
   wine
1 tablespoon sugar
¾ cup Madeira wine
¼ cup brandy

This is one of the most delectable of all the casseroles I have ever served. It makes a highly successful main dish for a party.

1. Heat 2 tablespoons of the butter and the bacon fat in a large, heavy skillet, and brown the beef well on all sides. Arrange in a large casserole.

2. Add to fat in the skillet the flour, salt, pepper, bay leaf, basil, orégano, and garlic, and stir until the flour begins to brown.

3. Drain liquid from vegetables and, if necessary, add water to make a *scant* 2 cups. Stir this into the skillet and keep stirring until it thickens.

4. Add the Burgundy to the skillet, stir until the sauce is smooth and thickened somewhat, and pour over the meat in the casserole. Cover and bake about 3 hours in a 300° oven.

5. Melt the remaining 2 tablespoons butter in the skillet and stir in the sugar. When this has melted add the drained vegetables and stir them frequently until they are slightly browned. Add them to the casserole with the Madeira and continue to cook, covered, 30 minutes longer.

6. Stir in the brandy just before serving. Serves 8.

*Serve with a wild rice casserole (see Index), a large tossed green salad, sliced tomatoes, and warm garlic bread.*

# BARBECUED MEAT LOAVES

*Loaves*

1 pound ground lean beef
1 egg lightly beaten
4 tablespoons fine bread crumbs or corn flake crumbs
1 tablespoon minced parsley
¼ cup water
2 tablespoons chopped onion
2 tablespoons prepared horse-radish
1 teaspoon salt
⅛ teaspoon pepper

*Sauce*

½ cup chili sauce
3 tablespoons catsup
1 teaspoon Worcestershire sauce
½ teaspoon dry mustard
Dash Tabasco

COMBINE all the ingredients for the meat loaves, mix well, and shape into 4 oblong loaves. Place these in a greased shallow casserole, not touching.

Combine the sauce ingredients and spread over the tops and sides of the loaves. Bake in a 350° oven about 45 minutes, basting the loaves two or three times with the drippings which accumulate. Serves 4.

*Serve with fluffy mashed potatoes and thinly sliced buttered carrots.*

# BARBECUED BEEF STRIPS

2 pounds top round ½-inch thick, cut in strips 1½ by 3 inches
3 tablespoons prepared mustard
Flour
4 tablespoons cooking oil
1 teaspoon minced garlic
½ cup minced onion
½ cup chopped green pepper
¼ cup chopped celery leaves
¼ cup minced parsley
8-ounce can tomato sauce
¼ cup cider or tarragon vinegar
1½ cups water
2 tablespoons brown sugar
½ teaspoon salt
¼ teaspoon cayenne pepper

THIS is a spicy and flavorful dish, especially welcome on a cold night.
1. Put the mustard in a large bowl, add the strips of beef, and stir
until they are well coated. Roll lightly in flour and brown well in a
heavy skillet in hot oil. Spread them in a 1½-quart casserole.
2. Add all the remaining ingredients to the fat remaining in the skillet,
stir well, and let simmer about 10 minutes, stirring frequently.
3. Pour this mixture over the steak strips in the casserole, cover
tightly, and bake 2-2½ hours in a 300° oven. Stir two or three times
while baking, and if it seems dry add a bit more water. Serves 5-6.

*Serve with buttered noodles (plain or spinach), and cut green beans.*

## BEEF CASSEROLE WITH POTATO TOPPING

2 cups leftover cooked beef cut in
  ½-inch cubes
2 cans condensed green pea soup
½ cup sliced mushrooms sautéed in
  a little butter or margarine
½ cup milk
1 teaspoon chopped parsley
½ teaspoon dried sweet basil or
  ½ tablespoon fresh, chopped

1 small onion chopped
  Salt and pepper
2 cups fresh hot mashed potatoes
1 cup cooked peas (optional)
1 egg well beaten
2 tablespoons melted butter or
  margarine

THIS casserole is almost a meal in itself, though you need an additional vegetable with it.
1. In a 2-quart casserole place the meat, soup, mushrooms, milk,
herbs, and onion. Season to taste. (The mixture will blend better if
you warm the soup first and stir in the milk.) Bake 25 minutes, covered, in a 350° oven.
2. Make fresh mashed potatoes (instant will serve well) and stir in
the peas and egg. Spread evenly over the casserole and drizzle the
melted butter over. Increase the heat to 425° and bake 10 minutes
more. Serves 6.

*Serve with scalloped tomatoes and cole slaw.*

## BEEF CASSEROLE WITH CORN MUFFIN TOP

1½ pounds ground lean beef
2 tablespoons butter, margarine, or salad oil
1 tablespoon chopped onion
10½-ounce can condensed consommé
1 teaspoon chopped parsley
1 teaspoon salt
⅛ teaspoon pepper
2 tablespoons A-1 or Worcestershire sauce
1 package corn muffin mix

1. Sauté the beef and onion in the hot fat in a heavy skillet. Stir in the consommé, parsley, salt, pepper, and A-1 or Worcestershire sauce. Spread the mixture in a casserole of a size that will leave at least an inch of space at the top.
2. Make your favorite corn muffin recipe or use a corn muffin mix, and spoon it carefully on top of the casserole, smoothing with a knife. Bake 25 minutes at 350°. Serves 5-6.

*Serve with fluffy mashed potatoes and buttered broccoli.*


## SPECIAL BEEF AND RICE CASSEROLE

3 pounds boneless chuck cut in 1½-inch cubes
12 slices bacon cut in ½-inch strips
2 large onions sliced
1 cup raw rice
1 cup dry red wine
2 cups consommé
1 clove garlic mashed
½ teaspoon dried thyme or 1 sprig fresh
1 teaspoon chopped parsley
1 small bay leaf
½ teaspoon saffron crumbled (optional)
1½ cups chopped fresh tomatoes (or canned)
1 cup grated Parmesan cheese
Salt and pepper to taste

THIS is truly a special casserole, the wine giving it delightful flavor. (If you do not want to use wine, use 3 cups consommé.)
1. Cook the bacon in a large heavy skillet. When it is crisp skim it out and spread it on the bottom of a large casserole.

2. In the accumulated fat brown the beef cubes well and transfer them to the casserole.

3. Brown the onions lightly in the fat remaining in the skillet and stir in the dry rice. Stir constantly until the rice is starting to brown and set aside for the moment.

4. Add to the casserole the wine, consommé, garlic, thyme, parsley, bay leaf, and saffron. Cover and bake 1 hour in a 325° oven.

5. Skim off any fat accumulated and stir the rice mixture and tomatoes into the casserole. Cover again and bake an additional hour. Check a couple of times to be sure there is enough liquid for the rice to absorb; you may have to add a bit more consommé.

6. Just before you are ready to serve check the seasoning and stir in the cheese. Heat long enough to melt the cheese. Serves 6.

*Serve with only a large tossed salad, to which you have added a grated carrot, thin tomato wedges, and sliced cucumbers (not peeled).*

## BEEF AND MACARONI

1 pound lean ground beef
8-ounce package macaroni
  cooked
2 tablespoons butter or margarine
2 tablespoons chopped green
  pepper

1 cup dairy sour cream
3 tablespoons onion soup mix
1 cup milk
¼ cup buttered crumbs, bread or
  corn flake

1. Melt the butter in a heavy skillet and in it sauté the beef and green pepper, stirring until the green pepper is soft and there is no more red in the meat.

2. Mix the sour cream and onion soup mix, heat just to the boiling point, and whip with a rotary egg beater. Stir in the milk gradually.

3. Combine this mixture with the meat and the macaroni, cooked according to package directions, and pour into a 1½-quart casserole. Top with buttered crumbs and bake about 20-25 minutes at 350°, covered.

4. Just before serving remove cover and brown under the broiler. Serves 6-8.

*Serve with buttered baby carrots and sliced tomatoes.*

# BEEF WITH DUMPLINGS

2 pounds lean chuck cut in 1-inch
   cubes
2 tablespoons flour
1½ teaspoons salt
¼ teaspoon pepper
3 tablespoons salad oil
3 medium onions, each stuck with
   1 clove

4 carrots cut in thin strips
   lengthwise
1½ cups consommé
1 tablespoon vinegar
3 tablespoons chopped chives
1 package biscuit mix

1. Shake up the flour, salt, and pepper in a paper bag and dredge
the pieces of meat by shaking them in it, a few at a time.
2. Heat the oil in a large heavy casserole and brown the meat well,
adding the onions as the meat starts to brown. Stir in the carrots,
consommé, and vinegar. Cover and bake the casserole 45 minutes
at 350°.
3. Shortly before the casserole is ready make the dumplings according to instructions on the package of biscuit mix. Uncover the casserole, drop the dumplings by spoonfuls on top, replace the cover at
once, and continue to bake 30 minutes more. Serves 4-5.

*Serve with chopped spinach into which slightly sautéed mushrooms
and a dash of nutmeg have been stirred, and with sliced tomatoes and
cucumber sticks.*

# BEEF AND EGGPLANT CASSEROLE

1½ pounds lean chuck ground
1 medium eggplant sliced in
   ½-inch slices
   Salt and pepper
2 tablespoons chopped onions
2 tablespoons salad oil
⅓ cup flour

¼ cup salad oil
½ teaspoon dried orégano or 1½
   teaspoons fresh, chopped
8-ounce can tomato sauce or
   tomato soup
   Mozzarella cheese

1. Wash the eggplant and slice it without peeling. Salt each slice and
pile them up for 15 or 20 minutes to take out the bitterness.

2. Mix the chuck, 1 teaspoon of salt and a little fresh-ground pepper, and the onions. Form into 8 patties, handling the mixture as little as possible.

3. Heat the 2 tablespoons oil in a heavy skillet and brown the patties on both sides. Arrange four of them on the bottom of a medium casserole and put the others on a plate for the moment.

4. Pat the eggplant slices dry with paper towels, dip them in the flour, and brown them lightly in the ¼ cup of the oil.

5. Arrange half of the slices on top of the beef patties in the casserole and sprinkle them with the orégano. Spread 1 tablespoon tomato sauce on each. Cover with the remaining patties, the remaining eggplant, and the remaining orégano. Pour the remaining tomato sauce on top and cover completely with slices of cheese.

6. Bake 30 minutes at 350°, or until the cheese is golden and bubbly. Serves 4-5.

## BEEF WITH HORSERADISH SAUCE

| | |
|---|---|
| 2 pounds round steak cut in 1½-inch cubes | ½ teaspoon salt |
| | ¼ teaspoon pepper |
| 2 tablespoons butter or margarine | 1½ cups water |
| 1 large onion sliced thin | 1 cup dairy sour cream |
| 1 teaspoon curry powder | 2 tablespoons prepared horse- |
| ½ teaspoon ground ginger | radish |
| 1 teaspoon sugar | 1 teaspoon minced parsley |
| 1 tablespoon Worcestershire sauce | |

THIS is a somewhat zippy casserole, but perfectly delicious. Even people who like their food pretty bland take to it.

1. Brown meat cubes well in hot butter in a heavy skillet and arrange in a medium casserole.

2. Add the onion, curry powder, ginger, sugar, Worcestershire, salt, pepper, and water. Cover and bake in a slow oven (300°) 2½-3 hours, or until the meat is fork tender.

3. When you are ready to serve stir in the sour cream, horseradish, and parsley. If you prefer the sauce somewhat thicker, thicken it with flour and butter or margarine kneaded together. Serves 4-5.

## BEEF AND MUSHROOM CASSEROLE

2 pounds top round sliced thin
  and cut in strips 1½" x 3½"
1 cup dried mushrooms soaked an
  hour or more in dry red wine
¼ cup flour
1½ teaspoons salt
⅛ teaspoon fresh-ground pepper
2 tablespoons salad oil
1-2 cups consommé
1½ cups chopped onions
Sour cream if desired

1. Put the flour, salt, and pepper in a paper bag, and shake the pieces of meat in it, a few at a time, to dredge them lightly.
2. Heat the oil to sizzling in a heavy skillet and brown the meat strips well on both sides. Arrange them in a medium casserole, add ¾ cup of the consommé, cover, and bake in a 300° oven. After 30 minutes begin to watch, and add more consommé as needed.
3. After an hour's cooking stir in the chopped onions, raw, cover again, and continue to cook.
4. About 15 minutes before you are ready to serve stir in the mushrooms and cover again. The overall cooking time for this casserole is about 2 hours, and there should be next to no liquid left at the end of that time. Serves 4-5.

*Serve with one of the noodle casseroles in this book (see Index), buttered green peas, and Brown-'n-Serve French bread.*


## BEEF AND NOODLES

1 pound lean beef ground
¼ pound medium noodles cooked
1 tablespoon butter or margarine
1 tablespoon salad oil
2 medium onions chopped
1 teaspoon salt
¼ teaspoon pepper
¼ teaspoon dried thyme or ¾
  teaspoon fresh, chopped
1 can condensed cream of
  mushroom soup
2 eggs beaten
¼ cup milk
¾ cup grated Cheddar cheese

1. Heat butter and oil together in a heavy skillet and sauté the onions

24

lightly. Move them to a bowl temporarily, while you brown the meat in the fat remaining in the skillet.

2. Break up the meat into rather loose chunks as it cooks. Add salt, pepper, and thyme. When the meat loses its color but is not browned, stir the cooked onions back in.

3. In a good-sized casserole make layers of ⅓ of the noodles, ½ of the meat, and ½ of the soup. Repeat the layers, with the last ⅓ of the noodles as the top layer.

4. Mix the beaten eggs with the milk and pour over the casserole. Top with cheese and bake in a 350° oven 35-40 minutes, or until golden brown and bubbly. Serves 8.

*Serve with shredded green cabbage cooked slowly, covered, in a heavy skillet, in butter, and sliced buttered beets.*

## BEEF WITH OLIVES

3 pounds chuck cut in 1½-inch cubes
1 cup pitted green olives
½ cup flour
Salt and pepper
3 tablespoons salad oil
12 little white onions peeled
1 clove garlic mashed
½ teaspoon dried thyme or
1 teaspoon fresh, chopped
1½ cups condensed consommé
¼ cup chopped parsley
2 tablespoons butter or margarine
2 tablespoons flour

1. Put the ½ cup flour, about 2 teaspoons salt, and pepper in a paper bag and dredge the beef cubes in it. Brown them in the hot oil and transfer to a large heavy casserole.

2. In the fat remaining in the skillet lightly sauté the onions and garlic. Add the thyme and the consommé and pour over the meat in the casserole, scraping up all the brown bits in the skillet.

3. Cover the casserole and bake about an hour in a slow oven, 300°.

4. Stir in the olives and parsley, cover again, and bake about 45 minutes longer, or until the meat is fork tender.

5. Knead the butter and flour together and stir in to thicken the sauce to taste. Check the seasoning before serving. Serves 6-8.

*Serve with buttered wide noodles and buttered baby Brussels sprouts.*

# BEER-BRAISED ROUND OF BEEF

2-pound slice of top round steak
¾ teaspoon salt
¼ teaspoon pepper
2 tablespoons flour
3 tablespoons butter or margarine
1 clove garlic crushed
1 large onion sliced thin

1½ cups beer
½ cup water
1 sprig parsley
1 sprig thyme
1 stalk celery cut in 3 or 4 pieces
1 bay leaf

COOKING with beer, as so much of the Flemish cooking is done, is almost always a highly successful way to add flavor to a dish, even for people who strongly dislike beer alone.

1. Mix the salt, pepper, and flour and pound it into the meat as you would for Swiss steak, with the blunt side of a butcher knife or the edge of a saucer.

2. Heat 1 tablespoon of the butter in a heavy skillet and brown the meat quickly on both sides. Remove it to a shallow casserole.

3. Add the remaining butter to the skillet and lightly sauté the garlic and onion.

4. Stir in the beer and water and bring to a boil. Pour over the meat in the casserole, add the parsley, thyme, celery, and bay leaf, cover, and bake in a 275° oven about 1½ hours, or until tender. (Use aluminum foil to make a cover.)

5. Drain the liquid into a saucepan and thicken it a bit if you prefer. Pour back over the meat and heat another 5 minutes if the meat has cooled a bit. Serves 4-6.

*Serve with small parsley-butter potatoes (you can buy small peeled potatoes frozen now) and Fordhook lima beans with butter and a tablespoon of heavy cream.*

# SPECIAL BOEUF BOURGUIGNON

2 pounds chuck or rump cut in
   ¼-inch slices
2 tablespoons salad oil
2 large slices salt pork
1½ cups thin-sliced carrots
   Salt and pepper
2 medium onions chopped
   coarsely

1 clove garlic mashed or minced
2 shallots minced (or green
   onions)
½ pound mushrooms chopped
½ bottle good Burgundy
⅓ cup cognac

THIS is quite a different Boeuf Bourguignon from the one found in most cookbooks, but equally delicious. I find it less trouble to make, too. Make it in a heavy casserole that can be started on top of the stove, like the French petite marmite or the newer porcelain-coated iron or stainless steel casseroles.

1. Pour oil in the bottom of the casserole and lay in one slice of pork. Add the carrots in an even layer and cover with ⅓ of the beef. Sprinkle with salt and pepper.

2. Cover this layer of meat with half the onions, garlic, shallots, and mushrooms. Repeat layers. Add the rest of the beef and lay on top the remaining slice of salt pork.

3. Pour over the Burgundy and cognac and season with additional salt and pepper.

4. Place the casserole over high heat until it begins to simmer and then place in a 250° oven for 3-3½ hours, or until the meat is fork tender. Check occasionally to be sure it is barely bubbling. Remove the top slice of salt pork before serving. Serves 6.

*Serve with mixed vegetables (lima beans, cut corn, green peas, cut asparagus, or any other combination), a plain tossed green salad, and warm garlic bread.*

## BOEUF EN DAUBE NIÇOISE

3-pound piece of top round
½ pound carrots cut in 1-inch pieces
1 tablespoon chopped parsley
1 tablespoon chopped fresh
orégano or 1 teaspoon dried

1 tablespoon chopped fresh
sweet basil or 1 teaspoon dried
Bacon
3 tomatoes skinned and chopped

*Marinade*

1 cup salad oil
1 medium onion chopped
4 shallots cut up
4-inch piece of celery
1 carrot split lengthwise and
crosswise
½ cup dry red wine
6 whole peppercorns

2 cloves garlic split
1 bay leaf
1 tablespoon fresh thyme or 1
teaspoon dried
1 tablespoon fresh marjoram or 1
teaspoon dried
2 sprigs parsley

THIS is rather like a French pot roast, and is so good that it is worth the trouble to make it.

1. Combine the marinade ingredients in a saucepan and simmer gently 15 to 20 minutes. Cool and pour over the beef in a large bowl. Marinate the meat 12-24 hours, part of the time in the refrigerator. Pierce the meat with a long-tined fork once in a while to let the marinade penetrate. Turn it 2 or 3 times.

2. Lay the meat in a casserole with about one cup of liquid from the marinade. Arrange the carrots and herbs around it and cover the top surface with bacon slices.

3. Cover the casserole first with brown paper and then with the casserole lid. Bake in a 275° oven about 2½ hours.

4. Add the tomatoes and continue baking another half hour. Remove the bacon slices, but slice the meat in the casserole at the table. Serves 6-8.

*Serve with buttered noodles and asparagus with a sauce made of melted butter, lemon juice, and fine bread or corn flake crumbs.*

# CHILI CON CARNE CABELL

3 pounds lean beef ground
1 pound black beans cooked
  Salad oil
2 medium onions chopped
1 green pepper chopped
1 clove garlic chopped
1 small can tomato paste

1 teaspoon celery salt
1 teaspoon Worcestershire sauce
½ teaspoon dry mustard
  Pinch cayenne
  Pinch cumin seed (optional)
2 tablespoons chili powder
  Salt and pepper to taste

THE usual chili is made with the red kidney beans. The use of the regular Mexican black beans here makes this an outstanding dish for chili fanciers.

1. To cook the beans soak them overnight in plenty of water and simmer them next day in just enough fresh water to cover with a generous teaspoon of salt. When they are almost soft enough so you can crush one between your fingers, remove them from the stove but do not drain.

2. Heat the oil in a large heavy casserole on top of the stove and brown the chopped vegetables and garlic very lightly, stirring often.

3. Stir in the beef and cook until there is no more red in it, stirring with a fork and leaving the meat in small chunks, about the size of an olive.

4. Add the beans with the water in which they were cooked, and all the remaining ingredients.

5. Cover and bake in a 300° oven about 25 minutes, or simmer gently on top of the stove, covered, for 20 minutes. Check seasoning before serving. Serves about 10, but this depends upon the number of servings per person!

*Serve with plenty of hot fluffy rice and garlic bread, and a large tossed salad.*

## BOEUF À LA BARONNE

2½-pound slice of top round
   Boiling water
1 bay leaf
3 small onions
3 tablespoons capers
1 sprig parsley

1½ cups dry red wine
½ teaspoon salt
⅛ teaspoon pepper
Flour-and-water thickening
(if desired)

1. Put the steak in a skillet just about its size, pour over boiling water just to the surface of the meat, cover, and simmer 30 minutes at extremely low heat.
2. Transfer the meat and the liquid to a shallow casserole a little larger than the meat.
3. Add the bay leaf, onions, capers, parsley, wine, salt, and pepper. Cover (with aluminum foil if you do not have a lid which fits), and bake at 375° about 30 minutes, or until tender.
4. Drain the liquid into a saucepan and thicken it slightly with flour-and-water paste if you prefer it that way. Pour back over the casserole. Serves 6.

*Serve with fluffy hot rice or buttered noodles to sop up the rich sauce, warm garlic bread, and baby carrots with butter and parsley stirred in.*


## BURGUNDY MEAT BALLS

¾ pound ground lean chuck
¾ cup bread or corn flake crumbs
1 small onion minced
1 egg beaten
½ cup light cream
1¼ teaspoons salt
¼ cup salad oil
3 tablespoons flour

2 cups consommé or half water
   and half consommé
1 cup Burgundy or other dry red
   wine
⅛ teaspoon pepper
½ teaspoon sugar
Kitchen Bouquet

1. Mix the meat, crumbs, onion, egg, cream, and ¾ teaspoon of salt. Shape into small balls and brown in a heavy skillet in the hot oil. Don't crowd the skillet. Transfer the meat balls to a medium casserole

as they are ready. (If the meat balls seem too soft as you shape them either add more crumbs or roll them in flour.)

2. Stir the flour into the fat left in the skillet and blend in the consommé, wine, ½ teaspoon salt, pepper, sugar, and just enough Kitchen Bouquet to give the sauce a good color—a few drops. Cook until smooth, stirring constantly.

3. Pour the sauce over the meat balls in the casserole and bake 30 minutes in a moderate oven, 350°. Stir two or three times. Serves 6.

*Serve with something to absorb the fine sauce—hot fluffy rice, buttered noodles, or spaghetti with cheese.*

## CANNELON OF BEEF

1½ cups cooked roast beef (rare)
1 cup cooked ham
1 medium onion peeled
2 stalks celery
1 tablespoon chopped parsley
¼ teaspoon dried thyme or ¾ teaspoon fresh, chopped
¼ teaspoon dried sweet basil or ¾ teaspoon fresh, chopped
¼ teaspoon sweet marjoram or ¾ teaspoon fresh, chopped
1¼ teaspoons salt
1 egg beaten slightly
1 can condensed tomato soup
1 tablespoon butter or margarine
½ cup minced onion
3 medium tomatoes peeled and chopped
½ teaspoon vinegar

THESE little individual meat loaves are as full of eye appeal as they are of taste appeal.

1. Put the beef, ham, peeled onion, and celery through the meat grinder. Mix in the parsley, thyme, basil, marjoram, ¾ teaspoon salt, egg, and ¼ cup of the soup. With your hands shape into six oblong meat loaves, and place them in a shallow, lightly greased casserole large enough to take them without touching.

2. Put the casserole in a moderate oven—350°—for 25 minutes.

3. While it bakes make the sauce. Heat the butter in a skillet and lightly brown the minced onion. Add the chopped tomatoes and simmer a few minutes. Then stir in the remaining soup, the remaining ½ teaspoon salt, and the vinegar. Cook until smooth and pour over the meat loaves. Continue to bake them about 10 minutes more. Serves 6.

# FLEMISH CARBONNADES OF BEEF

3-4 pounds of lean chuck or round
   cut in 1½-inch cubes
5 tablespoons butter or margarine
2 pounds onions sliced
   Flour
4-6 tablespoons beef fat, butter,
   margarine, or oil

1 teaspoon salt
1 teaspoon fresh-ground pepper
2 cloves garlic
1 pint beer
1 ounce cognac

LIKE so many Flemish dishes, the distinctive flavor here comes from the beer.

1. Melt the butter in a large heavy skillet and sauté the onions until they are just beginning to brown, stirring frequently. Transfer them to a large casserole—a large, old-fashioned bean pot is fine for this dish.

2. Roll the cubes of beef in flour to coat them well.

3. Heat the beef fat, or whatever fat you are using, in the skillet and brown the meat well on all sides. Don't crowd the skillet, or the meat won't brown well. As the pieces are browned move them to the casserole.

4. When all the meat is in the casserole add the salt, pepper, and garlic. Pour a little of the beer into the skillet to clean out all the brown bits and add to the casserole. Stir the contents of the casserole well and add enough beer just to cover.

5. Cover the casserole tightly and bake it in a very slow oven, 275°, about 3 hours, or until the meat is fork tender. If you like a thicker sauce thicken it somewhat with flour and butter kneaded together. Stir in the cognac just before serving. Serves 8-10.

*Serve with parsley-butter new potatoes or little potato balls scooped out of potatoes and sautéed gently in a heavy skillet, and steamed broccoli with a butter-lemon-bread-crumb sauce. A tossed green salad goes well with this meal.*

# GOURMET BEEF STROGANOFF

2 pounds fillet of beef sliced as thin
   as possible and cut in strips or
   squares
   Salt
5 tablespoons butter
3 tablespoons flour

2 cups consommé
½ cup sour cream
 2 tablespoons tomato paste
½ pound sliced mushrooms
 3 tablespoons grated onion

MANY recipes for this popular dish call for round steak and for considerably longer cooking than this one. This is truly a gourmet dish, a perfect choice for a party.

1. Salt the meat and let it stand a couple of hours in the refrigerator before you need it.

2. Melt 2 tablespoons of the butter in a heavy skillet and blend in the flour. Let it cook a moment and blend in the consommé. Cook until it begins to thicken, stirring constantly. Strain into a casserole heavy enough to cook on top of the stove.

3. Stir in the sour cream and tomato paste alternately over medium heat, stirring constantly.

4. Meantime, sauté the sliced mushrooms lightly in the remaining butter, skim them out, and add them to the casserole.

5. In the fat remaining in the skillet quickly brown the meat and onion, very lightly.

6. Pour the meat into the casserole, stir just enough to blend, and simmer over the lowest possible heat 20 minutes. *Do not overcook.* Serves 6.

*Serve with fluffy hot rice or plain boiled wild rice, buttered green peas, and a tossed salad of mixed greens, along with plenty of garlic bread with sesame seeds.*

# FRENCH BEEF CASSEROLE

2-pound slice of top round, cut
  thick
2 tablespoons butter or margarine
1 small carrot minced
2 shallots or scallions minced
1 small bay leaf

1 sprig of thyme, dried or fresh
½ cup dry red wine
¾ cup consommé
¾ teaspoon cornstarch
Pepper and salt to taste

THIS is a typically French stew, with all the flavor that implies.

1. Broil the steak under high heat until it is nicely browned on both sides. Divide into serving portions and arrange in a shallow casserole. Save the juice accumulated in the broiler pan.

2. Melt butter in a small skillet or saucepan and lightly sauté carrot and shallots. (Use a couple of slices of onion if neither shallots nor scallions are available.)

3. Add the steak juice, the bay leaf, thyme, wine, and consommé and pour over the casserole. Cover tightly and bake in a slow oven, 300°, 1½-2 hours, or until the meat is fork tender.

4. With a sharp-tined fork lift out the pieces of meat to a bowl for a moment and strain the sauce into a saucepan. Return the meat to the casserole and the casserole to the oven while you thicken the sauce with the cornstarch mixed to a thin paste with a little water.

5. Season the sauce to taste, pour over the casserole, and continue to cook about 10 minutes more, uncovered. Serves 4-5.

*Serve with parsley-butter new potatoes (or frozen peeled potatoes cooked barely tender) and buttered lima beans. A green salad is really called for, too.*

# HAMBURGER PIE

1 pound chopped lean beef
⅓ cup diced bacon
½ cup minced onions (or ¼ cup
  dehydrated onions soaked 20
  minutes in ¼ cup water)
1 cup water
2 teaspoons salt

⅛ teaspoon pepper
1 teaspoon prepared mustard
1 teaspoon minced parsley
⅓ cup catsup
3 tablespoons flour
Pastry for double-crust pie

34

1. Cook the bacon in a skillet a few minutes but not until it is crisp. Add onions and cook until they are lightly browned.
2. Stir in the beef and cook until the beef is lightly browned, stirring often to break it up.
3. Add the water, salt, pepper, mustard, parsley, and catsup, and bring to a brisk boil.
4. Mix the flour into a smooth paste with water and stir into the meat mixture, continuing to stir until it is fairly thick.
5. Line a 9-inch pie plate with your favorite pastry, pour in the mixture, and cover with the rest of the pastry. Slash to let steam escape and bake 40 minutes in a 425° oven, or until the top is golden brown. Serves 5-6.

## MEAT BALLS STROGANOFF

1 pound ground lean beef
1 teaspoon salt
¼ teaspoon pepper
¼ cup catsup
1 tablespoon Worcestershire sauce
¼ cup minced onion
½ cup bread or corn flake crumbs
1½ cups evaporated milk
2 tablespoons flour
2 tablespoons vegetable oil
1 can condensed cream of mushroom soup
1 tablespoon vinegar
1½ teaspoons Worcestershire sauce

1. Mix the beef, salt, pepper, catsup, the 1 tablespoon Worcestershire sauce, onion, and crumbs, together with ½ cup of the evaporated milk. Mix well and shape into 16 meat balls.
2. Roll the meat balls in the flour and brown in the hot oil in a heavy skillet. Arrange in a medium casserole and pour off any fat remaining in the skillet.
3. Mix the remaining cup of evaporated milk, the soup, the vinegar, and the 1½ teaspoons of Worcestershire sauce. Blend well and add to the skillet. When it is hot pour over the meat balls and bake 10 minutes in a 350° oven or finish on top of the stove over very low heat. Serves 4.

*With this good sauce, serve with buttered noodles or fluffy rice and buttered baby carrots with chopped parsley.*

# HAMBURGER POTATO ROLL

1 pound ground chuck
2 cups seasoned mashed potato
1 medium onion chopped
1 small clove garlic crushed
1 tablespoon drippings
1 egg lightly beaten
2 slices bread, crusts removed
1 teaspoon salt

¼ teaspoon dried orégano, rosemary, or basil, or ¾ teaspoon fresh, chopped
Fresh-ground black pepper
2 tablespoons dry bread crumbs
1 tablespoon minced parsley or green pepper (optional)
3 strips bacon (optional)

THIS recipe has appeared a number of times in the *New York Times'* food columns because it is so frequently requested. Try it once and you can understand its popularity.

1. Sauté the onion and garlic lightly in hot drippings, remove from the heat, and mix in the beef and egg.

2. Soften the bread in water a few minutes, squeeze out the water, and add the bread to the meat, along with the salt, orégano, and pepper. Mix well.

3. Spread out a piece of waxed paper and sprinkle it with the crumbs. Turn the beef out on the crumbs and pat it into a rectangle about ½ inch thick.

4. Beat the mashed potato with the parsley and spread it over the meat.

5. Roll up the meat by lifting the paper along the long side of the rectangle, as you would roll a jelly roll. Lift the roll carefully into a shallow casserole, greased if the meat is quite lean. Place bacon strips on top.

6. Bake about 1 hour in a moderate oven, 350°. Serve with gravy made from the pan drippings or with mushroom or tomato sauce. Serves 5-6.

*Serve with buttered baby carrots and fried tomatoes.*

# MOUSSAKA OF BEEF

1 pound lean ground beef
¾ cup salad oil
3 medium onions chopped
1 tablespoon minced parsley
⅓ cup water
1 tablespoon tomato paste
2 teaspoons salt
½ teaspoon fresh-ground black pepper
1 large or 2 medium eggplants
2 egg whites well beaten
½ cup bread or corn flake crumbs
1 cup medium cream sauce
1 cup grated Parmesan cheese

MOUSSAKA is a famous dish in the Middle East. The Turkish and Armenian versions are usually made with lamb, the Greek with beef, though either can be used. This is a delightful version with beef, far simpler than the traditional dish.

1. Heat a little of the oil in a heavy skillet and brown the meat lightly. Add to the skillet the onions, parsley, water, tomato paste, salt, and pepper. Simmer over the lowest possible heat for about 25 minutes, stirring occasionally.

2. Meantime, cut the eggplants in ¼-inch slices and sauté lightly in the rest of the oil.

3. Add the egg whites and crumbs to the meat mixture and blend until they are absorbed.

4. In a medium casserole, broad rather than deep, make alternate layers of eggplant slices and meat mixture, ending with eggplant.

5. Pour over the cream sauce (made with 2 tablespoons butter or margarine, 2 tablespoons flour, 1 cup milk, and seasoning to taste) and top with the cheese.

6. Bake in a medium oven, 350°, for half an hour, or until well browned. Serves 6.

*Serve with one of the vegetable casseroles at the beginning of the vegetable chapter and a large tossed salad. If you can get it, the flat Armenian bread, crisped in the oven a moment, is a nice accompaniment.*

## JAPANESE MEAT BALLS

1 pound ground lean beef
¼ cup fine bread or corn flake
  crumbs
⅔ cup chopped onion
1 teaspoon salt
⅛ teaspoon pepper
⅔ cup evaporated milk
2 tablespoons butter or margarine

1-pound-3-ounce can bean
  sprouts
¼ cup cornstarch
¼ cup water
½ cup soy sauce
1½ cups thin-sliced onions
1 cup thin-sliced mushrooms
1 cup shredded raw spinach

1. Mix beef, crumbs, chopped onion, salt, pepper, and milk well and shape into 12 balls.

2. Melt butter in a heavy skillet and brown the balls well on all sides, on medium heat.

3. Drain the bean sprouts but save the liquid; if necessary add water to make 1½ cups.

4. Mix the cornstarch and water into a smooth paste.

5. Stir the bean sprout liquid into the skillet with the meat balls and add the cornstarch, stirring constantly until it is smooth and thickened. Add the soy sauce.

6. Turn the mixture into a 2-quart casserole, cover, and bake 25 minutes in a 350° oven, or until the sauce is clear.

7. Remove from oven, stir in the bean sprouts, onions, mushrooms, and spinach. Cover and continue cooking about 10 minutes longer. Serves 6.


## SHEPHERD'S PIE FLORENTINE

1 pound lean beef ground
2¼ teaspoons salt
¼ teaspoon fresh-ground pepper
1½ tablespoons minced onion
¼ cup corn flake or bread crumbs
2 eggs
1 package frozen chopped
  spinach

1 cup water
1 cup milk
1 package instant mashed potato
  (4-serving size)
1 tablespoon butter or margarine
¼ teaspoon garlic salt
  Thin-sliced Cheddar cheese

1. Combine beef, 1 teaspoon of the salt, pepper, 1 tablespoon of the onion, the crumbs, and one egg. Mix lightly and pat gently into a 9-inch pie plate, covering the bottom and sides.
2. Bake this shell 15 minutes in a 425° oven. Pour off any fat that has accumulated.
3. Heat the spinach in a heavy skillet over low heat, covered, turning it often until it is completely thawed. Press out as much water as you can with a spatula.
4. In a saucepan bring the water to a boil, add milk, and beat in the instant potato, butter, garlic salt, remaining 1¼ teaspoons salt, the rest of the onion, and the other egg.
5. Fold in the spinach and pour into the cooked meat shell.
6. Cover the top with slices of cheese and put back in the oven for 10 minutes, or until cheese is melted and golden. Serves 6.

*Serve with crisp cole slaw and sesame party rolls.*

## TURKISH MEAT BALLS

| | |
|---|---|
| 1 pound ground lean chuck | ¼ cup pine nuts |
| ½ pound ground lean lamb | 1 teaspoon salt |
| ½ pound ground lean pork | ½ teaspoon fresh-ground pepper |
| 2 large garlic cloves mashed | Dash cayenne pepper |
| ¼ cup chopped parsley | 1 egg beaten lightly |
| 1 teaspoon dried orégano or | 2 tablespoons salad oil |
| 1 tablespoon fresh, chopped | ½ cup condensed consommé |
| 1 small bay leaf | ½ cup tomato purée |

HAVE the butcher grind the meats together. Mix with the garlic, parsley, orégano, bay leaf crumbled, pine nuts, salt and pepper, cayenne, and egg. Form this mixture into small balls, about the size of a walnut, and brown quickly in hot oil in a heavy skillet. Shake the skillet to keep them from sticking to the skillet and to keep them well rounded. Transfer them to a rather shallow casserole.

Mix the consommé and tomato purée, clean out the brown particles in the skillet with it, and pour over the meat balls. Bake an hour in a 350° oven, covering the casserole for the first half of the period. Serves 6-7.

## SAUERBRATEN

4-6-pound beef shoulder or rump roast, larded with strips of salt pork or bacon 2" x ¼"
Pepper
1 large clove garlic cut
Mild cider vinegar
½ cup sliced onion
2 small bay leaves
1 teaspoon peppercorns
¼ cup sugar
2 tablespoons salad oil
Flour-and-water paste
1 cup dairy sour cream
Salt

THIS is one of the classics of German cooking, and is widely popular in this country. Have the butcher lard the meat, or do it yourself by making gashes every 2 inches or so in the meat with a sharp-pointed knife and forcing the lardoons into the holes.

1. Rub the meat well with pepper and the cut clove of garlic and put in a large bowl.

2. Heat to the boiling point equal parts of vinegar and water, the onion, bay leaves, peppercorns, and sugar. Pour over the beef. There should be enough of the liquid so that the meat is more than half immersed in it. Cover the bowl and put in the refrigerator for anywhere from two to ten days—the longer the better. Turn the meat once a day.

3. Drain the meat, saving the marinade. Heat the oil to sizzling in a Dutch oven or heavy casserole and sear the meat well on all sides.

4. Add marinade to a depth of 1½-2 inches. Salt the meat, cover it, and bake 2-3 hours in a slow oven, 275°. Add more of the marinade if it becomes dry, but this is not likely to happen if the cover is tight.

5. Lift the meat from the casserole carefully and set aside for a moment while you thicken the gravy with flour-and-water paste, stir in the sour cream, and correct the seasoning.

6. Return the sauerbraten to the casserole.

7. Slice at the table, or, if you prefer, slice it before returning to the casserole. Serves 10-12.

*Serve with boiled potatoes and red cabbage.*

# SWISS STEAK WITH HORSERADISH SAUCE

3-pound slice of round steak
2 teaspoons salt
Fresh-ground black pepper
1 clove garlic cut
Flour

Salad oil
½ cup water
1 large onion sliced
½ cup dairy sour cream
1 tablespoon horseradish

THIS is really a delicious version of the popular Swiss steak.

1. Prepare the steak as usual, seasoning it well with salt and pepper, rubbing it with the cut clove of garlic, and pounding in all the flour it will take. (Use the edge of a saucer or the dull side of a butcher knife.) Treat both sides like this and brown the meat well in sizzling salad oil—the least amount that will keep it from sticking to the skillet.

2. Transfer the steak to an oval casserole—a shallow one—and add only the ½ cup of water and the onion. (See note below.) Under no circumstances increase the amount of water.

3. Cover the casserole tightly—with aluminum foil if you do not have a fitted cover—and bake in a slow oven, 275°, about 2 hours, or until the meat is very tender.

4. When it is done lift the steak onto a platter, using two spatulas, long enough to pour what sauce has accumulated into a small saucepan. Or drain sauce off by holding back steak with a spatula. Return the steak in the casserole to the oven while you stir the sour cream and horseradish into the sauce until it is smooth. Pour over the casserole and serve at once. Serves 6.

*Note:* If you prefer, cut the meat into serving portions before you lay it in the casserole. This makes it easier to use a round casserole with a fitted cover, and you can then drain off the sauce more easily.

*Serve with fluffy mashed potatoes, buttered green beans, and sliced ripe tomatoes.*

## SAVORY CORNED BEEF

2 cups canned or cooked corned
    beef, chopped (12-ounce can)
1½ cups cooked potatoes diced
    small
1 tablespoon prepared mustard
1 cup soft (fresh) bread crumbs
2 tablespoons minced onion

2 tablespoons minced green
    pepper
2 tablespoons butter or margarine
    melted
⅛ teaspoon fresh-ground pepper
    Garlic salt
1 cup milk
2 eggs beaten slightly

THIS is a simple way to make a corned beef casserole. It can also be made in a ring mold, and the center filled with vegetables.

1. Blend well the corned beef, potatoes, mustard, bread crumbs, onion, green pepper, butter, and pepper. Check seasoning—the chances are that you will not need salt with corned beef, but sometimes you do. If so, use garlic salt.

2. Shake the eggs and milk in a jar and stir into the corned beef mixture.

3. Arrange in a greased casserole or, as suggested above, in a greased 1-quart ring mold. Bake in a 350° oven about 30 minutes, or until a knife inserted in the center comes out clean. A ring mold will take only 20 minutes. Serves 6.

*Serve with one of the tomato casseroles given in this book (see Index) and wilted cucumbers in sour cream. If you make this into a ring, unmold on a hot platter and fill the center with creamed onions.*


## GYPSY HASH

2 large cans corned beef hash
    (4 cups)
1 large onion minced
1 small clove garlic mashed
½ cup dairy sour cream

2 eggs well beaten
¼ cup dry red wine
¼ teaspoon fresh-ground pepper
¼ teaspoon nutmeg
    Fine bread or corn flake crumbs

THIS is a very old recipe, but as good as any modern one.

42

Blend well all of the ingredients except the final crumbs. You may need to add a little salt, but the corned beef is likely to be salty enough. Spread in a fairly shallow greased casserole and top with a thin sprinkling of crumbs. Bake 20-25 minutes in a 350° oven, or until the center is firm to the touch. Serves 6.

*Serve with cut green beans and buttered corn.*

## DRIED BEEF AND MACARONI

4-ounce package of dried beef
6 ounces elbow macaroni
  Boiling water

1 can condensed cream of chicken
  soup
¼ cup grated Parmesan cheese
  Paprika

A SIMPLE and inexpensive main dish, out of the ordinary.
1. Tear the beef into moderate-size pieces and cover with boiling water. Let stand a minute or two and then drain well.
2. Cook the macaroni in a large pot of boiling water, salted, for 8 or 9 minutes. It should be what the Italians call *al dente,* not too soft. Drain well.
3. While the macaroni is cooking heat the soup and stir in the dried beef. Taste for seasoning—dried beef is usually salty enough so that no additional salt is required.
4. Mix the soup and the macaroni and pour into a medium casserole. Top with Parmesan cheese and paprika and bake about 30 minutes in a 350° oven, or until it is golden brown and bubbly. Serves 4-6.

*Serve with baked tomato halves (spread cut surfaces with salt, a bit of finely minced basil, and buttered crumbs), and small zucchini sliced (do not peel) and cooked slowly, covered, in butter or margarine.*

# BARBECUED TONGUE

1 fresh or smoked beef tongue
2 teaspoons salt
¼ cup flour

2 tablespoons butter, margarine,
  or salad oil

*Barbecue Sauce*

2 tablespoons flour
2 tablespoons prepared mustard
1 cup condensed tomato soup
¼ cup chopped onion
¼ cup chopped celery
½ teaspoon powdered cloves

1 teaspoon salt
½ teaspoon fresh-ground pepper
2 tablespoons Worcestershire
  sauce
2 tablespoons vinegar
½ cup water

IF you do not want to go to the trouble of cooking a tongue you can use this barbecue sauce with a canned whole tongue.

1. If you start with a fresh or smoked tongue, cover it with water, add the salt, and simmer from 2-4 hours, or until tender. Use only half the salt if the tongue is smoked.

2. Plunge the tongue immediately into cold water for several minutes and peel off the skin. Remove and discard the root end.

3. Dust the meat with flour, brown it delicately in the hot butter, and lay in a casserole.

4. To make the barbecue sauce, mix the flour and mustard, stir in the remaining ingredients, bring to a boil in a small saucepan, and pour over the tongue.

5. Bake in a moderate oven, 350°, for 30-40 minutes, basting often. Serves 8-10, depending upon size of tongue.

*Serve with fluffy hot rice and Frenched string beans.*


# BLACKBERRY TONGUE

1 cooked tongue (canned or fresh)
½ cup raisins
1 cup water

3 tablespoons lemon juice
1 cup blackberry jelly

44

IF you cook the tongue yourself, see the directions in the recipe for Barbecued Tongue.

1. Place the cooked tongue in a greased casserole.
2. Simmer the raisins in the water about 10 minutes. Drain and mix with the lemon juice and jelly in a small saucepan. Heat over very low heat until the jelly is melted.
3. Pour over the tongue in the casserole and bake, uncovered, 45 minutes in a 325° oven.
4. Serves 8-10, depending upon size of tongue.

*Serve with fluffy mashed potatoes and buttered broccoli.*


## SPICED BEEF TONGUE MARYLAND

1 fresh or smoked beef tongue
   weighing about 4 pounds
2 cups milk
3 strips lemon peel about ½" x 2"

1 teaspoon ground cinnamon
2 teaspoons brown sugar
½ teaspoon black pepper
2 cups dry white wine

FOR those who like spicy foods this is a wonderful way to cook a tongue.

1. Lay the smoked tongue in a small kettle and pour milk over it. Add enough water to cover the tongue and let it soak for an hour or two to remove the salt. (This is unnecessary if you start with a fresh tongue.)
2. Pour off the milk and water, cover the tongue with cold water, bring to a boil, and simmer, covered, 3-4 hours, or until the meat is tender. Let it cool in the stock.
3. Skin the tongue, remove the root end, and slice about ¼ inch thick. Arrange the tongue slices in a large shallow casserole.
4. Mix remaining ingredients and pour over the tongue.
5. Cover and bake in a moderate oven, 375°, 35 minutes. The tongue should have absorbed most of the wine by this time. If not, uncover the last 15 minutes. Serves 6-8.

*Serve with riced potatoes and corn pudding, together with a plain tossed green salad.*

## TONGUE WITH FRUIT SAUCE

12-ounce canned tongue, whole
½ cup brown sugar, packed
1½ tablespoons flour
½ teaspoon dry mustard

12-ounce can apricot nectar
¼ cup vinegar (scant)
⅓ cup seedless raisins

A QUICK and easy way to convert a canned tongue into a delicacy.

1. Slice the tongue thin (save the gelatin) and arrange the slices, over-lapping, in a shallow casserole.

2. Mix the sugar, flour, and mustard in a saucepan and stir in the remaining ingredients, including the gelatin from the tongue. Cook a minute or two, stirring constantly, until the sauce thickens.

3. Spread it over the tongue and bake in a 350° oven 15 minutes, or until well heated and bubbling. Serves 4.

*Serve with herbed rice and buttered wax beans.*

# HAM

## AVIGNON PANCAKE ROLLS

Pancake batter (your favorite or a mix)
1 cup cooked ham diced fine
3 tablespoons butter or margarine
3 tablespoons flour
1 cup chicken stock
1 cup rich milk
Salt and pepper to taste

½ teaspoon Worcestershire sauce
1 teaspoon dry mustard
1 large can sliced mushrooms, drained
2 tablespoons brandy
2 tablespoons chopped parsley
4 tablespoons grated sharp Cheddar

MANY delightful dishes are made with rolled-up thin pancakes. This is a good example.

1. Make the pancake batter first, quite thin, and let it stand while you make the filling.

2. Melt the butter in a medium saucepan, blend in the flour, and slowly stir in the stock and milk. Keep stirring until you have a smooth, velvety, thick sauce. Season it well with salt and pepper, Worcestershire, and mustard. Let it simmer on very low heat for about 10 minutes.

3. Remove the sauce from the stove and measure out ½ cup. To the remaining sauce add the mushrooms, ham, and brandy. Let it cool while you make the pancakes—about 5 inches in diameter, 18 in all.

4. Spread a tablespoon of the ham-mushroom mixture in the center of each pancake and roll up. Place, seam side down, close together in a buttered shallow casserole.

5. Mix the rest of the sauce (the ½ cup you reserved) with the parsley and spread it evenly over the pancakes. Bake 30 minutes in a 325° oven.

6. Five minutes before the dish is ready, sprinkle with grated cheese and brown under the broiler. Serves 6.

*Serve with buttered green peas and a salad of cooked vegetables (sliced or baby carrots, cut corn, Italian green beans, etc.).*

## BAKED HAM WITH GINGER PEARS

| | |
|---|---|
| 1 slice ham, about 2½ pounds | Grated rind of 1 lemon |
| 3 fresh pears, preferably Bartlett | ½ cup preserved ginger chopped |
| 1 cup water | 8-10 cloves |
| ½ cup sugar | ½ cup brown sugar |
| Juice of 1 lemon | |

1. Combine water, sugar, lemon juice and rind, and ginger in a saucepan and simmer 5 minutes. Add pears, peeled, halved, and cored, and simmer 5 minutes longer.

2. Lay the ham in a large but shallow casserole. Stick with cloves, and pat the brown sugar on top. Pour ¼ cup of the pear syrup around it.

3. Bake 20 minutes in a 350° oven, basting 2 or 3 times.

4. Arrange the pear halves around the ham with another ¼ cup of the pear syrup, and bake 20 or 25 minutes longer. Serves 6.

*Serve with a sweet potato casserole (see Index) and Italian green beans.*

# GERMAN HAM AND VEAL PÂTÉ

2 slices cold boiled ham ½-inch
  thick
2 slices cooked veal (leftover)
  ½-inch thick
  Pastry for 2-crust pie
4 tablespoons butter, margarine,
  or lard

2 shallots minced or one tablespoon
  minced onion
2 tablespoons minced parsley
½ cup mushrooms chopped (canned
  or fresh)
2 large eggs or 3 small
  Salt and pepper

1. Use your favorite recipe for the pastry. Roll out about ⅔ of it and line a 6-cup casserole with it, leaving a little rim around the edge.
2. Cut both meats into ¼-inch cubes.
3. Mix the meat trimmings with the butter or lard, shallots, parsley, and mushrooms. Grind this mixture very fine, beat in the eggs, and season to taste.
4. Fill the casserole with alternate layers of mixed ham and veal and the butter-mushroom mixture.
5. Cover with pastry gashed several times to allow steam to escape. Seal to lining pastry by moistening and pinching together.
6. Bake 1½ hours in a slow oven, 300°, or until the crust is golden. Serve hot or cold. Serves 4. (Can be doubled for larger casserole.)

*Serve with red cabbage and buttered carrots if hot, with a mixed vegetable salad if cold.*

# HAM, BROCCOLI, AND CHEESE PIE

2 cups cooked ham cut in ½-inch
  dice
1 package frozen broccoli or
  1 pound fresh, trimmed weight
2 cups shredded Swiss cheese

3 tablespoons chopped onion
1½ cups milk scalded
3 eggs beaten slightly
  Salt and pepper
  Unbaked 10-inch pastry shell

1. If you use fresh broccoli, clean it well and cut off all the flowerets.

48

Chop the stems coarsely. Cook separately in boiling water, the flowerets 5 minutes, the stems 10 minutes. If you use frozen broccoli, cook according to package directions, drain, and cut off the stems, chopping them coarsely also.

2. In the unbaked pie shell spread ½ the ham, the broccoli stems, the broccoli flowerets, and the cheese. Repeat the layers and spread the chopped onion on top.

3. Gradually stir the milk into the beaten eggs, add the seasonings (go slow on salt!), and pour carefully on top of the filled pie.

4. Bake in a 450° oven 10 minutes, lower the heat to 325°, and bake 25-30 minutes longer, or until the center is firm. Serves 4-6.

*Note:* You can make the pie more attractive looking by holding out 2 tablespoons of the cheese and sprinkling it on top of the pie before baking.

*Serve with herbed rice and a green salad.*


# HAM WITH CAULIFLOWER

2½ cups ground cooked ham
 2 small heads cauliflower broken
   into flowerets
 ¾ cup grated Parmesan cheese
 2 egg yolks
1½ cups dairy sour cream

2 tablespoons minced onion
1 tablespoon minced parsley
1 teaspoon paprika
 Salt
 Butter or margarine

1. Simmer the cauliflower flowerets in boiling salted water barely to cover for about 5 minutes. It should still be crisp. Drain.

2. In a greased casserole make alternate layers of cauliflower and ham, pressing them slightly together. Sprinkle each layer with part of the cheese, using ½ cup.

3. Beat the egg yolks with the sour cream. Stir in the onion, parsley, paprika, and a little salt if the ham is bland.

4. Pour this mixture over the casserole, spread with the remaining ¼ cup cheese, dot with butter, and bake in a 375° oven 20 minutes or until golden brown. Serves 5-6.

*Serve with buttered noodles or a rice casserole.* (See Index.)

# HAM CASSEROLE WITH SHERRY

4 cups ground cooked ham
2 eggs well beaten
2 tablespoons chopped green
  pepper
½ cup heavy cream or dairy sour
  cream
2 cups cooked rice
2 tomatoes peeled and chopped or
  1½ cups canned

1 teaspoon prepared mustard
1 teaspoon Worcestershire sauce
½ cup sherry
1 tablespoon grated or finely
  minced onion
2 tablespoons buttered bread or
  corn flake crumbs
Paprika

BLEND well all of the ingredients except crumbs and paprika and spread in a well-greased medium casserole. Sprinkle the top with buttered crumbs and paprika. Bake 30 minutes in a 350° oven. Serves 6.

*Serve with buttered baby carrots sprinkled with parsley and a tossed green salad.*


# HAWAIIAN HAM CASSEROLE

2 cups cooked ham cut in ½-inch
  dice
2 tablespoons butter or margarine
8½-ounce can pineapple chunks
  drained
3 tablespoons brown sugar

1 can condensed onion soup
Salt and pepper
4 large sweet potatoes boiled,
  peeled, and sliced thick, or
  10½-ounce can
½ cup chopped pecans

1. Heat butter in a heavy casserole and lightly brown the ham in it.
2. Stir in the pineapple chunks, 1 tablespoon of the brown sugar, and the onion soup. Season to taste. Cook just until it reaches the boiling point and remove from the heat.
3. Arrange the sweet potato slices on top of the ham-pineapple mixture, overlapping a little.
4. Mix pecans and remaining brown sugar and spread over the potatoes. Bake ½ hour at 400°. Serves 4.

*Serve with buttered baby Brussels sprouts and corn on the cob.*

# HAM JUBILEE

1 slice ham—about 2½ pounds
1 pound-4-ounce can pitted black
 cherries
¼ teaspoon each ground cloves,
 curry powder, cinnamon, dry
 mustard

1 tablespoon vinegar, preferably
 wine vinegar
1 cup currant jelly
½ cup orange juice
¼ cup grated orange rind

1. Combine in a saucepan the juice from the cherries, the spices, vinegar, jelly, and orange juice. Bring to a low boil. Remove from the stove and stir in the grated orange rind and the cherries.
2. Arrange the ham slice in a casserole a little larger than the ham but rather shallow. (Trim off some of the fat edge first and slash remaining fat several times to prevent the ham from humping up.)
3. Bake 30 minutes in a 350° oven.
4. Pour the syrup over the ham and continue to bake 30 minutes longer. Serves 4-5.


# SPICY HAM LOAF

1 pound lean ham ground
½ pound lean pork ground
1 can condensed tomato soup
⅓ cup chopped onion
½ cup fine dry crumbs
¼ cup minced celery

2 tablespoons minced parsley
1 egg slightly beaten
½ teaspoon dry mustard
 Dash fresh-ground pepper
2 teaspoons prepared horseradish

1. Mix thoroughly the meats, ½ cup of the soup, the onion, crumbs, celery, parsley, egg, mustard, and pepper (no salt). Shape into a firm loaf and put it in a shallow casserole.
2. Bake the loaf about 1¼ hours in a 350° oven. Hold the loaf back firmly with a spatula and drain off all the fat.
3. Heat the remaining soup in a small saucepan, stir in the horseradish, and pour over the loaf. Bake a few minutes longer before serving. Serves 6.

# HAM CASSEROLE WITH RAISINS AND PINEAPPLE

3 cups diced cooked ham
½ cup dark or golden raisins
¾ cup pineapple chunks
1 medium onion sliced and
separated into rings
1 small green pepper sliced in rings
1 cup pineapple syrup (from can of chunks)

⅓ cup vinegar
½ cup brown sugar (packed)
2 tablespoons cornstarch
2 teaspoons dry mustard
¼ teaspoon salt
1 teaspoon Worcestershire sauce
1 tablespoon soy sauce

1. Put ham in casserole and arrange onion and green pepper rings over it. Arrange pineapple and raisins on top.
2. In a small saucepan heat the pineapple syrup and vinegar. Mix the sugar, cornstarch, mustard, and salt. Add this to the hot liquid and stir until it thickens.
3. Add the Worcestershire and soy sauces and pour over the casserole.
4. Bake 45 minutes at 350°. Serves 5-6.


# HAM CASSEROLE WITH NOODLES AND SESAME SEEDS

3 cups diced cooked ham
8-ounce package medium noodles
cooked
2 tablespoons toasted sesame seeds

2 tablespoons butter or margarine
2 cups rich cream sauce or 1½ cans
condensed cream of chicken soup
3 tablespoons buttered crumbs

SESAME seeds give this casserole a special flavor.
1. Cook the noodles according to package directions, drain, and stir the butter in at once.
2. Toast the sesame seeds in the 400° oven where you will bake the casserole, 8-10 minutes.
3. Make the cream sauce, if you use that instead of the soup, with 3 tablespoons margarine, 3 tablespoons flour, and 2 cups top milk, with salt and pepper to taste.

4. Mix the ham and sesame seeds with this sauce.

5. In a medium casserole make alternate layers of the noodles and the ham-cream sauce, making 2 layers of each.

6. Top with buttered crumbs and bake 20 minutes in the 400° oven. Serves 6.

*Serve with cole slaw and purée of spinach.*


## HAM-AND-LEEK PIE WITH CHEESE

1½ cups cooked ham diced small
(or two 4½-ounce cans deviled
ham or 12 slices bacon cooked
crisp)
1⅞-ounce package dry cream of
leek soup mix
2½ cups coarsely grated Swiss
cheese
1½ cups milk

1½ cups light cream
4 eggs well beaten
1 teaspoon dry mustard
1 teaspoon salt (scant)
¼ teaspoon pepper
3 tablespoons bread or corn flake
crumbs
2 tablespoons Parmesan cheese
Unbaked 10-inch pie shell

1. Make the pie crust with 1½ cups flour, using your favorite recipe, and chill it while you make the filling.

2. Blend the soup mix with the milk in a saucepan and bring to a boil, stirring constantly. Cool a little, stir in the cream, and refrigerate until cold.

3. Mix well the eggs, mustard, salt and pepper, and blend in the soup mixture as soon as it has cooled.

4. If you use cooked ham, spread it on the bottom of the pie shell and add the crumbs to the soup mixture. If you use deviled ham or bacon, mix it with the crumbs and spread on the bottom of the shell. In either case, cover with the Swiss cheese.

4. Pour the milk-soup mixture over the cheese carefully, top with the Parmesan cheese, and bake at 375° about 50 minutes, or until a knife inserted in the center comes out clean. Serves 8.

*Serve with warm garlic bread or sesame seed rolls and a mixed vege-table salad.*

## BRAISED HAM STEAK IN WINE

1 center slice ham 2 inches thick
   Whole cloves
¼ cup brown sugar

1 teaspoon cornstarch
¾ cup dry red wine

ONE of the simplest possible ways of producing a delicious ham casserole.

1. Trim the fat from the ham, leaving not more than ¼ inch around it. Slash this a number of times. Insert a dozen or so cloves in the fat around the outside and in fat pockets in the ham itself. Lay the ham in a shallow casserole.

2. Mix sugar and cornstarch, spread evenly over the ham, and bake uncovered in a slow oven, 300°, about 30 minutes.

3. Add the wine to the casserole and continue to bake another 30-40 minutes, basting frequently with the wine. Serves 6.

*Serve with a sweet potato casserole (see Index) or whole sweet potatoes boiled 10-15 minutes and finished in the oven with the ham. Broccoli spears go well with this dinner.*


## HAM STEAK FLAMBÉ

1 center slice of ham 1 inch thick
¼ cup brown sugar
¾ teaspoon dry mustard

1 tablespoon orange juice
¼ cup Grand Marnier or Curaçao
   liqueur warmed slightly

NOT only good to eat but as spectacular to see as all flambé dishes are.

1. Trim excess fat from the edge of the ham and lay in a shallow casserole.

2. Mix the brown sugar, mustard, and orange juice into a thin paste and spread half of it in a thin layer on the ham.

3. Put under the broiler, about 3 inches, under medium heat if your broiler can be regulated. If not, put it about 5 inches from the heat. Broil about 10 minutes.

4. Turn the steak, spread with the remaining sugar mixture, and continue broiling about 5 minutes.

5. Just as you are ready to serve pour over the warmed liqueur and ignite. Serve flaming. (It is often easier to light liqueur in a pan or ladle and pour it blazing over the food.) Serves 4.

*Serve with buttered noodles dressed up with poppy seeds and slivered almonds, and a green salad with tomato wedges and cucumber slices added.*

## HAM AND SPAGHETTI PARMA

1 pound cooked ham julienned
8-ounce package spaghetti cooked
¾ cup grated Parmesan cheese
⅓ cup butter or margarine
1 large mushroom sliced
2 tablespoons minced or grated onion
¼ cup flour
2 cups light cream or top milk
¾ cup dry white wine
⅓ cup sliced green olives
1 pimiento cut in thin strips
¼ teaspoon dried orégano or ¾ teaspoon fresh, chopped
⅛ teaspoon fresh-ground pepper

1. Cook the spaghetti as directed on the package, but be careful not to overcook it—it should be *al dente,* as the Italians say.

2. Drain and immediately toss it with ½ cup of the cheese. Spread it out in a large shallow buttered casserole and keep barely warm.

3. Melt butter in a large skillet and cook the mushroom and onion in it, over medium heat, 3-4 minutes. Skim out of the skillet and set aside.

4. Into the fat remaining in the skillet blend flour and gradually stir in the cream. When it thickens stir in the wine, cooked mushroom and onion, ham, olives, pimiento, orégano, and pepper.

5. Spoon this mixture carefully over the spaghetti in the casserole, sprinkle with the remaining cheese, and broil 4-6 inches from the heat until golden. Serves 6-8.

*Serve with warm garlic bread and a salad made with separated leaves of Belgian endive and cooked beets julienned and tossed in French dressing.*

## SPICED HAM BALLS

1 can pork luncheon meat ground
⅔ cup uncooked oatmeal
1 egg beaten

½ cup milk
1 teaspoon Worcestershire sauce
1 tablespoon prepared mustard

*Sauce*

2 tablespoons flour
⅓ cup brown sugar or maple syrup

⅔ cup water
2 tablespoons vinegar

1. Mix thoroughly the meat, oatmeal, egg, milk, Worcestershire sauce, and mustard. Shape into small balls and lay in a shallow casserole.
2. Bake these ham balls 30 minutes in a 350° oven.
3. While the casserole is baking, combine the sauce ingredients in a saucepan and cook slowly until thick.
4. When the casserole has baked 30 minutes pour the sauce over and continue baking 15 minutes longer. Serves 5-6.


## SOUFFLÉ STRASBOURG

¾ cup ground ham
½ cup purée of foie gras
1 tablespoon chopped truffles
    (optional)
¼ cup butter or margarine

¼ cup flour
2 cups milk
Salt and pepper
3 eggs separated

1. Make a cream sauce of the butter, flour, and milk, seasoning it to your taste. Stir in the ham, foie gras, and truffles. Cool somewhat.
2. Stir in the well-beaten egg yolks and fold in the whites, beaten until they are stiff but not dry.
3. Pour gently into a buttered soufflé dish and bake in a 350° oven 50 minutes. Serves 4-5.

*A delicate soufflé like this calls for something light to accompany it, such as tiny green peas, sliced ripe tomatoes, and a simple salad of mixed greens.*

56

# LAMB

## BLANQUETTE OF LAMB

3 pounds boneless shoulder of
lamb cut in 1¼-inch cubes
6 tablespoons butter, margarine,
or salad oil
18 small white onions (canned
will do)

½ pound mushroom caps, halved
or quartered if large
½ cup Madeira or sherry
2 tablespoons flour
1½ cups light cream
Salt and pepper to taste

A FLAVORFUL combination, and a fine buffet dish for a party.

1. Heat 4 tablespoons of the butter in a heavy skillet and brown the lamb slightly. As the pieces are browned arrange them in a medium casserole. Cover the casserole and bake 20 minutes in a 300° oven.

2. In the fat remaining in the skillet sauté lightly first the onions and then the mushrooms, adding each to the casserole as they are ready. (If you use canned onions add them later, with the sauce.)

3. Pour the Madeira into the skillet, scrape up all the brown particles, and add this to the casserole.

4. Blend the remaining 2 tablespoons of butter and the flour in a medium saucepan and cook over medium heat. Slowly stir in the cream and keep stirring until the sauce is somewhat thickened. Season to taste.

5. Add this to the casserole at the end of the 20 minutes it has cooked. Stir gently to blend ingredients, cover again, and bake 30 minutes longer. Serves 6.

*Serve with an herbed or curried rice, warm garlic bread with sesame seeds added to the garlic butter, and succotash.*

# LAMB CHOP CASSEROLE

4 thick shoulder lamb chops
2 tablespoons flour
¾ teaspoon salt
⅛ teaspoon pepper
2 tablespoons butter, margarine,
  or salad oil
8 small white onions
2 medium carrots diced small
¼ cup diced celery

½ cup currant jelly
½ cup condensed consommé
½ teaspoon dried chervil or 1½
  teaspoons fresh, chopped
½ teaspoon dried orégano or 1½
  teaspoons fresh, chopped
1 small bay leaf
¼ cup orange juice

1. Shake the flour, salt, and pepper together in a bag and dredge the chops in it.
2. Heat the butter in a shallow casserole large enough to hold all the chops flat and brown them on both sides.
3. Add all remaining ingredients except the orange juice, cover the casserole, and bake one hour in a 375° oven, basting several times.
4. Add the orange juice and bake 15 minutes more, uncovered. Serves 4.

*Serve with riced potatoes and asparagus with butter-lemon-juice-bread-crumb sauce.*

# GREEK LAMB CASSEROLE

3 pounds stewing lamb cut in
  1-inch cubes
¼ cup salad oil
¼ cup chopped onion
2½ cups solid-pack tomatoes
2 teaspoons salt
¼ teaspoon dried thyme or ¾
  teaspoon fresh, chopped
¼ teaspoon dried orégano or ¾
  teaspoon fresh, chopped

¼ teaspoon dried sweet basil or
  ¾ teaspoon fresh, chopped
1 large or 2 medium carrots diced
  small or sliced thin
1 or 2 leeks (white part only)
12 small white onions peeled or
  1 medium can
1 package frozen okra partly
  thawed
1 teaspoon lemon juice

1. Brown the meat well in hot oil in a heavy skillet and transfer to a medium casserole with a slotted spoon.
2. In the fat remaining in the skillet cook the chopped onion until soft but not browned and add to the casserole.
3. Pour the tomatoes into the skillet and stir to pick up all the browned particles. Add herbs and salt and pour over the casserole. Cover and bake 1 hour in a 325° oven.
4. Remove cover and stir in carrots, leeks, and onions. (If you use canned boiled onions do not add them until later.) Cover again and bake 25 minutes longer.
5. Uncover and add the okra and lemon juice. If you use boiled onions add them at this time also. Bake 15 minutes longer, uncovered. Serves 6.

*Serve with fluffy hot rice, cole slaw, and buttered baby Brussels sprouts.*

## LAMB CHOPS FARM STYLE

6 shoulder lamb chops cut rather thick
3 tablespoons flour
2 teaspoons salt
⅛ teaspoon fresh-ground pepper

2 tablespoons butter, margarine, or salad oil
2 tablespoons water
1 can condensed cream of mushroom soup

1. Shake up the flour, salt, and pepper in a paper bag and dredge the chops in it.
2. Heat the butter in a large heavy casserole or electric fry pan and brown the chops well. Arrange in a shallow casserole.
3. Stir the water into the soup until well mixed and pour over the casserole.
4. Bake at 375° one hour, uncovered, or until chops are tender. Serves 6.

*Serve with a baked rice casserole (see Index) and sliced zucchini gently sautéed in butter, covered, about 8-10 minutes.*

## LAMB WITH EGGPLANT

1 pound ground raw lamb
1 medium eggplant cut in ½-inch slices (unpeeled)
⅓ cup butter, margarine, or salad oil
¼ cup chopped onion

½ teaspoon salt
Dash fresh-ground pepper
8-ounce can tomato sauce
¼ cup grated Parmesan cheese
Mozzarella cheese sliced

1. Heat the butter in a heavy skillet and brown the eggplant slices lightly on both sides. Arrange part of it as a layer on the bottom of a medium casserole and reserve the rest on a plate. You may have to add a bit more butter to brown all the eggplant.
2. In any fat remaining in the skillet put the lamb, onion, and seasonings. Cook until the lamb is lightly browned, stirring several times.
3. Spread the lamb on top of the eggplant layer in the casserole. Arrange the remaining eggplant slices on top, cut in halves or quarters.
4. Pour tomato sauce over, sprinkle Parmesan cheese on top, and bake 20 minutes in a 350° oven.
5. Arrange mozzarella cheese slices to cover top of casserole and bake 10 minutes more, or until cheese is bubbly. Serves 6.

*Serve with buttered noodles and a tossed green salad.*


## LAMB WITH BEANS

2 pounds boneless lamb cut in good-sized chunks, 1½-2 inches
1 cup dried white beans
4 slices bacon diced
½ cup chopped onion
3 tablespoons flour
1½ cups chicken broth
Salt and pepper to taste
½ clove garlic mashed

½ teaspoon dried thyme or 1½ teaspoons fresh, chopped
½ teaspoon dried orégano or 1½ teaspoons fresh, chopped
½ teaspoon dried marjoram or 1½ teaspoons fresh, chopped
¾ cup scallions chopped (green onions)
8 tiny white onions or 1 small can whole boiled onions

60

1. If you use old-style beans soak them overnight, drain, cover with fresh cold water, bring to a boil, and simmer until tender (when the skin cracks when you put a bean in a spoon and blow on it). If you use the newer quick-cooking beans follow package directions in cooking. Drain beans, but save water in which they were cooked.

2. In a heavy skillet sauté the bacon and chopped onion together lightly and put in a medium casserole with the cooked beans.

3. In the fat left in the skillet brown the lamb pieces lightly and transfer to the casserole.

4. Stir the flour into the fat left in the skillet, adding a bit of butter or margarine if necessary to make a smooth paste.

5. Add the chicken broth slowly, season to taste, and add to the casserole with the garlic, herbs, scallions, whole onions, and enough of the bean water to come about ¾ of the way up.

6. Cover and bake 2 hours in a 300° oven. If sauce is too thin at this time, thicken with flour-and-water paste. Serves 4.

*Serve with spaghetti tossed well with Parmesan cheese and Italian green beans well buttered.*

## LAMB AND MACARONI

2 cups cooked lamb diced rather small

8-ounce package shell macaroni cooked

1 can condensed cream of celery soup

4-ounce can sliced mushrooms with liquid

½ teaspoon dried rosemary, basil, or orégano, or 1½ teaspoons fresh, chopped

Salt and pepper to taste

⅓ cup grated Parmesan cheese

1. Cook the macaroni according to package directions. Be sure not to overcook it. Drain.

2. Combine lamb, soup, mushrooms, herb, and seasonings. Add the cooked and drained macaroni and mix well.

3. Pour into a medium casserole, buttered, and sprinkle with cheese.

4. Bake 35 minutes in a 350° oven. Serves 5-6.

# DE LUXE LAMB HASH

2 cups cold roast lamb chopped
  rather fine, not ground
5 tablespoons brandy
1 garlic clove cut in half
½ teaspoon dried orégano or
  1½ teaspoons fresh, chopped
1 teaspoon chopped parsley

1 generous teaspoon meat glaze
1 can condensed consommé
2 tablespoons butter or margarine
1 good-sized onion sliced thin
2 cups fresh bread crumbs
  slightly packed
Salt

1. Pour the brandy over the lamb, stir to be sure it is all moistened, and let stand an hour.
2. Add the garlic clove, herbs, and meat glaze to the consommé and let it stand until the meat is ready to use. Remove the garlic clove at that time.
3. Heat the butter in a skillet and lightly sauté the onion.
4. Add consommé and bread crumbs to the meat, and add the onion. Let stand briefly, until the liquid is all absorbed by the bread. Check seasoning and add a little salt if needed. Spread in a rather shallow casserole.
5. Bake 15 minutes in a 350° oven and then brown under the broiler. Serves 4-5.

*Serve with asparagus Hollandaise and Frenched green beans.*


# SWEDISH LAMB SHANKS

4 lamb shanks
2 tablespoons salad oil
1 teaspoon paprika
1 large onion sliced
1 cup sliced mushrooms
1 cup water or ½ cup each water
  and dry white wine

1 tablespoon prepared horseradish
¾ teaspoon mixed herbs: rosemary,
  parsley, sweet basil, and orégano
1 teaspoon salt
¼ teaspoon fresh-ground pepper
1 cup dairy sour cream

1. Heat oil in a heavy skillet. Sprinkle the lamb shanks with paprika and brown them in the oil, along with the onion and mushrooms.

2. When the lamb is browned on all sides transfer it to a large casserole. Add the water or water-wine mixture to the skillet, scrape up all the brown particles, and add this to the casserole, along with the horseradish, herbs, and salt and pepper.

3. Cover and bake in a 325° oven 1½ hours, or until lamb is fork tender.

4. Remove the shanks and cut off the meat.

5. Stir the sour cream into the casserole, return the meat to it, and just reheat to serving temperature. Serves 4.

*Serve with buttered noodles and buttered beets.*

# LAMB AND SPAGHETTI PARMESAN

1 pound ground lean lamb
6 ounces spaghetti cooked and
   drained
5 tablespoons butter or margarine
2 cups chopped onion
¾ cup tomato paste
1 cup warm water

½ teaspoon cinnamon
⅛ teaspoon nutmeg
   Salt and pepper
¼ cup grated Parmesan cheese
3 eggs
3 tablespoons flour
1½ cups milk

1. Heat 2 tablespoons of the butter in a medium casserole and brown the lamb and onion.

2. Stir in the tomato paste and water, cinnamon, nutmeg, and salt and pepper to taste.

3. Cover and bake 25-30 minutes in a slow oven, 300°.

4. Combine the cheese and one of the eggs, beaten with a fork. Stir this into the drained spaghetti and spread on top of the lamb mixture in the casserole.

5. Melt the remaining 3 tablespoons of butter, blend in the flour, and slowly stir in the milk. Cook until thickened, stirring constantly. Season to taste.

6. Beat the other two eggs well. Stir a little of the hot cream sauce into them and stir back into the sauce. Simmer a couple of minutes but do not let it boil.

7. Pour the sauce over the spaghetti in the casserole, increase the heat to 400°, and bake 15 minutes more. Serves 4.

## LAMB STEAKS WITH VEGETABLES

4 lamb steaks ¾-inch thick
2 cloves garlic mashed
1 cup sliced mushrooms
1 cup chopped green pepper
1 cup choped onions
2 medium tomatoes sliced

1 teaspoon salt
¼ teaspoon fresh-ground pepper
2 teaspoons paprika
½ teaspoon dried rosemary or 1½
teaspoons fresh, chopped
¼ cup dry sherry

SPREAD mashed garlic on the steaks and arrange them in a fairly shallow casserole that will hold them in one layer.

Arrange the remaining ingredients on top of the steaks, and bake in a 325° oven 40 minutes, or until the steaks are very tender. Cover for the first 25 minutes, then remove cover. Serves 4, or more if the steaks are very large.

*Serve with riced potatoes and a plain green salad.*


## LAMB STEW WITH WINE

2 pounds lean lamb shoulder cut
in 1½-inch cubes
2 medium onions sliced
1 medium clove garlic, peeled
1½ cups dry white wine

Seasoned flour
4 tablespoons salad oil
½ cup water
1 teaspoon chopped parsley

THE wine gives this stew a lot of flavor, particularly because it is used for marinating.
1. Put the lamb in a deep bowl with onions and garlic and stir well. Pour the wine over it, cover, and let marinate 2-3 hours, or put in the refrigerator overnight.
2. Drain the meat cubes well (save the marinade) and roll them in seasoned flour or shake them in a paper bag. (Use ¼ cup flour, 2 scant teaspoons salt, and ¼ teaspoon pepper.)
3. Heat oil in a heavy skillet, brown the meat, and remove to a medium casserole.

4. Add water and parsley to the leftover marinade and pour over the casserole.

5. Cover and bake 1½ hours in a 325° oven, or simmer an hour over very low heat on top of the stove. Serves 4-5.

Note: *If you want to make this a complete meal, add vegetables when you put the casserole in the oven: carrots and celery sliced, a dozen little white onions, and 2 good-sized potatoes diced or 15-20 small potato balls. Otherwise, serve with little new potatoes and buttered Italian beans.*

## LAMB TERRAPIN

2½ cups cooked lamb cut in small
slices or diced
2 tablespoons butter, margarine,
or salad oil
2 tablespoons flour
½ teaspoon dry mustard
1 cup condensed consommé or
½ cup consommé and ½ cup
dry red wine

½ cup cream or top milk
1 tablespoon Worcestershire
sauce
2 hard-cooked eggs chopped
½ cup sliced mushrooms lightly
sautéed
½ cup buttered crumbs
1 teaspoon minced parsley

LEFTOVER lamb should meet a royal welcome if dressed up in this way, especially if you use the wine.

1. Melt the butter in a medium casserole on top of the stove, stir in flour and mustard, and blend in the consommé gradually, stirring constantly.

2. Cook 2-3 minutes and then stir in the cream, Worcestershire sauce, eggs, mushrooms, and meat.

3. Top with buttered crumbs and parsley mixed.

4. Bake the casserole 20-25 minutes in a moderate oven, 350°, uncovered, until it is bubbly and golden. Serves 5-6.

*Serve with buttered noodles, buttered Brussels sprouts, and sliced ripe tomatoes topped with chopped chives and French dressing.*

# LAMBROSIA

2 pounds lamb stewing meat cut
   in medium cubes
¼ cup flour
1½ teaspoons curry powder or to
   taste
3 teaspoons salt

¼ teaspoon pepper
2 tablespoons butter or margarine
2 cups water (or ½ chicken broth
   or white wine)
8 medium carrots cut in strips
1-pound can boiled whole onions

## Topping

¾ cup sifted cornmeal
1½ cups flour
  2 teaspoons baking powder
¾ teaspoon salt

½ cup shortening
1½ cups canned or cooked frozen
   whole-kernel corn
¾ cup milk

THIS dish is well named, especially if you use boned lamb or bone it yourself.

1. Combine the flour, curry powder, salt, and pepper in a paper bag and shake the lamb pieces in it. Brown well in hot fat and put in a medium casserole.

2. Pour the water or broth into the skillet, scrape out the browned particles, and add to the casserole.

3. Cover the casserole and bake 30 minutes in a 325° oven.

4. Add the carrots and bake 25 minutes more.

5. Remove the casserole from the oven and stir in the onions. Increase oven heat to 425°.

6. For the topping, sift together the cornmeal, flour, baking powder, and salt. Cut in the shortening until the mixture is uniform. Stir in the corn (drained if you use canned corn). Add the milk all at once and stir just enough to dampen the mixture.

7. Drop on top of the casserole by tablespoonfuls and bake 25 minutes. Serves 5-6.

*Serve with French-cut string beans to which sliced and lightly sautéed mushrooms have been added.*

# NOISETTES D'AGNEAU

8 fillets cut from saddle of lamb,
 1½ inches thick
2½ tablespoons clarified butter
 Salt and pepper
¼ cup dry sherry
¼ cup dry vermouth

1 cup veal or chicken stock
2 tablespoons butter
1 truffle peeled and minced
 (optional)
1 cup Soubise sauce
 Grated Parmesan cheese

THIS is a delectable French dish, something to make for very special people.

To clarify butter melt it, preferably over hot water, and after it settles pour it carefully through a fine cloth or folded cheesecloth wrung out in warm water. This filters out the scum.

1. Heat the clarified butter in a heavy skillet. Season the fillets and brown them lightly on both sides.

2. Add the sherry and vermouth and cook until the wines are greatly reduced.

3. Add the stock and cook slowly over low heat until the sauce becomes slightly thickened. Transfer fillets and sauce to a shallow serving casserole.

4. Cream the butter with the truffle and place a nut-sized piece on each chop.

5. Top with Soubise sauce. (This is a cream sauce strongly flavored with onion. Make the cream sauce with 2 tablespoons butter, 2 tablespoons flour, and 1 cup top milk. Boil ¾ cup chopped onions in water 5 minutes. Drain, add more water, just to cover, and cook until they are soft. Drain well and press through a sieve into the cream sauce. Season to taste.)

6. Sprinkle the Soubise sauce topping of the fillets with a generous coating of Parmesan cheese, put under the broiler, and broil until golden brown. Serves 4.

*This is a rich dish, and needs only something like fat asparagus stalks with butter-lemon-juice-bread-crumb dressing and a salad of Belgian endive with French dressing.*

## ROQUEFORT LAMB CHOPS

4 loin lamb chops cut 2 inches thick
¼ pound Roquefort cheese crumbled
1 clove garlic cut
Salt and pepper

2 teaspoons Worcestershire sauce
½ can condensed consommé or
½ consommé and ½ red wine

1. Trim the chops of excess fat and rub well all over with the cut garlic. Sprinkle with salt and pepper.
2. Mix cheese and Worcestershire sauce and spread on the chops. Lay them in a shallow casserole just large enough to hold them.
3. Pour the consommé around the chops and bake 45 minutes in a 350° oven, basting occasionally. Serves 4.

*Serve with scalloped potatoes and scalloped apples, if your oven can take 3 casseroles. If not, substitute cut green beans for the apples.*


## SHOULDER LAMB CHOPS BERMUDA

6 shoulder lamb chops cut 1½
  inches thick
  Salt and pepper
2 tablespoons butter, margarine,
  or salad oil

6 medium onions sliced
2 cups chicken stock or water
12 tiny new potatoes sliced
2 teaspoons chopped parsley

1. Season the chops well and brown in hot butter in a large heavy skillet or directly in the casserole in which they will be baked, if you have one that large. Drain off excess fat.
2. Add the onions and stock or water to the casserole and bake 25-30 minutes in a 325° oven, covered.
3. Add the potatoes and parsley to the casserole, check seasoning, cover again, and continue to bake 25-30 minutes longer, or until potatoes are tender. Serves 6.

*Serve with young zucchini, sliced but not peeled, and sautéed gently in sweet butter until done—8-10 minutes.*

# PORK

## CALIFORNIA PORK CHOPS

6 loin or rib pork chops 1 inch thick
Salt and pepper
¼ cup flour
Salad oil
2 oranges peeled and sliced
5 tablespoons brown sugar
2 teaspoons cornstarch

½ cup chicken stock, white wine, or water
1 cup orange juice
½ teaspoon dried marjoram or 1½ teaspoons fresh, chopped
2 medium onions sliced
2 tablespoons chopped parsley

ORANGES and pork make a delightful combination, and this recipe makes the most of it.

1. Trim excess fat from chops and try out the pieces in a heavy skillet. Skim out and discard the scraps when they are brown.

2. Season the chops to taste, roll lightly in the flour, and brown well in the hot fat, adding a little oil if there is not enough fat from the pork fat pieces.

3. Arrange the browned chops in a large shallow casserole, preferably one that will enable you to crowd them in one layer.

4. Sprinkle the orange slices with 3 tablespoons of the brown sugar and let them stand.

5. Blend the cornstarch with the stock or wine, the orange juice, marjoram, and the rest of the brown sugar. Pour this mixture over the chops in the casserole and arrange the onions on top.

6. Sprinkle the onions with parsley, cover, and bake 1 hour in a 350° oven.

7. Arrange the orange slices on top and bake 15 minutes more, uncovered. Serves 6.

*Serve with creamy mashed potatoes and buttered French-cut string beans, along with a plain tossed salad.*

# CARBONNADES OF PORK

3 pounds shoulder of pork, boned
½ cup flour
¼ teaspoon fresh-ground pepper
6 tablespoons butter, margarine,
    or salad oil

3 pounds medium onions sliced
½ teaspoon dried thyme or 1½
    teaspoons fresh, chopped
1 small bay leaf
1 pint beer

1. Trim off excess fat from the pork, cut in 2-inch cubes, and shake in a paper bag with the flour, 2 teaspoons salt, and the pepper. Shake off excess flour, leaving a thin coating on the meat.
2. Try out the fat trimmings in a heavy casserole and skim out the pieces when they are brown. Brown the pork cubes well in the fat.
3. In a skillet melt the butter and lightly brown the onions in it. Salt sparingly. Stir in the thyme, bay leaf, and beer and pour over the pork in the casserole.
4. Cover and bake 1½-2 hours in a slow oven, 300°.
5. If the sauce is too thin for your taste, drain it into a small saucepan and thicken slightly with either flour and water paste or beurre manié (flour and butter kneaded together). Return the sauce to the casserole. Serves 6-8.

*Serve with fluffy rice and scalloped apples.*

# CHINESE PORK PIE

2 cups cold roast pork cut in
    1-inch dice
1 clove garlic minced
1 leek minced (white part only) or
    1 tablespoon minced onion
2 tablespoons butter or margarine
1½ cups leftover pork gravy
    Salt and pepper
1 small bay leaf crushed

2 cloves
1 medium carrot sliced thin
½ cup sliced water chestnuts
1 cup canned bean sprouts
1 apple pared and chopped
2 cups hot mashed sweet potatoes
1 tablespoon brown sugar
2 teaspoons butter or margarine

1. Sauté garlic and leek or onion in hot fat until lightly brown. Stir in pork cubes and brown lightly.
2. Add gravy, seasonings, and carrot. If gravy is pretty thick thin it out a bit with water or dry white wine.
3. When the gravy comes to a boil stir in water chestnuts, bean sprouts, and apple. All of this can be done in a medium casserole, but if it has been done in a skillet pour into a casserole now and put in a moderate oven, 350°, for 10 minutes.
4. Remove casserole from the oven and carefully top with hot mashed sweet potatoes, adding them by small tablespoonfuls and then smoothing over to make a solid top. Sprinkle with the brown sugar, dot with butter, and bake 10 minutes more. Serves 6.

*Serve with glazed carrots and a tossed green salad.*

## FLANDERS PORK AND APPLES

2 pounds pork shoulder or loin
   sliced ½-inch thick
12 small white onions
2 tablespoons flour
½ cup dry white wine
½ cup chicken broth or condensed
   consommé

Salt and pepper to taste
1 teaspoon dried orégano and
   rosemary mixed or 1 tablespoon
   fresh, chopped
1 teaspoon minced parsley
1 pound tart cooking apples
   peeled and quartered

1. Trim fat off the pork slices and try out in a heavy skillet. Skim out the brown particles, and sauté in the fat the pork and onions. Remove to a medium casserole.
2. If there is much fat left in the skillet pour it out and measure back 2 tablespoons. Stir in the flour and slowly add the wine and broth, stirring until the sauce is smooth and thick.
3. Season the sauce to taste with salt and pepper, add the herbs, and pour over the casserole. Cover tightly and bake 2 hours in a slow oven, 300°. (If your casserole lid does not fit tightly cover the casserole first with heavy brown paper and then put on the lid.)
4. When the casserole has baked 1½ hours stir in the apples, cover again, and finish baking. Serves 6.

*Serve with mashed sweet potatoes and buttered cut green beans.*

# FRENCH MEAT PIE

1 pound lean pork shoulder ground
½ pound lean veal shoulder ground
¾ teaspoon salt
½ teaspoon dry mustard
½ clove garlic mashed
1 small bay leaf crumbled

¼ teaspoon dried marjoram or
   ¾ teaspoon fresh, chopped
¼ teaspoon dried thyme or ¾
   teaspoon fresh, chopped
Pastry for 10-inch 2-crust pie

1. Mix the ground meats (have the butcher grind them together) with salt, mustard, garlic, and bay leaf. Brown in a hot, dry skillet 2-3 minutes, stirring constantly.
2. Cover, reduce heat, and simmer over lowest possible heat about 25 minutes, stirring occasionally.
3. Stir in marjoram and thyme, correct seasoning, and cool a little.
4. Roll out a bit over half the pastry to ⅛ inch thickness and line a 10-inch pie plate with it. Spread the meat mixture evenly in it. Roll out the remaining pastry and lay over the meat.
5. Seal the edges by moistening and pinching together to form a rim and gash the crust several times to permit steam to escape.
6. Bake the pie 40-45 minutes in a hot oven, 425°, or until pastry is golden. Serve hot or cold. Serves 6-8.

*If hot, serve with buttered beets cut in julienne strips and fresh corn on the cob or buttered cut corn. If cold, serve with hot mixed vegetables and a tossed green salad.*

# PORK CHOPS IN CIDER

6 loin pork chops cut 1 inch thick
2 tablespoons butter, margarine, or
   salad oil
¾ cup cider
½ cup water
3 medium onions chopped fine

½ teaspoon dried sweet basil or
   1½ teaspoons fresh, chopped
½ teaspoon dried sweet marjoram
   or 1½ teaspoons fresh, chopped
Salt and pepper to taste
Paprika

1. Heat the butter in a large heavy casserole and brown the chops well on both sides. (If you do not have a casserole large enough to take them all do them three at a time and arrange in 2 overlapping layers.)

2. Pour over the chops the cider and water and spread over the chopped onions, pushing them into the spaces where you can.

3. Sprinkle with herbs, salt and pepper, and paprika, cover, and bake 45 minutes to an hour in a 350° oven. Serves 6.

*Note:* If you want a thicker sauce than this provides, drain off the liquid into a small saucepan, thicken it to taste with flour-and-water paste, and pour back on the chops.

*Serve with hot fluffy rice and glacé carrots.*


## PORK CHOPS NICOISE

6 pork chops 1 inch thick
4 medium ripe tomatoes, peeled, seeded, and chopped
3 small cloves of garlic mashed
1 medium green pepper minced

1 teaspoon dried basil or 1 table-spoon fresh, chopped
Salt and pepper
½ cup ripe olives pitted or cut off pits

This is a different way of cooking pork chops that should prove popular for the Mediterranean flavor.

1. Remove excess fat from chops, try out in a heavy skillet, skim out the browned pieces, and brown the chops well in the fat, on both sides. Arrange in a rather shallow casserole large enough to hold them in one layer.

2. Mix the remaining ingredients, except the olives, season to taste, and spread over the chops. Cover and bake 35 minutes in a slow oven, 325°.

3. Stir in the olives and bake 10 minutes longer, uncovered. Serves 6.

*Serve with plenty of fresh hot rice, buttered and mixed with a lot of coarsely chopped parsley. Buttered green peas and a tossed green salad will complete the meal.*

# PORK NORMANDY

1½ pounds pork shoulder cut in
   1-inch cubes
   Salt and pepper
1 cup chopped onion
1 clove garlic crushed

2 cups applesauce
2 tablespoons tomato purée
¼ teaspoon dried rosemary or
   ¾ teaspoon fresh, chopped

As in other recipes in this section, the flavor of the pork is brought out by apples.

1. Remove what excess fat you can from the pork and try it out in a heavy casserole. Remove the browned bits and brown the pork cubes well on all sides in the fat. Season with salt and pepper and arrange in medium casserole.

2. In the fat remaining in the skillet brown the onion and garlic very lightly.

3. Stir in the applesauce, tomato purée, and rosemary, season to taste, and spread over the meat in the casserole.

4. Cover and bake in a 350° oven about 50 minutes. Uncover and continue baking 15-20 minutes longer. Serves 4-6.

*Serve with buttered noodles and buttered broccoli.*

# ORANGE-GLAZED STUFFED PORK CHOPS

4 double loin pork chops

Salt and pepper

*Stuffing*

½ cup seasoned crumbs
2 teaspoons minced parsley
1 teaspoon grated orange peel

½ teaspoon salt
½ teaspoon Worcestershire sauce
¼ teaspoon pepper

*Glaze*

½ cup orange juice
4 tablespoons brown sugar

4 tablespoons orange marmalade
2 tablespoons cider vinegar

1. Trim off excess fat from the chops, wipe them, and cut a pocket in each one clear to the bone—or have the butcher cut the pocket.
2. Mix the stuffing ingredients in a small bowl and fill the pockets in the chops. Fasten the edges together with several toothpicks and secure them by running a piece of twine in and out and tieing it around the back of each chop.
3. Salt and pepper the chops lightly and arrange them in a casserole which will hold them comfortably.
4. Put the casserole in a 375° oven, bake it for 15 minutes, turn the chops, and bake 15 minutes more.
5. Mix the glaze ingredients and simmer, uncovered, 10 minutes while the chops are baking. Pour over the chops and bake an additional 30 minutes, basting with a baster every 10 minutes. Serves 4.

*Serve with riced potatoes, buttered baby Brussels sprouts, and a green salad.*

## PORK CHOPS WITH WHITE WINE

| | |
|---|---|
| 6 loin pork chops 1 inch thick | 4 tablespoons butter or margarine |
| ¾ teaspoon dry mustard | 1 large onion sliced |
| 1 teaspoon salt | ¾ cup dry white wine |
| ½ teaspoon fresh-ground pepper | |

1. Blend the mustard, salt, and pepper and season the chops with the mixture.
2. Heat 2 tablespoons of the butter in a heavy skillet and brown the chops well on both sides. Remove them to a casserole, preferably one that will hold them in a single layer.
3. Add remaining butter to the skillet and sauté the onion until soft but not brown. Spread over the chops and fill spaces with them.
4. Clean out the skillet with the wine and pour over the chops. Cover and bake 1 hour in a 325° oven.

The sauce is very good as is but, if you prefer, drain the liquid from the casserole into a small saucepan and thicken slightly with flour-and-water paste. Serves 6.

*Serve with rice, and corn pudding, plus a tossed green salad.*

# SOUTH SEAS PORK

2 pounds pork loin cut in 1-inch
  cubes
2 tablespoons flour
3 tablespoons cornstarch
6 tablespoons soy sauce
½ cup salad oil
1 green pepper sliced
2 medium onions sliced thin
1 carrot sliced thin

4-ounce can bamboo shoots
8½-ounce can pineapple chunks
  (or 1 package frozen)
¼ cup sugar
2 tablespoons vinegar
¼ cup tomato sauce
¾ cup condensed consommé
  or ½ water and ½ consommé
Salt and pepper

THIS is a delectable casserole, spicy and mouth-watering.

1. In a good-sized bowl put the flour, 2 tablespoons of the cornstarch, and 1 tablespoon of the soy sauce. Mix them well. Add the meat cubes and stir until the flour mixture is evenly distributed on them.

2. Heat the oil in a heavy skillet and brown the pork pieces all over. Arrange in a medium casserole.

3. Drain off the remaining oil and measure back 2 tablespoons into the skillet. In this sauté lightly the green pepper, onions, carrot, bamboo shoots, and pineapple. Stir in the sugar, the rest of the soy sauce, vinegar, tomato sauce, consommé, and salt and pepper to taste.

4. Add this mixture to the pork in the casserole, cover, and bake 30 minutes in a 350° oven.

5. Mix the remaining tablespoon of cornstarch with a little water and stir into the casserole. If the sauce is not as thick as you like, add a bit more cornstarch-water paste. Correct seasoning and bake another 15 minutes, uncovered. Serves 4-6.

*Serve with corn on the cob and buttered lima beans.*


# SAUSAGE-APPLE-NOODLE CASSEROLE

1 pound pork sausage links
3 cups noodles cooked
1 cup sweetened applesauce

2 teaspoons lemon juice
⅛ teaspoon nutmeg
½ cup grated Cheddar cheese

1. Prick the sausages well with a sharp-tined fork, lay them in a pan, and bake in a 400° oven 25 minutes. Turn once or twice to brown evenly. Drain on paper toweling.
2. Stir 2 tablespoons of the pork drippings into the noodles and arrange half of them in a greased medium casserole.
3. Combine the applesauce, lemon juice, and nutmeg and pour on top of the noodles. Add the rest of the noodles and lay the sausages on top.
4. Sprinkle with cheese and bake 20 minutes at 350°, uncovered. Serves 4-5.

*Serve with buttered green peas and warm garlic bread.*


## SAUSAGE PUDDING

| | |
|---|---|
| 1½ pounds country sausage meat | ¼ teaspoon dried thyme or |
| 1 tablespoon salad oil | ¾ teaspoon fresh, chopped |
| 3 eggs | Dash cayenne pepper |
| 1½ cups milk | ¼ teaspoon salt |
| 1½ cups flour | |

A REMARKABLY simple and delicious dish, especially for luncheon or Sunday-night supper.
1. Roll the sausage meat into small balls, about the size of a walnut.
2. Heat the oil in a heavy casserole of medium size and brown the sausage balls lightly on all sides. If the sausage meat is unusually fat, drain the fat from the casserole and pour back 3 tablespoons of it.
3. Make a batter by combining the eggs, milk, flour, thyme, cayenne, and salt. Pour over the sausages and bake in a hot oven, 450°, 15 minutes.
4. Lower the heat to 350° and continue to bake 15-20 minutes, or until the pudding is puffy and brown. Serves 5-6.

*Serve with mixed vegetables and a plain tossed green salad.*

# VEAL

## BAKED VEAL CUTLETS

2 pounds veal cutlets ½ inch thick
6 slices bacon
1 egg
2 tablespoons water
½ cup bread or corn flake crumbs

½ cup minced onions
1 teaspoon Worcestershire sauce
2 cans condensed cream of
   mushroom soup
Buttered crumbs

1. Wipe the veal and cut it into 8 serving pieces.
2. Cook the bacon in a heavy skillet until crisp. Skim out and reserve.
3. Combine the egg and water and beat lightly with a fork. Dip the pieces of veal first into this and then into the crumbs.
4. Brown the veal quickly on both sides in the bacon fat left in the skillet. Arrange in a casserole, crumble the bacon over it, and scatter the onions on top.
5. Stir the Worcestershire sauce into the soup and pour over the casserole.
6. Top with buttered crumbs and bake, covered, in a 350° oven 30-40 minutes, or until the veal is tender. Serves 8.

*Serve with buttered noodles with poppy seeds and slivered almonds added and buttered whole young green beans.*

## BALKAN VEAL STEW WITH ALMONDS

2 pounds shoulder veal cut in
   1-inch cubes
½ cup flour
2 teaspoons salt
½ teaspoon fresh-ground pepper
¼ cup salad oil
1 large onion chopped

¼ pound mushrooms sliced or
   4-ounce can drained
1½ cups dry white wine
2 tablespoons paprika
¼ cup water
1 cup dairy sour cream
½ cup blanched and toasted
   slivered almonds

1.  Put half of the flour, half of the salt, and the pepper in a paper bag and shake the pieces of veal well in it.
2.  Heat the oil in a large skillet and brown the veal well on all sides. Remove to a medium casserole.
3.  In the fat remaining in the casserole brown the onion and mushrooms slightly. Stir in the wine, paprika, and remaining salt. Pour over the casserole and bake 1 hour at 375°, covered.
4.  Make a paste of the remaining ¼ cup of flour and the water. Remove the casserole from the oven and thicken the sauce with the paste.
5.  Stir in the sour cream and almonds and return to the oven for 5 minutes. Serves 6.

*Serve with fresh boiled rice, green peas, and a green salad.*

## BRAISED VEAL CHOPS À LA CHARTRES

6 veal chops 1 inch thick
3 tablespoons butter, margarine, or salad oil
   Salt and pepper
4 tablespoons minced onion
2 cups fine bread or corn flake crumbs
1 cup grated Parmesan cheese
1 cup dry white wine

HERE is an extremely simple way to make veal chops outstanding fare.
1.  Melt the butter in a heavy skillet, season the chops well, and brown them well on both sides. Arrange in a shallow casserole, preferably in one layer.
2.  Sauté the onion lightly in the fat remaining in the skillet. Stir in crumbs and cheese. If the mixture seems very dry blend in 1-2 tablespoons of the wine.
3.  Pat this mixture carefully onto the chops, heaping it smoothly. Pour in the wine carefully, so as not to disturb the topping.
4.  Cover and bake 1½ hours at 375°. Baste the chops every 15 or 20 minutes and add a bit of water if they dry out. Serves 6.

*Serve with a rice casserole (see Index), buttered cut string beans, and a tossed green salad.*

# BLANQUETTE OF VEAL

2 pounds rump of veal cut in
1-inch cubes
12-15 small white onions peeled,
or 1-pound can
3 medium carrots cut in large
pieces
1½ teaspoons salt
Herb bouquet (2 pieces celery,
3 sprigs parsley, small bay
leaf, and ¼ teaspoon dried

thyme tied loosely in
cheesecloth)
1 pound mushrooms (halved
or quartered if large)
Juice of 1 lemon
2 tablespoons butter
2 tablespoons flour
2 egg yolks
1 cup light cream

1. Cover the veal with water and parboil it 5 minutes. Drain, rinse
in cold water, and spread in a medium casserole.
2. Add the onions if raw (add later if canned), the carrots, 1 teaspoon of the salt, the herb bouquet, and 1 quart of water. Bring to a
boil on top of the stove and simmer 1-1½ hours, or until tender.
3. Put the mushrooms in a saucepan with ½ cup of water, the lemon
juice, and the remaining ½ teaspoon salt. Bring to a boil and remove
from the heat at once. Let them stand a few minutes to marinate.
4. When the veal is done, drain the liquid in which it was cooked
into a saucepan and boil hard until it is reduced to about ⅓ of the
original quantity.
5. In a separate saucepan melt the butter, blend in the flour, and cook
until it begins to color. Blend in both the reduced veal liquid (discard
the herb bouquet) and the liquid drained from the mushrooms. Cook
until smooth and thickened, stirring constantly.
6. Beat the egg yolks slightly with the cream and blend into the
sauce. Do not allow it to boil. Add sauce and mushrooms to casserole
and check seasoning. Serves 6-8.

*Serve with plenty of hot fluffy rice to take up the wonderful sauce and
buttered baby green peas. A tossed green salad and warm garlic bread
will complete an outstanding meal.*

# EXOTIC VEAL

2 pounds veal shoulder cut in
  1-inch cubes
2 teaspoons Kitchen Bouquet
2 tablespoons butter, margarine,
  or salad oil
¾ cup chopped onions
¼ pound mushrooms sliced or
  6-ounce can
1 cup water, white wine, or
  chicken broth
2 tablespoons light brown sugar
¼ cup vinegar

1 teaspoon ground ginger
1 teaspoon dry mustard
1 teaspoon salt
¼ teaspoon fresh-ground pepper
1 tablespoon cornstarch
2 tablespoons water
2 tablespoons dry red wine
1½ cups moist flaked coconut
  (optional)
5-ounce can water chestnuts
  sliced thin

THIS is a fussy casserole that you might not tackle for an ordinary family dinner, but it is delicious beyond words, and is a wonderful company dish, especially since it can be put together except for the last step even a day ahead.

1. Spread out the cubes of veal on waxed paper and brush all of them with Kitchen Bouquet, using a pastry brush.

2. Heat the butter in a heavy skillet and brown the veal on all sides, a few pieces at a time so as not to crowd the skillet. Transfer the pieces to a good-sized casserole as they are browned.

3. In the fat remaining in the skillet lightly sauté the onions and mushrooms and spread them over the meat in the casserole.

4. Add the 1 cup liquid, sugar, vinegar, ginger, mustard, salt, and pepper to the skillet. Clean out all the brown particles and pour over the casserole.

5. Cover and bake 1 hour in a 325° oven, or until the meat is very tender.

6. Mix the cornstarch with the 2 tablespoons water and stir in.

7. Add the wine, coconut, and water chestnuts and bake 10-15 minutes longer. Serves 5-6, but can be doubled or tripled.

*Serve with lots of hot fluffy rice and a salad made of cold cooked vegetables: peas, corn, lima beans, cut green beans, asparagus, etc.*

# CÔTES DE VEAU FOYOT

4 veal cutlets
½ cup chopped onion
3 tablespoons butter or margarine
¼ cup dry white wine
¼ cup chicken broth

Salt and pepper
¼ cup each Parmesan and Gruyère
cheese, grated (scant)
Bread or corn flake crumbs

THIS is an adaptation of a classic French dish, from a famous restaurant.

1. Cook the onion slowly in butter until golden. Stir in the wine and chicken broth.

2. Season the veal with salt and pepper. Mix the grated cheeses and roll the chops first in the cheese and then in the crumbs.

3. Put a thin layer of crumbs in a shallow casserole. Lay the cutlets on them and cover with the cooked onion and their liquid. Cook uncovered in a very slow oven, 275°, about an hour, adding a bit of chicken broth occasionally. Serves 4.

*Serve with fluffy mashed potatoes and buttered baby green peas.*


# HUNGARIAN VEAL

1½ pounds veal steak cut in
   1-inch pieces
¼ cup flour
3 tablespoons butter, margarine
   or salad oil
1 clove garlic crushed
2 tablespoons minced onion

1 tablespoon chopped parsley
½ teaspoon salt
½ teaspoon paprika
¼ teaspoon celery salt
1 cup chicken stock
½ cup sour cream

Roll or shake the veal pieces in flour and brown well in butter in a heavy skillet. Add the garlic and onion while the veal is browning. Stir in remaining ingredients except sour cream and pour into a medium casserole. Cover and bake 45-50 minutes in a slow oven, 325°.

Just before serving stir in the sour cream and reheat. Serves 4.

*Serve with buttered noodles to which you have added poppy seeds and slivered almonds. For a vegetable, slice unpeeled zucchini and sauté gently, with a bit of minced onion, in a covered skillet, until tender but still crisp, 10-12 minutes.*

## HUNGARIAN VEAL ROLLS

8 veal cutlets about 5" x 2½" x ¼"
¼ pound lean beef ground
¼ pound lean pork ground
2 tablespoons bread or corn
  flake crumbs
¼ cup light cream
1 egg
1½ teaspoons salt
¼ teaspoon pepper
1 tablespoon minced onion

3 tablespoons minced parsley
3 tablespoons butter, margarine,
  or salad oil
4-ounce can sliced mushrooms
1 cup condensed consommé and
  red or white wine mixed
¾ cup dairy sour cream
1 teaspoon sugar
1 teaspoon Worcestershire sauce

THIS looks like a lot of ingredients, but is actually an easy casserole to make and an especially good one.

1. Mix the ground beef and pork with the crumbs, light cream, egg, salt and pepper, onion, and parsley.

2. Trim the cutlets, pounding them between sheets of waxed paper if more than ¼ inch thick.

3. Divide the ground meat mixture among them, roll up, and skewer with toothpicks or tie with twine.

4. Heat the butter in a heavy skillet and brown the rolls well. Transfer them to a medium casserole, stir in mushrooms and their liquid, as well as the consommé mixture, cover, and bake 45 minutes in a 325° oven. Remove the cover 15 minutes before the time is up.

5. Remove the rolls from the casserole and unskewer or untie them.

6. Before returning them to the casserole stir into the sauce the sour cream, sugar, and Worcestershire sauce. Reheat. Serves 4.

*Serve with buttered noodles to which a tablespoon of poppy seeds have been added, and buttered cut green beans.*

# ROQUEFORT VEAL BIRDS

1½ pounds veal cutlet
  ¼ inch thick
½ cup butter or margarine
1 tablespoon minced onion
1 cup dry bread or corn flake
  crumbs
1 teaspoon minced parsley
½ teaspoon dried orégano or
  1½ teaspoons fresh, chopped
½ teaspoon dried basil or
  1½ teaspoons fresh, chopped

½ teaspoon salt
⅛ teaspoon pepper
4 tablespoons finely crumbled
  Roquefort or other blue cheese
3 tablespoons flour
2 tablespoons paprika
½ medium green pepper coarsely
  chopped
3½-ounce can sliced mushrooms
1 cup chicken broth or water

THERE are many ways of making veal birds. This one, with its deli-cate blue cheese flavor, is quite unusual.

1. Cut the veal into 6 pieces, about 5 by 3 inches. However, if it has been sliced more than ¼ inch thick, cut it a little smaller, lay the pieces between sheets of waxed paper, and pound them thinner, using a wooden mallet or a rolling pin.

2. Heat half the butter in a skillet and cook the onion just until it begins to color, stirring frequently.

3. Stir in the crumbs, herbs, salt, pepper, and cheese, mixing well.

4. Lay out the pieces of veal and divide the crumb mixture among them, placing it toward one end. Roll up and tie with twine or fasten with toothpicks.

5. Dredge the rolls with flour and brown in the rest of the butter. Arrange in a casserole large enough to take them in one layer but not too deep.

6. Sprinkle with paprika and spread the green pepper and mushrooms on top.

7. Clean out the skillet with the chicken broth, and pour over the rolls. Cover and bake 45 minutes in a 350° oven. Serves 6.

*Serve with herbed rice and cole slaw.*

# TARRAGON VEAL

4 pounds shoulder veal cut in
   1-inch cubes
¼ cup butter, margarine, or
   salad oil
⅓ cup flour
1½ cups dry white wine
1¾ cups boiling water
2 teaspoons salt

¼ pound sliced mushrooms
   lightly sautéed
4 teaspoons dried tarragon or
   4 tablespoons fresh, chopped
2 medium onions chopped
4 egg yolks
1 cup sour cream
4 tablespoons tarragon vinegar
¼ cup chopped parsley

A HEARTY dish for a buffet meal.

1. Melt butter in a large heavy skillet and brown the meat cubes, removing them as they brown, and being careful not to fill the skillet too full at a time. Return all the meat to the skillet when the last pieces are browned.

2. Sprinkle the flour over, stir well, and when the flour is all absorbed add the wine and water slowly, stirring constantly.

3. Add the salt, mushrooms, tarragon, and onions, cook a moment, and transfer to a large heavy casserole. Cover tightly and bake 2 hours in a slow oven, 275°.

4. Mix the egg yolks with the sour cream. Remove the casserole from the oven briefly and stir in the sour cream mixture and the vinegar.

5. Return to the oven for 5-10 minutes, uncovered, long enough to thicken the sauce. Sprinkle with parsley just before serving. Serves 10-12.

*Serve with lots of fluffy hot rice, a large salad with grated carrot, tomato wedges, sliced unpeeled cucumbers, and a sliced avocado, plus greens. Have plenty of warm garlic bread available.*

# SAVORY VEAL

4 pounds veal cut in 2-inch cubes
½ cup flour
2 teaspoons salt
½ teaspoon fresh-ground pepper
¼-½ cup salad oil
2 large onions chopped
4 medium carrots diced
4 sticks celery cut in diagonal
   ¼-inch slices
Bouquet garni (2 sprigs parsley,
¼ teaspoon each orégano, basil,
   and rosemary tied in cheesecloth)
2 cups chicken broth
½ cup dry white wine
4 medium tomatoes skinned and
   chopped or 1 can Italian-style
1 large clove garlic mashed
2 tablespoons chopped parsley
2 teaspoons grated lemon rind
2 tablespoons lemon juice

THIS big hearty casserole is a good choice for a buffet dinner.

1. Shake the veal pieces in a paper bag in which you have put the flour, salt, and pepper—a few pieces at a time.

2. Heat half the oil to sizzling in a heavy skillet and brown the meat, being careful not to crowd the skillet too much at a time. Add more oil as you need it. Arrange the meat in a large casserole.

3. In the same skillet sauté lightly the onions, carrots, and celery, and spread them over the meat.

4. Add to the skillet the herb bouquet, chicken broth, wine, tomatoes, and garlic. Let cook 2-3 minutes and pour over the meat.

5. Cover the casserole and bake 1¾ hours in a slow oven, 300°. Uncover the last 20 minutes. About halfway through, check the seasoning and stir.

6. Just before serving stir in the parsley, lemon rind and lemon juice and remove the herb bag. Serves 10-12.

*Serve with plenty of fluffy rice to absorb the good sauce, succotash, a tossed green salad, and warm garlic bread.*

# VEAL CUTLETS WITH COINTREAU

2 pounds veal cutlets
   Salt and pepper
3 tablespoons butter, margarine,
   or salad oil
2 tablespoons flour
1 cup chicken broth
4 teaspoons Cointreau liqueur
1 tablespoon lemon juice

THE Cointreau here performs real magic on the veal.

1. Divide the cutlets into 6 pieces. They should be quite thin, and can be made so by laying the pieces between sheets of waxed paper and pounding them with a wooden mallet or a rolling pin.

2. Season the cutlets and brown them quickly in sizzling fat in a heavy skillet. Lay them in a shallow casserole.

3. Stir the flour into the fat left in the skillet and brown it lightly. Slowly stir in the chicken broth, Cointreau, and lemon juice. Check seasoning and pour over cutlets.

4. Bake 20 minutes in a 350° oven. Serves 6.

*Serve with a rice casserole (see Index), green peas, and a tossed green salad.*

## VEAL CASSEROLE WITH WHITE WINE

| | |
|---|---|
| 2 pounds veal cutlet cut in strips 2" x ½" | 1 cup chicken broth |
| | 1 cup dry white wine |
| 1 tablespoon salad oil | 2 dozen little white onions, or |
| 3 tablespoons butter or margarine | 1-pound can |
| 3 tablespoons flour | 1 small bay leaf |
| ¾ teaspoon salt | ¼ cup minced parsley |
| ⅛ teaspoon pepper | ½ pound small whole mushrooms |

1. Heat the oil and 1 tablespoon of the butter in a heavy skillet and brown the meat strips well in it. Skim the pieces out with a slotted spoon and arrange them in a medium casserole.

2. Blend the flour into the butter remaining in the casserole, stir in the salt, pepper, and chicken broth, and keep stirring until the sauce is thick and smooth.

3. Add the wine, onions (if raw), bay leaf, and parsley, season to taste, and pour over the casserole.

4. Cover and bake in a 325° oven one hour, or until the meat is very tender. (If you use the canned little white onions add them about halfway through the cooking.)

5. Melt the rest of the butter in the skillet and gently sauté the mushrooms. Stir them into the casserole about 15 minutes before you are ready to serve. Serves 6.

## VEAL CHOPS IN CREAM

6 veal chops 1 inch thick
6 tablespoons butter
3 tablespoons warmed brandy
  (optional)
¾ cup sliced mushrooms
3 tablespoons flour
1 cup chicken broth or water
1 teaspoon meat glacé

1 cup heavy cream
Salt and pepper
1 small bay leaf
¼ teaspoon dried thyme or
  ¾ teaspoon fresh
Parmesan cheese
Butter or margarine

1. Brown the chops quickly in hot butter, pour over them the barely warmed brandy, and flame them. (Or light the brandy before you pour it, pouring it flaming.) Arrange the chops in a shallow casserole.
2. In the fat left in the skillet sauté the mushrooms lightly. Sprinkle with flour, and gradually add the chicken broth and glacé. Let it come to a boil.
3. Stir in the cream, salt and pepper to taste, bay leaf, and thyme.
4. Pour over the meat in the casserole, cover, and bake in a slow oven, 300°, 1 hour.
5. Sprinkle with Parmesan cheese, dot with butter, and brown under the broiler. Serves 6.

*Serve with fluffy mashed potatoes and buttered green peas.*


## VEAL MARENGO

2½ pounds veal shoulder cut in
  1½-inch cubes
3 tablespoons flour
1½ teaspoons salt
3 tablespoons salad oil
2 tablespoons minced onion
6 small white onions
1 clove garlic mashed
1-pound-4-ounce can tomatoes,
  drained

1 cup chicken broth
1 cup dry white wine
¼ teaspoon pepper
12 mushroom caps lightly sautéed
  in butter
½ cup heavy cream or dairy
  sour cream
3 tablespoons flour
6 tablespoons water

1. Put the flour and salt in a paper bag and shake the veal pieces in it. Brown them on all sides in hot oil and arrange in a good-sized casserole.
2. In the fat remaining in the skillet lightly brown the minced onion, the whole onions, and the garlic. Stir in the tomatoes, chicken broth, wine, and pepper. Bring to a boil and pour over the casserole.
3. Cover and bake 1½ hours in a 300° oven.
4. Stir in the sautéed mushroom caps and bake 20-25 minutes longer.
5. Stir in the cream. Transfer the casserole to the top of the stove, over low heat.
6. Mix the flour and water into a paste and stir in to thicken the sauce. Serves 8.

*Serve with plain spaghetti mixed with grated Parmesan or Romano cheese and a large tossed green salad mixed with grated carrots and sliced unpeeled cucumber. Warm garlic bread goes well with this meal.*

## VEAL ROLLS WITH ANCHOVIES

| | |
|---|---|
| 1 pound veal cutlets cut as thin as possible | ½ cup butter |
| | ½ cup condensed consommé |
| ¼ pound mozzarella cheese | 1 teaspoon chopped parsley |
| 2-ounce can anchovy fillets | |

1. Cut the veal into 3″ x 5″ pieces, lay between sheets of waxed paper, and pound thinner with a wooden mallet or a rolling pin.
2. Cut the cheese into as many pieces as you have veal pieces. On each veal piece lay a piece of cheese and an anchovy fillet. Roll up and tie with a string or fasten with toothpicks.
3. Heat half the butter in a heavy skillet and brown the rolls lightly in it. Add 2 tablespoons consommé and let the rolls simmer in it about 10 minutes. Arrange in a shallow casserole.
4. Add remaining butter to the skillet and remaining consommé, bring to a boil, and pour over the veal rolls.
5. Bake, uncovered, about 15 minutes in a 325° oven. Serves 4.

*Serve with buttered noodles and broccoli with a butter-lemon-crumb sauce.*

# VEAL CHOPS WITH NOODLES

4 veal chops 1 inch thick
1 egg beaten a little with
  1 tablespoon water
  Bread or corn flake crumbs
¼ cup butter, margarine, or
  salad oil

3 cups Mornay sauce
3 cups hot buttered green noodles
6 tablespoons grated Parmesan
  cheese

*Mornay Sauce*

6 tablespoons butter
4 tablespoons flour
2½ cups milk scalded

3 egg yolks lightly beaten
6 tablespoons heavy cream
  whipped

1. With a sharp knife cut the bones from the chops. Lay the meat between sheets of waxed paper and pound to ⅛-inch thickness with a wooden mallet or a rolling pin.
2. Dip the chops in the egg and then in the crumbs. Cook them to a golden brown in sizzling butter in a heavy skillet. They should be very tender.
3. To make the Mornay sauce, melt the butter, stir in the flour, and gradually add the scalded milk. Season to taste. When the sauce is thick and smooth remove it from the heat and stir in the egg yolks and whipped cream.
4. Spread the cooked noodles in a large casserole. Lay the chops on top and cover with the Mornay sauce.
5. Top with cheese and broil until well browned. Serves 4.


# VEAL SCALOPPINI

1½ pounds veal cutlets
  ¾ cup grated Parmesan and
    Romano cheeses mixed
  3 tablespoons flour

¼ teaspoon dried marjoram or
  ¾ teaspoon fresh, chopped
  ⅛ teaspoon pepper
  4 tablespoons salad oil
1½ cups condensed consommé

1. Cut the meat into 8 pieces, lay them between sheets of waxed paper, and pound very thin with a wooden mallet or rolling pin.
2. Mix in a large soup plate half the cheese, the flour, the marjoram, and the pepper (salt is usually unnecessary). Coat the veal pieces with the mixture as heavily as you can.
3. Heat the oil in a heavy skillet and sauté the veal pieces to a golden brown on both sides, a few at a time.
4. Arrange in a casserole, in 2 layers, and pour over the consommé. Cover and bake 15 minutes in a 325° oven.
5. Sprinkle the casserole with the remaining cheese and put under the broiler until well browned, watching carefully to avoid burning. Serves 4.

*Serve with spinach noodles and buttered baby carrots.*

## VEAL MAYACAMAS

1 pound veal steaks cut
 ½-inch thick
1-pound slice ready-to-eat
 ham ½ inch thick
1 cup rosé or white wine
¼ cup butter, margarine, or
 salad oil
4 carrots cut in 1-inch rounds

¼ pound mushrooms sliced
2 tablespoons capers
2-ounce can anchovy fillets
 drained and halved
½ teaspoon rosemary and
 orégano mixed
1 cup dairy sour cream

1. Cut the veal in 1-inch squares. Trim fat from the ham and cut it into strips 1½ inches by ½ inch. Put both in a bowl, pour the wine over, and let them marinate at least 1 hour. Drain and save the marinade.
2. Heat the butter in a heavy skillet and brown both meats lightly.
3. Add the marinade, carrots, mushrooms, capers, and anchovies, stirring gently.
4. Pour into a medium casserole, sprinkle the herb mixture on top, and bake, uncovered, in a 300° oven 30 minutes.
5. Pour the liquid from the casserole into a saucepan, blend in the sour cream, and thicken with a flour-and-water paste if you so desire. Pour back on the casserole. Serves 6.

# VEAL SCALOPPINI WITH SOUR CREAM AND WINE

2 pounds veal cutlets
3 tablespoons flour
1 teaspoon salt
⅛ teaspoon pepper
¼ cup butter, margarine, or
 salad oil
1 cup chopped onion

½ pound coarsely chopped
 mushrooms
1 teaspoon dried marjoram or
 1 tablespoon fresh, chopped
1 cup dry white wine
1 cup dairy sour cream
Chopped parsley

1. Cut the veal into small serving portions, lay them between sheets of waxed paper, and pound very thin with a wooden mallet or rolling pin. Shake them well, a few at a time, in a paper bag containing the flour, salt, and pepper. Save the leftover seasoned flour.
2. Heat butter in a heavy skillet and brown the veal pieces well on both sides. Arrange them in 2 or 3 layers in a medium casserole or a large shallow one.
3. In the fat remaining in the skillet cook the onion and mushrooms until the onion takes on some color and the mushrooms begin to look transparent. Add to the casserole, with the marjoram.
4. Add the wine, cover, and bake in a 325° oven 25-30 minutes, or until veal is very tender.
5. Remove the casserole from the oven and drain the sauce into a saucepan. Mix the reserved seasoned flour with a little water and thicken the sauce. Stir in the sour cream and pour back over the casserole. Reheat to the bubbling point and sprinkle with parsley. Serves 6.

*Serve with hot fluffy rice, a salad of cold cooked vegetables (peas, corn, carrots, lima beans, and torn-up lettuce mixed with mayonnaise thinned out considerably with French dressing), and warm garlic bread.*

# VEAL SWEETBREAD CASSEROLE

2 pairs sweetbreads
1 teaspoon salt (scant)
¼ cup lemon juice (scant)
¼ cup flour
4 tablespoons butter or margarine
2 small onions minced
2 slices bacon diced
½ cup coarsely chopped mushrooms
2 small carrots diced in
   ¼-inch pieces

½ teaspoon dried thyme or
   1½ teaspoons fresh, chopped
½ small bay leaf
1 tablespoon tomato paste
½ cup sherry
½ cup boiling water
½ cup condensed cream of
   mushroom soup

IF you like sweetbreads there are few greater delicacies, and this recipe brings out all their flavor.

1. Soak the sweetbreads 1 hour in cold water just as soon as you get them home. Cover with boiling water, add the salt and lemon juice, and simmer 12-15 minutes. Plunge them at once into very cold water and when they are cold remove all gristle and membrane. After this you can refrigerate them and prepare the casserole at your convenience.

2. Slice each sweetbread in half lengthwise, roll in flour, and brown delicately in sizzling butter. Lift out and set aside.

3. In the fat remaining in the skillet sauté lightly the onions and bacon. Add the mushrooms and cook 2-3 minutes longer. Stir in the carrots, thyme, and bay leaf. Pour into a small casserole and lay the sweetbreads on top.

4. In the same skillet mix the tomato paste, sherry, boiling water, and soup and pour over the sweetbreads. Bake 15-20 minutes in a 350° oven. If you like, sprinkle the top with 2 tablespoons of buttered crumbs before baking. Serves 4.

*Serve with fluffy mashed potatoes and buttered baby green peas.*

# VEAL SCALLOPS ALMONDINE

2½ pounds veal cutlets
4 tablespoons flour
1 teaspoon salt
6 tablespoons salad oil
4 tablespoons butter or
    margarine
2 large onions sliced thin

⅛ teaspoon thyme
½ bay leaf crushed
¾ cup dry sherry
1 cup chicken broth
1 teaspoon minced parsley
½ cup toasted slivered almonds

1. Cut the veal into 12 portions, and pound very thin between sheets of waxed paper. Shake the pieces in a paper bag containing flour and salt.
2. Sauté in hot oil until brown on both sides. Arrange in a casserole.
3. Heat the butter in a skillet and sauté the onions until they have just begun to color. Add to the casserole.
4. Add thyme, bay leaf, sherry, and chicken broth. Cover and bake in a 325° oven about 45 minutes, or until the veal is very tender.
5. Scatter almonds and parsley on top before serving. Or, if you prefer, drain off the liquid into a saucepan, thicken it somewhat with flour-and-water paste, stir in the almonds, and pour back over the meat; scatter parsley on top. Serves 6.

*Serve with plain spaghetti mixed with plenty of grated Parmesan or Romano cheese (or a mixture of both) and Italian green beans.*

# POULTRY

# CHICKEN

## BAKED CHICKEN BREASTS DE LUXE

3 chicken breasts boned and
  halved
4 tablespoons butter or
  margarine
¼ cup brandy slightly warmed
  (optional)
1 tablespoon minced shallots or
  2 teaspoons minced onion

¾ cup toasted slivered almonds
1 tablespoon tomato paste
2 tablespoons flour
½ cup chicken broth
¾ cup dry white wine
1 teaspoon dried tarragon or
  1 tablespoon fresh, chopped
Salt and pepper

THIS is a truly de luxe dish, and not difficult to make. It is improved
by being flambéed in brandy, but this is not indispensable.

1. It is surprisingly easy to bone chicken breasts yourself if you have
a sharp knife, but the butcher can easily do it. Flatten the boned
breasts with the flat side of a cleaver or a rolling pin, and brown them
in 3 tablespoons of the butter, in a heavy skillet.

2. Pour over them the warmed brandy and ignite (or ignite the brandy
and pour it over flaming). When the flames die down arrange the
chicken breasts in a shallow casserole.

3. Add the remaining butter to the skillet and lightly sauté the shallots. Add ½ cup of the almonds and slowly stir in the tomato paste
and flour.

4. Gradually stir in the chicken stock and wine, and when the sauce
is smooth and velvety add the tarragon. Season to taste and pour over
the chicken in the casserole.

5. Cover and bake in a 325° oven 35-40 minutes, or until the chicken
is very tender. Scatter the remaining almonds on top. Serves 6.

*Serve with fluffy mashed potatoes, buttered baby green peas, a plain
tossed green salad, and warm garlic bread.*

# REGENCY CHICKEN BREASTS

3 chicken breasts halved and
  preferably boned
6 tablespoons butter or
  margarine
¼ cup Cointreau liqueur
¼ cup brandy
  Salt and pepper

½ pound mushrooms sliced
1 tiny can truffles chopped
  (optional)
1½ cups heavy cream whipped
2 tablespoons grated Parmesan
  cheese

HERE is a true gourmet dish, with its truffles, cream, and liqueurs.
1. Heat 4 tablespoons butter to sizzling in a heavy skillet and brown
the chicken breasts on both sides. Arrange in a large shallow casserole and season to taste.
2. Flambé the chicken with the Cointreau and brandy mixed in a
small saucepan and slightly warmed. When the flames die down cover
the casserole and bake about 30 minutes in a 375° oven, or until
chicken is tender.
3. Add the remaining 2 tablespoons butter to the skillet and lightly
sauté the mushrooms. Stir in the truffles and whipped cream and heat
almost to boiling point, stirring constantly.
4. Pour over the chicken breasts, sprinkle with cheese, and brown
under the broiler. Serves 6.

*Serve with buttered noodles to which you have added generous
amounts of poppy seeds and slivered toasted almonds, and a tossed
green salad with grated carrots, sliced scallions, and thin tomato
wedges added. Warm garlic bread with toasted sesame seeds added
to the garlic butter is good with this.*

# CHICKEN BREASTS WITH BLACK CHERRIES

3 good-sized chicken breasts halved
6 tablespoons butter or margarine
1 cup port wine
½ cup chicken broth
2 teaspoons meat glaze (Maggi, Bevo, etc.)
1 teaspoon cornstarch
1 cup pitted black Bing cherries

BLACK cherries make a company dish out of almost anything. Here they add greatly to both flavor and appearance.

1. Brown the breasts in sizzling butter in a large skillet and arrange them in a large casserole that will hold them on one layer, even though crowded. Cover and bake 20 minutes at 350°.

2. To the skillet add the port, chicken broth, and meat glaze. Stir well and simmer 10 minutes.

3. Dissolve the cornstarch in a bit of water, stir into the skillet, and simmer until the sauce is clear, stirring constantly.

4. Add the cherries and pour over the chicken breasts.

5. Cover the casserole again and continue to bake 20 minutes longer. Serves 6.

*Serve with well-whipped potatoes and asparagus with lemon-butter-crumb sauce.*


# CHICKEN BREASTS WITH KIRSCH

2 chicken breasts halved, boned, and skinned
Salt
3 tablespoons butter or margarine
¼ cup cognac
¼ cup kirsch
½ cup heavy cream
2 egg yolks

1. Salt the chicken breasts lightly and sauté them to a golden brown in sizzling butter.

2. Arrange them in a shallow casserole, cover, and bake 20 minutes in a 375° oven.

3. Mix the cognac and kirsch in a small saucepan and warm a little. Remove the chicken from the oven, ignite the liqueurs, and pour over the chicken. Let flame until flames die down.

4. Whip the cream until it begins to thicken. Add the egg yolks and beat a moment more, until well blended. Heat the mixture in a saucepan, stirring constantly. When it is hot, but not boiling, pour over the chicken breasts gently and continue to bake 15-20 minutes, or until the meat is very tender. Serves 4.

## BREAST OF CAPON WITH WILD RICE

| | |
|---|---|
| Breast of 5-6-pound roasting capon cut in two and skinned | ¼ pound mushrooms sliced |
| | 2 cups heavy cream |
| 1 cup wild rice | ¼ cup dry sherry |
| 4 cups boiling water | 1 tablespoon brandy |
| Salt | ½ cup Hollandaise sauce |
| 3 tablespoons butter or margarine | (canned will do) |

1. Wash the wild rice in several waters and cook in the boiling water and salt for 30-40 minutes, or until tender. Drain it and let it dry out 10 minutes or so over very low heat.

2. With a sharp knife slice the two halves of the capon breast in two and brown them in butter slowly until a golden brown. Salt lightly and remove to a plate for a few minutes.

3. In the fat remaining in the skillet cook the mushrooms 2-3 minutes over low heat. Reserve ½ cup of cream and stir the rest of the cream, the sherry, and the brandy into the mushrooms.

4. Blend well, replace the chicken breasts, and simmer over the lowest possible heat, covered, until the chicken is tender and the sauce thickened. Season to taste and keep warm on an asbestos plate.

5. In a well-greased shallow casserole spread out the rice. Lay the chicken breasts on top, and cover with the mushroom sauce.

6. Whip the remaining ½ cup of cream, blend it with the Hollandaise sauce, and spread smoothly over the casserole.

7. Brown well under the broiler. Serves 4.

# BALTIMORE CHICKEN WITH CRABMEAT

¾ cup cooked chicken diced
   (or 6-ounce can)
¾ cup cooked crabmeat flaked
   coarsely (or 6½-ounce can)
1 can condensed cream of
   mushroom soup
1 can condensed cream of
   chicken soup

½ cup top milk
1 tablespoon grated onion
½ teaspoon paprika
½ cup mushrooms sliced and
   lightly sautéed (or canned)
½ cup buttered bread or corn
   flake crumbs

1. In a saucepan mix the two soups, the milk, onion, and paprika, and heat to just under boiling. Stir in the chicken, crabmeat, and mushrooms and blend well.
2. Pour into a medium casserole, top with buttered crumbs, and bake 15 minutes in a 325° oven, or until brown and bubbly. Serves 4.

*Serve with fresh hot rice to take up the sauce, or serve on hot baking powder biscuits or waffles. Buttered green peas and tossed green salad complete the meal.*


# BRANDIED CHICKEN

2 fryer-broilers, cut up
   Salt and pepper
¼ pound butter (1 stick) melted
6 tablespoons brandy
5 medium shallots minced
1 tablespoon chopped parsley

1 teaspoon fresh chopped
   tarragon or ⅓ teaspoon dried
½ cup dry white wine
4 tablespoons Cointreau liqueur
½ cup heavy cream

1. Season the chicken pieces well and brown them lightly all over in sizzling butter in a large skillet or electric fry pan.
2. Warm 4 tablespoons of the brandy in a small saucepan, pour over the chicken, ignite, and let it burn off. (Or ignite the brandy in the saucepan and pour flaming over the chicken.) Arrange the chicken in a large casserole.

3. To the fat remaining in the pan add the shallots, parsley, and tarragon, cooking briefly.
4. Add the remaining 2 tablespoons brandy, the wine, and the Cointreau. Blend well and stir in the cream.
5. Pour over the chicken, cover the casserole, and bake 45 minutes in a 375° oven. Serves 6-7.

*Serve with riced potatoes and asparagus spears with lemon-butter-crumb sauce, a tossed green salad, and warm garlic bread.*


## CHICKEN ALMONDINE

3½-4 cups cooked chicken diced
  3 tablespoons butter or
    margarine
  2 tablespoons flour
  1 cup top milk
  Salt and pepper
  1 tablespoon minced onion
  ½ cup dry white wine
  1 cup chicken broth

  1 clove
  1 small bay leaf
  ½ cup toasted slivered almonds
  3 egg yolks
  ¼ cup heavy cream
  ¼ cup dry sherry
  1 tablespoon Angostura bitters
  2 tablespoons bread or corn
    flake crumbs

1. Make a white sauce of 2 tablespoons of the butter, the flour, and the milk. Season to taste.
2. Lightly sauté the onion in ½ teaspoon of butter.
3. Stir in the white sauce, wine, chicken broth, clove, and bay leaf. Simmer about 5 minutes and stir in the chicken and almonds.
4. Mix the egg yolks with the cream, sherry and Angostura bitters. Blend well, stir into the chicken mixture, and pour into a medium casserole.
5. Melt the remaining butter, stir in the crumbs, and sprinkle on top of the casserole.
6. Bake 15 minutes in a 325° oven, uncovered, and brown under the broiler. Serves 10.

*Serve with plenty of hot fluffy rice to absorb the wonderful sauce, buttered baby carrots, and a tossed green salad.*

# CHICKEN WITH AVOCADO

3-pound broiler-fryer cut up
1 large avocado peeled and sliced
6 tablespoons butter, margarine,
  or salad oil
2 small onions chopped
1 chicken bouillon cube or
  1 teaspoon chicken stock base

Salt and pepper
½ teaspoon chili powder
Dash cinnamon
3 tablespoons flour
1 cup orange juice (or ½ cup
  and ½ cup dry white wine)
2 tablespoons grated orange rind

THE avocado here makes this a real party dish. The recipe can be doubled easily, still using just the one large avocado.

1. Brown the chicken in half the butter in a large skillet and arrange in a large casserole.

2. In the fat remaining in the skillet lightly sauté the onions.

3. Stir in the bouillon cube, mashed, seasoning to taste, chili powder, and cinnamon.

4. Spread over the chicken, cover the casserole, and bake 20 minutes in a 350° oven.

5. Heat the remaining fat in the same skillet, stir in the flour and cock until smooth and lightly browned.

6. Blend in the orange juice or mixture of orange juice and wine. When smooth and somewhat thickened pour over the chicken in the casserole, cover, and bake 25 minutes longer.

7. Check seasoning, cover entire top with avocado slices, salt very lightly, and bake 10 minutes longer, uncovered.

8. Sprinkle the top with the grated orange rind before serving. Serves 4.

*Serve with riced potatoes and fresh corn on the cob (in season) or buttered cut corn.*

# CHICKEN CACCIATORE À LA FRED HARVEY

2 broiler-fryers cut in quarters
  (about 2½ pounds each)

1 medium onion sliced
½ pound fresh mushrooms sliced

½ cup flour
1 teaspoon salt
⅛ teaspoon pepper
¼ cup butter, margarine, or
   salad oil

1 clove garlic minced
12 pitted ripe olives
1 can tomato paste or 1 cup
   canned tomatoes
½ cup dry red wine or sherry

Put the flour, salt, and pepper in a paper bag and shake the chicken quarters in it. Sauté in hot fat until well browned. Arrange the chicken pieces in a large casserole. Mix the remaining ingredients and pour over them. Cover and bake 30-40 minutes in a 375° oven. Serves 4.

*Serve with buttered broccoli and a hearty green salad. If you want something to soak up the wonderful sauce serve with fresh hot rice or buttered noodles.*

## CHICKEN CASSEROLE WITH HERBS

4-pound broiler-fryer cut up
   (or two 2½-pound ones)
2 tablespoons salad oil
2 tablespoons butter or
   margarine
6 tablespoons flour
2¾ cups milk scalded
2½ teaspoons salt

⅛ teaspoon pepper
¾ teaspoon dried thyme or
   1 tablespoon fresh, chopped
¾ teaspoon dried tarragon or
   basil or 1 tablespoon fresh,
   chopped
¼ cup dry white wine

1. Cook the chicken in sizzling oil in a skillet until it is golden all over. Lay the pieces in a large shallow casserole.
2. Add the butter to the oil left in the chicken skillet and blend in the flour. Add a bit more butter if necessary to absorb the flour.
3. Stir in the milk, salt and pepper, and herbs, stirring until the sauce is smooth and thick.
4. Thin it out somewhat with the wine, pour over the chicken, and bake about 1 hour, or until the chicken is tender, in a 325° oven. Serves 6.

*Serve with fresh hot rice, buttered green peas with a couple of fresh mushrooms chopped and sautéed stirred in, and Brown-'n-Serve French bread.*

# CHICKEN CASSEROLE WITH WALNUTS

2 cups cooked chicken cut in
  large pieces
3 cups cooked rice
½ cup stuffed olives coarsely
  chopped
½ cup coarsely broken walnut
  meats

1 can condensed cream of
  mushroom soup
1 cup chicken broth or leftover
  chicken gravy thinned a bit
1 teaspoon parsley chopped
2 tablespoons grated Parmesan
  cheese

1. Mix the rice, olives, nuts, and chicken in a bowl.
2. In another bowl mix the soup, chicken broth, and parsley.
3. In a medium casserole spread half the chicken mixture, half the sauce, and repeat the layers.
4. Top with grated cheese and bake, uncovered, 30 minutes in a 350° oven. Serves 6.

*Serve with riced potatoes and buttered French-cut string beans.*


# CHICKEN CONTINENTAL

2½-3-pound fryer-broiler cut up
  ¼ cup lime juice (2 limes)
  ¼ cup lemon juice (1 lemon)
  ⅓ cup dry white wine
  1 clove garlic mashed

1 teaspoon salt
¼ teaspoon dried tarragon or
  ¾ teaspoon fresh, chopped
⅛ teaspoon fresh-ground pepper
¼ cup butter or margarine

1. Put the chicken pieces in a bowl and pour over them a mixture of the lime and lemon juice, the wine, garlic, salt, tarragon, and pepper. Let them stand at room temperature half an hour or put them in the refrigerator for 2-3 hours. Stir occasionally.
2. Remove the chicken from the marinade (save it) and arrange the pieces in a shallow casserole. Crowd them as much as you please, but keep them on one layer.
3. Dot the chicken with the butter and bake, uncovered, 30-40 minutes in a 425° oven. Using a baster, baste with the reserved marinade

every 10 minutes. When you serve (from the casserole, of course) pour some of the sauce over each serving. Serves 4.

*Serve with fluffy mashed potatoes and corn on the cob—in season— or buttered cut corn with chopped green pepper and chopped pimiento.*

## SPECIAL CHICKEN CURRY

2 cups cooked chicken (or turkey) diced large
2 cups diced cooked ham
½ cup butter, margarine, or salad oil
⅔ cup mushrooms sliced
4 tablespoons green and sweet red peppers chopped
1 medium onion minced

2 cups chicken or turkey broth
5 tablespoons flour
2 teaspoons curry powder (or to taste)
2 cups top milk
Salt and pepper
½ cup slivered toasted almonds
½ cup flaked coconut

1. Melt 3 tablespoons of the butter in a large casserole and cook the mushrooms, peppers, and onion a few minutes, until the onion is transparent.
2. Stir in the broth and simmer gently a few minutes.
3. Blend the remaining butter with the flour and curry powder and slowly stir it into the casserole, continuing to stir until the sauce is velvety smooth and thickened. Add the milk and season to taste.
4. Stir in the chicken and ham and simmer, uncovered, over the lowest possible heat until almost boiling, stirring occasionally to prevent sticking.
5. Add the almonds and coconut just before serving. Serves 10-12.

*Serve with plenty of flaky hot rice, a large tossed green salad, and the usual curry accompaniments: chutney, fresh coconut, chopped salted peanuts, preserved or candied ginger, poppadums (large thin wafers imported from India, for which toasted and buttered pilot crackers do very well), and Bombay duck, which belies its name by being a dried fish from India, for which one can easily use shredded dried codfish.*

# CHICKEN (OR TURKEY) DIVAN WITH NUTS

Cooked sliced chicken
enough to serve 6
Cooked broccoli for 6
(2 packages frozen)
½ cup sliced toasted Brazil
nuts or almonds
6 tablespoons butter or
margarine

6 tablespoons flour
3 cups milk
1½ teaspoons salt
3 egg yolks slightly beaten
¼ teaspoon Tabasco sauce
4 tablespoons grated Parmesan
cheese

1. Make a cream sauce of the butter, flour, and milk, and season to taste. Stir until it is smooth and thick. Add a little to the egg yolks and blend back into the cream sauce. Cook a minute or two more, but do not let it boil. Stir in the Tabasco and cheese.
2. Arrange the cooked broccoli on the bottom of a large but fairly shallow casserole (if you use fresh broccoli cut off a good part of the stems, chop them, and cook them for another day).
3. Pour a thin layer of the cream sauce on the broccoli and cover with half of the nuts.
4. Arrange the chicken slices on top in a thick layer, overlapping them. Cover with the rest of the sauce.
5. Bake the casserole 20 minutes in a 375° oven.
6. Sprinkle with the remaining nuts and bake 5 minutes longer.
7. Put under the broiler for a moment to brown. Serves 6.

*Serve with a salad of cold cooked vegetables (green peas, corn, lima beans, diced carrots), thinly sliced raw mushrooms, and thinly sliced avocado, tossed with a small head of iceberg lettuce cut in rather small cubes. Warm garlic bread goes well with this meal.*

# CHICKEN AND LOBSTER CASSEROLE

Cooked chicken slices enough
to serve 4

Salt and pepper
2 egg yolks

½ pound cooked lobster diced
  (canned will do)
3 tablespoons butter or margarine
3 tablespoons flour
2 cups chicken broth (or
  ½ dry white wine)

½ cup heavy cream
½ cup sliced mushrooms
  (canned will do)
1 cup cooked peas
¼ cup grated Parmesan cheese
Paprika

1. Melt the butter in a saucepan, stir in the flour, and slowly blend in the chicken broth, stirring until it is smooth and thickened. Season to taste and remove from heat.
2. Beat the egg yolks and ¼ cup of the cream together lightly and stir into the sauce. Add the mushrooms, peas, and lobster.
3. Whip the remaining ¼ cup heavy cream and fold into sauce.
4. Lay the chicken slices in a large flat casserole, overlapping them a little, and pour the lobster sauce over.
5. Sprinkle with cheese and paprika, and bake about 15 minutes in a 325° oven, or until golden brown. Serves 4.

*Serve with wild rice and buttered cut green beans.*


## CHICKEN AND NOODLE CASSEROLE WITH MUSHROOMS

1½ cups cooked chicken diced
¾ pound mushrooms sliced
½ pound medium noodles cooked
½ green pepper diced
1 cup stuffed olives chopped

½ pound sharp Cheddar or
  Swiss cheese grated coarsely
2 hard-cooked eggs chopped
2 cups rich white sauce,
  well seasoned
Chopped parsley

THIS is a flavorful dish, especially easy when you have leftover chicken.
  Stir all the ingredients except the parsley together in a large casserole, cover, and bake 1 hour at 325°. Remove the cover after ½ hour. Sprinkle with parsley before serving. Serves 8.

*Serve with a tossed green salad and a dish of mixed vegetables: cut corn, green peas, cut green beans, diced carrots, and cut asparagus.*

# CHICKEN ELEGANTE

2 cups cooked chicken diced
¼ cup butter or margarine
¼ cup flour
1 can condensed cream of
chicken soup
¼ cup blue cheese, crumbled
½ teaspoon dried marjoram or
1½ teaspoons fresh, chopped

½ cup grated Parmesan cheese
1 package frozen broccoli
cooked and chopped
1 cup dairy sour cream
¼ cup buttered bread or corn
flake crumbs
Paprika
Salt and pepper

1. Melt the butter in a large saucepan, stir in the flour and cook a minute or two. Gradually stir in the soup, blue cheese, marjoram, half of the Parmesan cheese, and the chicken and broccoli. Heat to just under boiling, remove from the heat, and stir in the sour cream. Season to taste.

2. Pour into a casserole and top with the remaining Parmesan cheese mixed with the buttered crumbs.

3. Sprinkle with paprika and bake in a 350° oven 20 minutes, or until browned and bubbly. Serves 6.

*Serve with fried rice, fresh asparagus with lemon-butter-crumb sauce, and a tossed green salad.*

# CHICKEN-ALMOND PIE

2 cups cooked chicken cut in
good-sized pieces
¼ cup butter or margarine
¼ cup flour
1 cup light cream or top milk
Salt and pepper
1 cup chicken broth

¼ teaspoon dill weed
1 teaspoon chopped parsley
¼ pound mushrooms sliced and
sautéed (or 4-ounce can)
½ cup toasted slivered almonds
Pastry for 1-crust 9-inch pie

1. Make a cream sauce of the butter, flour, and cream, and season to taste.

2. Stir in the chicken broth, dill weed, and parsley, and cook, stirring, until the sauce is velvety and thick.

3. Stir in the chicken, mushrooms, and almonds.

4. Pour into a deep pie plate and top with pastry, slashed to permit steam to escape. Bake in a 400° oven 25-30 minutes, until golden brown. Serves 5-6.

*Serve with well-buttered baked potatoes and buttered cut green beans. Serve a bowl of dairy sour cream and chives to go with the baked potatoes.*

## CHICKEN PILAFF

3½-pound broiler-fryer cut up
1½ cups raw rice
4 tablespoons salad oil
1 cup chopped onion
1½ cups light cream
1 tablespoon lemon juice

2 teaspoons salt
¼ teaspoon pepper
½ teaspoon ground allspice
2 cups chicken broth heated
1 green pepper seeded and sliced thin

PILAFS are everyday fare throughout the Middle East, and we are tending to use them more in this country. This recipe is a slight modification of the usual type.

1. Cover the rice with water (don't rinse if it is converted rice), bring to a boil, turn off heat, and let stand 15-20 minutes. Drain.

2. Heat the oil in a large heavy casserole and brown the chicken pieces in it. Stir in the onion before the chicken is finished.

3. Remove the larger chicken pieces for a moment and stir into the casserole the cream, lemon juice, salt, pepper, and allspice. Stir rapidly to prevent the cream from curdling.

4. Stir in the rice and hot chicken broth.

5. Put back the chicken pieces and lay the green pepper rings on top.

6. Cover and bake about 35 minutes in a 325° oven, or simmer gently on top of the stove about 25-30 minutes.

7. Check 2 or 3 times while cooking. Pilaf should be on the dry side, but you may have to add a bit of water or broth. Serves 4-6.

*Serve with young zucchini, sliced and slowly sautéed in butter or margarine with a bit of onion.*

# CHICKEN AND OYSTER PIE

3 cups cooked chicken,
  diced coarsely
½ pint raw oysters, fresh or frozen
2 hard-cooked eggs, sliced
½ cup minced celery
2 cups chicken broth

4 tablespoons flour
  Salt and pepper
½ recipe biscuits
1 tablespoon softened butter
  or salad oil

1. In a medium casserole make alternate layers (2 each) of chicken, oysters, and eggs, scattering some of the celery on each layer.
2. Heat the chicken broth, but first mix a little of it with the flour and use to thicken the broth. Season to taste and pour over the casserole.
3. Mix the biscuit dough and pat it out on a lightly floured board to a thickness of ½ inch. Cut out small biscuits and lay them close together as a topping for the casserole. Spread with the softened butter or brush with oil.
4. Bake in a 425° oven 25 minutes or until the biscuits are golden and the pie bubbly. Serves 6.

*Serve with mixed vegetables and sliced ripe tomatoes spread with chopped chives and parsley mixed with French dressing.*


# CHICKEN RAPHAEL

2 two-and-a-half-pound fryer-
  broilers cut up
1½ teaspoons salt
⅛ teaspoon pepper
2 tablespoons flour
½ cup butter or margarine
  (1 stick)

1 small onion chopped
¾ cup sliced mushrooms
½ cup dry white wine
1 tablespoon lemon juice
1 cup light cream
¼ teaspoon grated nutmeg (scant)
1 tablespoon minced parsley

1. Mix the salt, pepper, and flour in a paper bag and shake the pieces of chicken in it. Sauté lightly in a heavy skillet in hot butter and ar-

110

range in a medium casserole, just large enough to hold them spread out.

2. In the fat remaining in the skillet cook the onion and mushrooms for 3-4 minutes and add them to the casserole.

3. Clean out the casserole with the wine and pour that over the casserole.

4. Cover and bake 20 minutes in a 375° oven.

5. Mix the lemon juice, cream, nutmeg, and parsley, and pour this over the chicken, stirring it in as best you can. Cover again and bake 20 minutes longer. Remove cover the last 5 minutes. Serves 4.

*Serve with fluffy mashed potatoes and buttered green peas.*

## CHICKEN AND RICE ALMONDINE

2 cups cooked chicken diced
1½ cups raw rice
3 cups chicken broth (or half dry white wine)
1 teaspoon saffron
1 can pitted black Bing cherries
¼ cup slivered almonds or ½ cup whole almonds

¼ cup white raisins (sultana)
½ teaspoon dried rosemary or 1½ teaspoons fresh, chopped
½ teaspoon dill or dill weed
½ cup salad oil
4 small white onions sliced
Salt and pepper
1 tablespoon chopped parsley

1. Put the rice, the chicken broth, and the saffron (which you can omit if you don't care for yellow rice) in the top of a double boiler and cook it over boiling water, without stirring, 30-35 minutes, or until it is flaky and all the liquid is absorbed.

2. Stir in the cherries, raisins, almonds, and herbs.

3. Heat the oil in a heavy casserole and slightly brown the onions.

4. Stir the chicken in, continue cooking for a minute or two, and then add the rice mixture.

5. Correct the seasoning and bake, covered, in a 350° oven about 20 minutes.

6. Sprinkle with parsley before serving. Serves 6.

*Serve with buttered julienned beets, warm garlic bread, and a tossed salad.*

# CHICKEN AND RICE CURRY

2 cups cooked white meat of
  chicken (generous)
¼ pound butter or margarine
4 tablespoons flour
3 cups top milk
  Salt and pepper

2 teaspoons curry powder
¼ cup dry sherry
2 cups cooked rice
1 tablespoon minced parsley
  Grated Parmesan cheese

1. Slice chicken and cut the slices into squares about 1 by 1 inch.
2. Melt half the butter in a saucepan, blend in the flour, and gradually stir in the milk. Season to taste.
3. Melt the rest of the butter in a medium casserole and lightly sauté the chicken pieces.
4. Stir in the cream sauce, curry powder, and sherry. Cook a moment and blend in the rice and parsley.
5. Top with cheese and brown under the broiler. Serves 4.

*Note:* If you have made this casserole early and kept it in the refrigerator, let it come to room temperature and then bake it 10 minutes in a 350° oven before you broil it.

*Serve with buttered wax beans and buttered baby carrots.*


# CHICKEN AND SHRIMP WITH RICE

5-pound roasting chicken
  cut up
1½ pounds shrimp cooked,
  cleaned, and shelled
1 cup raw rice
1 medium onion sliced
1 medium carrot sliced thin

1½ quarts salted water
  Salt and pepper
½ teaspoon dried dill or
  1½ teaspoons fresh
12 small white onions or
  1 small can boiled
1 lemon sliced thin

MANY good dishes combine chicken, shrimp, and rice, especially Spanish dishes.
1. Simmer the chicken pieces in a kettle with the onion, carrot, and

the water, for 25-30 minutes, covered. Remove the chicken and strain the broth.

2. Skin the chicken pieces and arrange them in a large casserole, with the shrimp, a little salt and pepper, and the dill. Add the dry rice, whole onions, and lemon slices.

3. Boil the broth hard to reduce it to 2 cups and pour over the casserole.

4. Cover and bake 40 minutes in a 350° oven, or until chicken is tender and rice has absorbed all the broth. Stir a little with a long-tined fork to release steam. Serves 6.

*Serve with mixed vegetables and a tossed green salad.*

## CHICKEN STROGANOFF

| | |
|---|---|
| 2½-3-pound fryer-broiler cut up | 3 tablespoons lemon juice |
| ¼ cup flour | 1 cup chicken broth |
| 1 teaspoon salt | ½ pound mushrooms sliced and |
| ⅛ teaspoon pepper | sautéed or 2 four-ounce cans |
| 3 tablespoons butter, margarine, | 8-ounce package medium |
| or salad oil | noodles broken up |
| 1 medium onion chopped | 1 cup sour cream |
| 1 clove garlic mashed | ¼ teaspoon paprika |

1. Coat the chicken pieces with the flour, salt, and pepper mixed and brown in hot butter. Drain on paper towels and pour off any fat remaining in the skillet.

2. Mix in the skillet the onion, garlic, lemon juice, chicken broth, and mushrooms (and their liquid, if canned). Cook 3-4 minutes.

3. Stir in the chicken, pour into a medium casserole, cover, and bake 30 minutes in a 325° oven.

4. Stir in the uncooked noodles and bake 15 minutes longer, covered.

5. Just before serving stir in the sour cream and paprika and blend well. (Blending is easier if you remove a few pieces of chicken while you do it.) Serves 4-5.

*Serve with fluffy hot rice, succotash, and a tossed salad.*

# CHICKEN WITH SPAGHETTI AND NUTS

2 cups chicken slices cut
  rather small
1 pound thin spaghetti cooked
½ cup pine nuts or slivered almonds
1 can condensed cream of
  chicken soup

1 can condensed cream of
  mushroom soup
¾ cup light cream
½ cup grated sharp Cheddar or
  Swiss cheese
1 pimiento sliced thin
  Paprika

HEAT together the soups, cream, and cheese. Mix in the spaghetti, nuts, and pimiento. Stir in the chicken lightly. Spread in a medium casserole, sprinkle with paprika, and bake 20 minutes in a slow oven, 325°. Serves 6.

*Serve with buttered green peas and a tossed salad.*


# CHICKEN TARRAGON

2 two-and-a-half-pound broiler-
  fryers cut up or 3 whole
  chicken breasts halved
½ cup flour
1 tablespoon salt
½ teaspoon pepper

½ cup butter, margarine, or
  salad oil
1 medium onion minced
1 teaspoon crushed dried tarragon
  or 1 tablespoon fresh
1 cup white wine

1. Dredge the chicken pieces by shaking them in a paper bag containing the flour, salt, and pepper.
2. Heat the fat in a heavy skillet and cook the onion 3-4 minutes, until it is soft but not brown. Skim out and put in a large casserole.
3. In the same skillet brown the chicken well and arrange in the casserole.
4. Sprinkle the tarragon evenly on the chicken and pour in the wine. Cover and bake about 45 minutes, or until chicken is tender, in a 350° oven.
5. If you like a thickened sauce, drain off the liquid from the casserole

into a small saucepan and thicken it to your taste with flour-and-water paste. Season, and stir in a little sour cream if you like. Pour back over the chicken. Serves 6.

*Serve with a rice casserole* (see Index) *and buttered broccoli.*

## COQ AU VIN

2 three-pound fryer-broilers cut up
2 teaspoons salt
¼ teaspoon ground cloves or allspice
¼ teaspoon pepper
2-3 tablespoons tarragon vinegar
½ pound salt pork diced small
12 small white onions peeled
3 tablespoons brandy warmed
1 bottle dry red table wine

1 tablespoon sugar
¼ teaspoon dried thyme or orégano or ¾ teaspoon fresh, chopped
1 tablespoon minced celery leaves
8-10 baby carrots cooked barely tender
24 button mushrooms lightly sautéed in butter or 6-ounce can
Chopped parsley

1. Use the backs, necks, wing tips, and giblets to make chicken broth for another time, and use only the better parts here. Rub them with a mixture of the salt, cloves, and pepper. Sprinkle with vinegar and let stand 20-30 minutes.
2. Try out the salt pork in a large heavy skillet. Brown the onions lightly in this fat and skim out both pork bits and onions, spreading them in a large casserole.
3. Brown the chicken pieces in the remaining fat and arrange them in the casserole.
4. Ignite the warmed brandy and pour it flaming over the chicken.
5. When the flames die down add the remaining ingredients to the casserole, except the mushrooms and parsley.
6. Cover the casserole and bake 1 hour in a 325° oven.
7. Add the mushrooms 15 minutes before the time is up.
8. Sprinkle with parsley before serving. Serves 8-10.

*Serve with plenty of rice, buttered broccoli, and warm garlic bread. A tossed green salad goes well, too.*

# CHICKEN TERIYAKI

3-pound fryer-broiler cut up
⅔ cup soy sauce
¼ cup dry white wine

2 tablespoons sugar
½ tablespoon ground ginger
1 small clove garlic mashed

THIS is a simple dish with outstanding flavor.
1. In a small bowl mix the soy sauce, wine, sugar, ginger, and garlic.
2. Put the chicken in a large bowl and pour the marinade over it. Let it marinate from 1 to 3 hours.
3. Remove the chicken pieces from the marinade and lay them in a large casserole.
4. Bake, uncovered, 1 hour in a 325° oven. Baste with the marinade every 15 minutes. Serves 4.

*Serve with riced potatoes, glazed onions, and buttered asparagus.*


# CHINESE CHICKEN CASSEROLE

3-pound chicken cut up
1 tablespoon salad oil
½ teaspoon salt
2 teaspoons ginger
1 tablespoon whiskey
1 cup boiling water
1 can bamboo shoots
    (1 pound 4 ounces)
½ pound mushrooms sliced

8-ounce can water chestnuts
    sliced in two
4 scallions cut in 1-inch pieces
    (green onions)
2 tablespoons cornstarch
2 teaspoons soy sauce
1 teaspoon sugar
¼ cup water

LIKE most Chinese dishes, this one is full of flavor and quite out of the ordinary.
1. Heat the oil in a large skillet and brown the chicken pieces well. (You may have to add a bit more oil.) Sprinkle with salt and ginger and arrange in a casserole.
2. Drizzle the whiskey over them. Add the boiling water, cover the casserole, and bake 40 minutes in a 325° oven.

**116**

3. Drain the liquid from the casserole into a saucepan and to it add the bamboo shoots, mushrooms, water chestnuts, and scallions. Bring to a boil.

4. Blend the cornstarch, soy sauce, sugar, and ¼ cup of water and stir this into the hot mixture. Cook until slightly thickened, stirring constantly, and pour over the chicken. Continue baking about 10 minutes. Serves 6.

*Serve with plenty of fresh hot rice, creamed spinach, and a tossed green salad.*

## CREAM OF CHICKEN MARENGO

4½-pound chicken cut up
¼ pound fresh mushrooms
¼ cup dry white wine
1 large onion quartered
2 cloves garlic cut up
¼ cup parsley sprigs
½ cup flour
1½ teaspoons salt

¼ teaspoon fresh-ground pepper
¼ teaspoon dried tarragon or
  ¾ teaspoon fresh
½ teaspoon dried rosemary or
  1½ teaspoons fresh
3 tablespoons butter or
  margarine

This delectable dish owes its texture and its ease of making to a blender.

1. Put in the blender the stems of the mushrooms, wine, onion, garlic, parsley, flour, salt, pepper, tarragon, and rosemary. Cover and blend on high speed 40 seconds. Stop two or three times to scrape the sides down if necessary.

2. Melt the butter in a large skillet and brown the chicken pieces on all sides. Arrange in a casserole with the mushroom caps.

3. Pour over the sauce from the blender. Cover and bake about 45 minutes in a 350° oven, stirring occasionally. Serves 5-6.

*Serve with fluffy mashed potatoes, braised celery with slivered almonds, and buttered asparagus spears.*

## CREAMY CHICKEN HASH À LA LOUIS DIAT

2 cups cooked chicken
  coarsely cut up
1 cup light cream
2 teaspoons flour
½ teaspoon grated lemon rind
⅛ teaspoon mace (optional)

¼ teaspoon salt
⅛ teaspoon fresh-ground pepper
1 teaspoon grated onion
3 tablespoons grated Parmesan
  cheese

PUT in a skillet the chicken, cream and flour mixed, lemon rind, seasonings, and onion. Cook over low heat, stirring constantly, until thickened. Pour into a shallow casserole, sprinkle with Parmesan cheese, and brown 5 inches from the broiler heat. Serves 4.

*Serve with buttered noodles, green pepper squares cooked tender in butter, and a tossed green salad.*

## GOURMET CHICKEN SAUTÉ

3-4-pound fryer-broiler cut up
  Salt and pepper
3 tablespoons butter or margarine
2 ounces brandy warmed (¼ cup)

2 ounces Madeira wine
1 dozen small whole mushrooms
  or ½ dozen large, quartered
1 cup sweet or dairy sour cream

THIS delicious casserole is surprisingly easy to make.

1. Season the chicken pieces with salt and pepper and brown them in sizzling butter in a heavy skillet. Lay them in a large casserole and bake in a 350° oven 45-50 minutes. Baste frequently with the butter left in the skillet, adding a little more if necessary.

2. After the chicken has baked 20 minutes or so remove it from the oven, light the warmed brandy, and pour it flaming over the chicken. Return to the oven when the flames die down.

3. Ten minutes later pour the Madeira over the chicken, add the mushrooms, and continue to cook ten minutes longer.

4. Drain off the liquid into a saucepan at this point, stir in the cream,

and when it is well blended and almost boiling pour back over the chicken. Continue to bake until chicken is very tender. Serves 5-6.

*Serve with plenty of fluffy rice to absorb the wonderful sauce. Buttered little green peas, a tossed green salad, and warm garlic bread will complete a fine meal.*


# INDIA CHICKEN WITH SESAME SEEDS

2 two-and-a-half- to three-pound fryer-broilers cut up
½ cup flour
2 teaspoons salt
½ teaspoon fresh-ground pepper
1 teaspoon paprika
3 tablespoons butter, margarine, or salad oil

2 tablespoons brown sugar
½ teaspoon ground ginger
1 cup red wine (or ½ cup and ½ cup water)
2 tablespoons soy sauce
⅓ cup toasted sesame seeds

THIS tangy chicken casserole will appeal to those who like savory foods.
1. Shake the chicken pieces in a paper bag containing the flour, salt, pepper, and paprika.
2. Brown lightly in hot butter in a large heavy skillet and arrange in a large casserole.
3. To the fat remaining in the skillet add the brown sugar, ginger, wine, and soy sauce. Clean out all the brown particles in the skillet and pour over the chicken in the casserole.
4. Toast the sesame seeds to a golden color in the oven or in another skillet (stir them constantly in the skillet) and sprinkle over the chicken pieces.
5. Cover the casserole and bake 45 minutes to an hour in a 350° oven. Serves 6-8.

*Serve with fresh hot rice, purée of spinach, and a large tossed green salad.*

E

# GEORGIA CHICKEN

2 three-and-a-half-pound broiler-
 fryers cut up
1 cup butter or margarine
2 cups fine bread or corn
 flake crumbs
¾ cup grated Parmesan cheese
¼ cup chopped parsley
1 clove garlic minced
1 tablespoon salt
⅛ teaspoon fresh-ground pepper

THIS oven-fried chicken is one of the easiest ways imaginable to prepare chicken, and one of the best.
1. Melt the butter in a small skillet.
2. Combine the crumbs, cheese, parsley, garlic, salt, and pepper.
3. Wipe the pieces of chicken with a damp cloth, dip in the melted
butter, roll in the crumb mixture, and arrange in a shallow casserole.
4. Drizzle the remaining butter over the chicken, cover, and bake in a
350° oven for 1 hour, or until tender. Uncover the last half hour.
Serves 8.

*Serve with Dutch potato salad (warm) or, in hot weather, with regular
potato salad. Mixed vegetables (cooked peas, cut beans, cut corn,
diced carrots, and asparagus spears cut up) and a tossed salad go well
with this dish.*


# HAWAIIAN CHICKEN

3-3½ pound broiler-fryer cut up
¼ cup flour
1 teaspoon paprika
1 teaspoon salt
⅛ teaspoon pepper
¼ cup butter, margarine, or
 salad oil
1 tablespoon grated orange rind
½ cup orange juice
9-ounce can crushed pineapple
1 large orange sliced

1. Shake the chicken pieces in a paper bag containing the flour, paprika, salt, and pepper, and sauté them until golden on all sides in hot
butter. Arrange in a large casserole.

120

2. Sprinkle the chicken pieces with the grated orange rind and pour in the orange juice.

3. Spread the crushed pineapple (not drained) on the chicken. Cover and bake 45 minutes to 1 hour in a 350° oven, or until chicken is very tender.

4. Five minutes before serving poke the orange slices (cut in two) into all the crevices. Continue to bake 5 minutes, uncovered. Serves 5-6.

*Serve with herbed rice and steamed cauliflower covered with melted sharp Cheddar cheese.*

## PARISIAN CHICKEN

2½-pound fryer-broiler quartered
   Salt and pepper
3 tablespoons butter, margarine,
   or salad oil
3 shallots or ½ small onion
   sliced thin

2 ounces cognac warmed
¼ cup dry vermouth
¾ cup heavy cream
4 large mushroom caps scored and
   sautéed lightly in butter

VERMOUTH adds flavor to many dishes. This French dish uses it with chicken, to excellent effect.

1. Season the chicken pieces and brown them well in hot butter. (It is easier to brown the wing quarters if you cut off wing tips and run short skewers through to hold the rest of the wing flat.) Arrange in a rather shallow casserole.

2. In the fat remaining in the skillet sauté the shallots a moment and add to the chicken.

3. Light the warmed cognac and pour flaming over the chicken.

4. When the flames die down add to the casserole the vermouth and cream mixed. Cover and bake 30-40 minutes at 300°, or until chicken is tender.

5. Lay a mushroom cap on each piece before serving. (Scoring the caps, or cutting into them a pattern of parallel lines merely adds to their decorative effect.) Serves 4.

*Serve with wild rice and broccoli Hollandaise.*

## HERBED CHICKEN CASSEROLE

2 three-pound broiler-fryers cut up
1 teaspoon rosemary
1 teaspoon orégano
1 teaspoon chopped marjoram

2 tablespoons butter
⅓ cup lemon juice
¾ cup dry white wine

1. Remove all skin from the chicken pieces and lay them out on waxed paper. Mix the herbs and sprinkle over the chicken.
2. Brown the chicken in butter in a heavy skillet and arrange in a large casserole.
3. Combine the lemon juice and wine and pour over.
4. Cover and bake about 40 minutes in a 375° oven.

If you cook this chicken on top of the stove you may have to add a bit more wine to keep it from getting dry. Serves 6-8.

*Serve with buttered noodles dressed up with poppy seeds and slivered almonds, and buttered lima beans.*

## POLYNESIAN CHICKEN-PEACH CASSEROLE

3½-pound fryer-broiler cut up
3 tablespoons butter, margarine,
  or salad oil
1 large white onion quartered
1 green pepper cut in 1-inch strips

1 No. 2½ can sliced peaches
  (1 pound 13 ounces)
1 tablespoon cornstarch
1 tablespoon soy sauce
3 tablespoons vinegar
2 medium tomatoes cut in wedges

1. Brown the chicken pieces in sizzling butter. Cover the skillet, reduce the heat to very low, and simmer about 20 minutes, or until the chicken is somewhat tender. Arrange in a large casserole.
2. Separate the onion quarters into their layers, and sauté onion and green pepper in the fat remaining in the skillet until the onion is transparent.
3. Drain the peaches well, but reserve the syrup. Mix 1 cup of the syrup with the cornstarch, soy sauce, and vinegar, and add to the

skillet. Cook until the sauce is clear and somewhat thickened, stirring frequently.

4. Stir in peaches and tomatoes and pour over the chicken in the casserole.

5. Cover the casserole and bake 20 minutes in a 375° oven. Remove the cover the last 5 minutes. Serves 6.

*Serve with wild rice to which sliced sautéed mushrooms are added, and buttered green peas.*

## POULET CINTRA

3-pound broiler-fryer cut up or
    2 chicken breasts halved
2 tablespoons butter, margarine,
    or salad oil
1 clove garlic
1 shallot minced or 1 slice of onion
    Salt and pepper
½ cup port wine

½ cup dry white wine
1 liqueur glass brandy
1 liqueur glass cherry brandy or
    kirsch
1 cup cream
2 egg yolks slightly beaten
2 tablespoons chopped parsley

EVEN though the alcohol is burned off, the various liquors nevertheless impart a subtle and wonderful flavor to this delightful French dish. It is of course better when chicken breasts are used.

1. Heat the butter in a heavy skillet or directly in a large heavy casserole.

2. Add the garlic clove and shallot. Brown a moment, and then remove the garlic. Brown the chicken pieces well. Arrange compactly in the casserole and sprinkle with salt and pepper.

3. Put both wines and both brandies in a small saucepan and warm them slightly. Light and pour flaming over the chicken.

4. When the flames die down cover the casserole tightly and bake in a slow oven, 325°, about 40 minutes, or until tender.

5. Pour whatever liquid remains into a small saucepan, bring it almost to a boil, and stir in the cream mixed with the egg yolks, stirring over low heat until thick. Pour over the casserole, sprinkle with parsley, and serve. Serves 4.

*Serve with wild rice and buttered asparagus.*

## RACHEL'S CHICKEN DELIGHT

5-pound fowl cut up
Salt
2-3 slices onion
1 carrot cut in several pieces
1 small bay leaf
2 sprigs parsley
3 tablespoons butter or margarine
3 tablespoons flour
½ cup heavy cream

½ cup top milk
¼ cup dry sherry
Fresh-ground black pepper
½ pound salted almonds (whole)
1 large can button mushrooms,
drained
Buttered bread or corn flake
crumbs

THIS is a sinfully rich dish, but makes a wonderful treat for a very special occasion.

1. Put the chicken in a large pot, with 1 teaspoon salt, onion, carrot, bay leaf, and parsley. Cover with water, bring to a boil, and simmer until the meat almost falls off the bones—1½-2 hours.

2. Lift out the chicken pieces, skin them, and tear off the meat in quite large chunks. Strain the liquid and discard the vegetables.

3. Melt the butter in a large saucepan, blend in the flour, cook 3-4 minutes over low heat, and blend in the cream, milk, sherry, and 1 cup of the chicken broth. (Save the rest for another day.)

4. Season the cream sauce very mildly and stir in the chicken, almonds, and mushrooms.

5. Pack the mixture into a shallow casserole, top quite thickly with buttered crumbs, and bake 30-40 minutes in a very slow oven, 250°, or until it is golden brown and bubbly. Serves 8.

*Serve with buttered French-cut string beans and buttered corn.*


## SESAME CHICKEN

3-pound broiler-fryer cut up
¼ cup toasted sesame seeds
½ cup flour
1 egg slightly beaten

½ cup milk
¼ cup butter melted
1 teaspoon salt
¼ teaspoon fresh-ground pepper

1. For practically all sesame seed recipes the seeds should be toasted before using. Toast them over slightly higher than medium heat in a heavy skillet, stirring constantly, until they begin to brown. Or spread them in a cake pan or pie plate and toast them 12-15 minutes in a hot oven, 400°.
2. Blend the toasted sesame seeds with the flour.
3. In separate soup plates put the egg blended with the milk, the flour-sesame seed mixture, and the melted butter. Dip the pieces of chicken first in the egg-milk plate, then in the flour plate, and then roll in melted butter.
4. Sprinkle with salt and pepper and lay in a well-buttered shallow casserole and bake, uncovered, about 1 hour in a 350° oven, or until tender. Serves 4.

*Serve with a rice casserole* (see Index) *or wild rice with mushrooms added, and buttered asparagus.*

## CHICKEN-SPAGHETTI CASSEROLE

3 cups chicken (or turkey) diced rather small
1 pound spaghetti cooked and drained
3 tablespoons salad oil
1 medium onion chopped
1 small green pepper chopped
1 cup sliced mushrooms
2 cans tomato sauce (8-ounce)
1 teaspoon salt
⅛ teaspoon pepper
½ teaspoon dried orégano or 1½ teaspoons fresh, chopped
½ pound mozzarella cheese coarsely grated or sliced thin

1. Heat the oil in a skillet and sauté the onion and green pepper until the onion begins to color.
2. Stir in the mushrooms, tomato sauce, salt, pepper, and orégano.
3. Cover and simmer over the lowest possible heat for 25-30 minutes, stirring frequently. Check seasoning.
4. In a good-sized casserole arrange layers of spaghetti, chicken, and cheese—at least 2 layers of each, ending with cheese.
5. Bake about 30 minutes in a 375° oven. Serves 8.

*Serve with a mixed vegetable salad and warm garlic bread.*

# ROCK CORNISH GAME HENS

| | |
|---|---|
| 4 small Rock Cornish hens, thawed | 1½ cups dry white wine |
| 4 tablespoons butter or margarine | ¼ teaspoon dried rosemary or |
| 1½ teaspoons Kitchen Bouquet | ¾ teaspoon fresh, chopped |
| ½ pound mushrooms sliced or | 2 tablespoons cornstarch |
| 1 large can | 3 tablespoons cold water |

ROCK Cornish game hens make an attractive addition to American cooking, and are now almost universally available frozen. They require close to 24 hours to defrost in the refrigerator, so have to be planned well in advance.

1. Bring the hens to room temperature before starting this dish— about an hour. Remove the giblets from the cavity. They are not used in this recipe.

2. Blend the butter, well softened, with the Kitchen Bouquet and spread over the hens with a pastry brush.

3. Place the hens on a rack in a shallow baking pan and roast them in a slow oven, 325°, about 45 minutes, or until tender.

4. Place the mushrooms, wine, and rosemary in a saucepan and bring to a boil.

5. Blend the cornstarch with the water and stir into the saucepan, stirring until the sauce is smooth and thickened. Keep warm.

6. When the chickens are about done arrange them in a large casserole and pour the sauce over and around them. Cover and bake about 15 minutes longer. Serves 4.

*Serve with herbed or curried rice and steamed cauliflower blanketed with melted sharp Cheddar.*


# ROCK CORNISH GAME HENS ROYALE

| | |
|---|---|
| 6 small Rock Cornish hens | 8 shallots minced or |
| (one pound each) thawed | 2 tablespoons minced onion |
| 3 tablespoons butter or margarine | 3 cloves |

3 tablespoons salad oil
2 cups dry white wine
  Salt and pepper

2 cups tiny mushrooms
  (canned button ones will do)

1. Allow the hens to defrost 24 hours in the refrigerator, and bring them to room temperature before cooking, about an hour.

2. Remove the giblets from the cavities and simmer in a little salted water with a sprig of parsley and a bit of onion. Chop the livers and discard the other giblets. Use the broth another day, or substitute it for part of the wine.

3. Heat the butter and oil in a large heavy skillet and brown the hens all over. Salt and pepper them lightly and arrange in a large casserole, crowded closely together.

4. Add the wine to the skillet to clean out the brown particles and pour over the hens. Cover and bake 25 minutes in a 325° oven.

5. Add the livers, the shallots, the cloves, and the mushrooms.

6. Cover loosely with a piece of aluminum foil and bake another 20 minutes. Serves 6.

*Serve with fluffy mashed potatoes and buttered asparagus.*

## CURRIED TURKEY (OR CHICKEN)

3 cups cooked turkey diced large
6 tablespoons margarine or oil
1 medium onion minced
2 tablespoons diced green pepper
4 tablespoons flour
1½ cups turkey or chicken broth
1¼ cups sliced mushrooms lightly
  sautéed, or 6-ounce can

1 large tart apple cored and
  diced
5-ounce can water chestnuts
  drained and sliced
3 tablespoons chopped pimiento
1 tablespoon minced parsley
  Salt and pepper
1½ teaspoons curry powder or
  to taste

THIS is an especially good curry. The water chestnuts give it a nice crunchy quality.

1. Heat the fat in a large casserole and sauté the onion and green pepper until soft. Stir in the flour, cook a moment, and blend in the turkey or chicken broth and the mushrooms, with their liquid if you use canned mushrooms. Simmer the mixture 15-20 minutes.

2. In a large bowl mix the turkey, apple, water chestnuts, pimiento, parsley, and salt and pepper.

3. Stir the curry powder into the sauce—as much as you like—and check seasoning.

4. Stir in the turkey mixture, heat slowly, and simmer 10-15 minutes over the lowest possible heat. Serves 6-8.

*Note:* Remember that curry always improves with time. Make this in the morning or the day before, bring to room temperature, and merely reheat at serving time.

*Serve with plenty of fresh hot rice and the usual curry accompaniments: chutney, fresh coconut grated or broken in chunks, chopped salted peanuts, preserved or candied ginger, poppadums (large thin wafers from India, for which toasted and buttered pilot crackers substitute), and Bombay duck—a dried Indian fish, for which shredded salt cod serves about as well. A large tossed green salad is almost a must.*

# LEMON-TURKEY CASSEROLE WITH RICE

3 cups coarsely diced turkey
2 cups cooked rice
 Salt and pepper
½ teaspoon whole celery seed
8-ounce can tomato sauce
1 cup chicken broth

4 slices lemon
5 thin slices onion (or more)
⅓ cup dry white wine
2 tablespoons butter
1 teaspoon paprika

THIS casserole is out of the ordinary in both flavor and texture.

1. Spread the rice in a good-sized but shallow casserole and arrange the turkey evenly over it.

2. Sprinkle with salt, pepper, and celery seed.

3. Mix the tomato sauce and chicken broth well and pour over the turkey.

4. Cut the lemon and onion slices in two and cover the top with them, adding more if needed.

5. Cover the casserole and bake 1¼ hours in a 350° oven. Check halfway through, and add a little broth if it seems quite dry.

6. When done, uncover the casserole, pour the wine over, dot with butter cut in bits, sprinkle with paprika, and broil until browned and sizzling. Serves 6.

*Serve with slices of eggplant dipped first in slightly beaten egg and then in bread or corn flake crumbs and sautéed until golden brown on both sides and tender. A tossed salad is in order, too.*

# TURKEY ALMONDINE

2 cups cooked turkey diced coarsely
4 tablespoons butter or margarine
4 tablespoons flour
2 cups milk
1¼ teaspoons salt
2 tablespoons dry white wine
1 cup cooked peas
⅓ cup toasted slivered almonds
2 egg yolks
2 tablespoons bread or corn flake crumbs
1 tablespoon butter
2 tablespoons Parmesan cheese

1. Make a cream sauce by melting the butter, stirring in the flour, and blending in the milk. Season to taste.

2. Stir in the wine, and keep stirring until the sauce is smooth.

3. Stir in the turkey, the peas, and half of the almonds.

4. Beat the egg yolks a little with a fork, add a little of the sauce, and rapidly stir it back into the turkey mixture.

5. Pour the mixture into a small casserole. Scatter the remaining almonds on top, then the crumbs, the butter, and finally the Parmesan cheese.

6. If you make the casserole just before serving, so that it is already hot, merely brown it well under the broiler. However, if you make it early in the day and refrigerate it, bring it to room temperature (1 hour) and bake 10 minutes in a 375° oven before broiling it. Serves 4.

*Serve with riced potatoes and broccoli with lemon-butter-crumb sauce.*

# TURKEY SHEPHERD'S PIE

2 cups cooked turkey diced medium small
½ cup chopped celery
¼ cup chopped onion
¼ cup sliced and lightly sautéed mushrooms or 4-ounce can
1 tablespoon minced parsley
1½ tablespoons dry sherry
2 cups hot mashed potatoes or 4-serving portion instant potatoes made with 1 cup water and 1 egg

2 tablespoons butter, margarine,
   or salad oil
1 can condensed cream of
   mushroom soup

1 egg (if raw potatoes are used)
2 tablespoons buttered crumbs
Paprika

1. Sauté the celery, onion, and mushrooms in hot fat in a skillet until the onion is transparent. Stir in the turkey.
2. Mix the soup with the parsley and sherry and blend it smoothly with the turkey mixture. Spread in a shallow casserole.
3. Beat the hot mashed potatoes well with the egg and spread over the turkey mixture.
4. Top with crumbs and sprinkle with paprika. Bake 25 minutes in a 350° oven, or until golden. Serves 4.

*Serve with buttered cut green beans and cole slaw.*

## TURKEY-SPAGHETTI CASSEROLE

1½-2 cups cooked turkey diced
   rather small
1¼ cups spaghetti
¼ cup pimiento diced fine
¼ cup green pepper chopped
½ medium onion minced

1 can condensed cream of
   mushroom soup
½ cup turkey broth, water,
   dry white wine, or a
   combination of these
¾ cup grated sharp cheese
Salt and pepper

1. Cook the spaghetti in boiling salted water until it is barely tender—about 7 minutes—and drain well.
2. Mix the turkey, pimiento, green pepper, and onion and spread in a medium casserole.
3. Heat the soup and stir in the turkey broth.
4. Stir in the cooked spaghetti. Pour this over the turkey in the casserole and blend the two mixtures. Season to taste.
5. Top with the grated cheese and bake, uncovered, about 45 minutes in a 350° oven, or until bubbling and browned. Serves 5-6.

*Serve with buttered baby Brussels sprouts and a tossed green salad with grated carrot, cucumber slices, and tomato wedges added.*

## TURKEY WITH WILD RICE

2 cups cooked turkey diced
medium small
1 cup raw wild rice
½ pound mushrooms sliced and
sautéed lightly
1½ cups heavy cream

2½ cups turkey stock or gravy
thinned with chicken broth
2 tablespoons chopped chives
Salt and pepper
½ cup grated Parmesan cheese
1 tablespoon butter

1. Wash the rice in several waters and let it soak in cold water for an hour or two.

2. Drain the rice well and mix with the turkey, mushrooms, cream, 1½ cups of the turkey stock, chives, and seasoning to taste.

3. Put in a buttered casserole, cover, and bake 1 hour in a 350° oven.

4. Add the remaining cup of turkey stock and bake 25-35 minutes longer, or until the liquid is absorbed and the rice is tender and fluffy when stirred with a fork.

5. Sprinkle the top with cheese, dot with bits of butter, and broil to a golden brown. Serves 6.

*Serve with sliced tomatoes topped with chopped chives and parsley mixed with French dressing, and wilted cucumbers in sour cream, together with a tossed green salad.*

# DUCK

## DUCKLING ALMONDINE

2 four-pound ducklings cut up
½ cup flour
1 teaspoon salt
⅛ teaspoon pepper
¼ cup margarine, butter, or
salad oil

½ cup scallions sliced
(green onions)
½ cup slivered toasted almonds
2 cups dry white wine
Minced parsley

132

1. Put the flour, salt, and pepper in a paper bag and dredge the duckling pieces in it.
2. Sauté to a golden brown in hot fat and arrange in a large casserole, crowding the pieces.
3. Scatter the scallions and almonds over the duck, pour on the wine, cover tightly, and bake in a moderate oven, 375°, about 1 hour, or until the duck is very tender. Remove the cover the last 15 minutes.
4. Sprinkle with parsley before serving. Serves 6-8.

*Serve with small parsley-butter boiled potatoes (or potato balls) and buttered tiny green peas.*

## DUCK AND PINEAPPLE CANTON

5-pound duck cut in pieces
¼ cup soy sauce
1 tablespoon sugar
½ teaspoon ginger or
   ground ginger root
1 clove garlic cut in 2 pieces
4 tablespoons salad oil

1 cup pineapple juice
1¾ cups water
2 tablespoons cornstarch
2 cups pineapple chunks
   (frozen or canned) well drained
Salt and pepper

1. Mix the soy sauce, sugar, ginger, and garlic in a bowl and dip the pieces of duck in the mixture, draining each one as you remove it and laying the pieces on paper toweling.
2. Heat the oil in a heavy skillet and brown the duck pieces well all over. Arrange in a large casserole.
3. Mix the pineapple juice with 1½ cups of the water and clean out the skillet with it. Pour over the duck, cover, and bake about an hour in a 300° oven.
4. Drain the liquid from the casserole into a saucepan and stir into it the cornstarch and the remaining ¼ cup water mixed to a paste. Simmer about 10 minutes, stirring constantly.
5. When the sauce is thickened and clear stir in the pineapple. Pour back over the duck in the casserole and bake about 10 minutes longer, uncovered. Serves 4-5.

*Serve with plenty of hot fluffy rice, glazed onions, and a tossed green salad.*

# SPANISH DUCK

5-pound duck cut up
¼ cup salad oil
1 tablespoon paprika
1 medium onion chopped
¼ cup flour

2 cups chicken broth
½ cup dry sherry
1 medium tomato sliced
¼ cup chopped stuffed olives

1. Thoroughly mix the oil and paprika, heat in a heavy skillet, and brown the pieces of duck on all sides. Arrange in a large casserole.
2. In the fat remaining in the skillet sauté the onion until it begins to be transparent.
3. Blend in the flour and gradually add the chicken broth and sherry, stirring constantly until smooth and thickened.
4. Add the sliced tomato and chopped olives to the sauce and pour over the duck in the casserole.
5. Cover and bake in a slow oven, 325°, about an hour, or until the duck is tender. Serves 4.

*Serve with small parsley-butter potatoes and purée of spinach.*


# SWEET AND SOUR DUCKLING

6-pound duckling cut up
1½ teaspoons salt
1 teaspoon pepper
2 teaspoons paprika
2 cups water

½ cup sugar
2 tablespoons cornstarch
½ cup vinegar
1 teaspoon soy sauce
12-ounce can pineapple chunks

THIS is an exceptionally flavorsome dish, as most sweet-sour dishes are.
1. Cut off as much fat as possible and season the duck pieces well with salt, pepper, and paprika. Arrange them in a large casserole, closely packed together.
2. Cover the casserole and bake 1 hour in a 350° oven, turning the pieces 2 or 3 times. Uncover the last 15 minutes.

3. Simmer the giblets in the water until tender, cutting the gizzard into several pieces so that it will cook in the same time as the other giblets.
4. Strain the broth from the giblets into a small saucepan, and add the liquid that has accumulated in the casserole from the duck.
5. Combine the sugar, cornstarch, vinegar, and soy sauce and stir into the saucepan. Cook until thickened and smooth, stirring constantly.
6. Add the pineapple and pour over the duck. Bake fifteen minutes longer, uncovered. Serves 4.

*Serve with fresh hot rice and whole tiny buttered green beans.*


## DUCKLING CASSEROLE

5-6-pound duckling cut up
¼ cup butter, margarine, or
   salad oil
2 small onions sliced
2 carrots sliced thin
1 cup dry white wine
3 cups chicken broth

1 teaspoon minced parsley
½ teaspoon dried orégano or
   1½ teaspoons fresh, chopped
½ small bay leaf crumbled
   Salt and pepper
1-2 tablespoons cornstarch
¼ cup water

1. Brown the duckling pieces in hot fat in a heavy casserole. When half browned add the onions and carrots.
2. Stir in the wine, chicken broth, herbs, and salt and pepper to taste.
3. Cover and bake in a slow oven, 300°, 1½ hours.
4. Pour the liquid from the casserole into a saucepan and boil hard until it is reduced to 1½ cups.
5. Reduce the heat and stir in the cornstarch mixed to a paste with the water, continuing to stir until the sauce is thickened and smooth.
6. Pour the sauce back over the duck and bake 5 minutes longer, uncovered. Serves 4-6.

*Serve with hot fluffy rice and buttered baby lima beans.*

# DUCKLING NIPPONESE

4-5-pound duckling cut up
1 egg slightly beaten
1 teaspoon soy sauce
½ cup flaked coconut
¼ cup flour

1½ teaspoons salt
⅛ teaspoon fresh-ground pepper
3 tablespoons cognac slightly
warmed

*Nipponese Sauce*

11-ounce can mandarin orange
segments
½ cup maple syrup
1½ tablespoons cornstarch
(generous)
2 tablespoons lemon juice

3 tablespoons frozen orange
juice, undiluted
1 tablespoon grated orange rind
1 tablespoon grated lemon rind
2 firm bananas sliced
2 tablespoons butter

1. Cut off as much fat from the duckling pieces as you possibly can. Prick the skin well with a sharp-tined fork and arrange the pieces on a rack in a large casserole or baking pan. Bake 30 minutes in a hot oven, 400°.

2. Pour off all the fat and arrange the pieces in the casserole, without using the rack.

3. Brush the pieces well with the egg and soy sauce blended.

4. Combine the coconut, flour, salt, and pepper and sprinkle evenly over the duckling. Return to the oven and bake another 25-30 minutes, or until golden brown.

5. Remove the casserole from the oven, ignite the warmed cognac, and flambé the duckling.

6. When the flames die down, spread the sauce over and let stand in the oven, heat off, 5 minutes or so. Serves 4.

*Sauce:* Combine the juice of the mandarin oranges, the maple syrup, cornstarch, lemon and oranges juices and rinds, and bring to a boil, stirring constantly until somewhat thickened. Stir in the orange segments, bananas, and butter and simmer about 5 minutes. The sauce can be held in a double boiler a long time, and hence can be made long ahead of time. This recipe is a generous one, and there is actually enough sauce for two ducks.

*Serve with a rice casserole* (see Index) *and a large tossed salad.*

136

# FISH

# FISH FILLETS AU GRATIN

1 pound any white or light
  fish fillets
1 can condensed cream of celery
  or cream of mushroom soup
½ cup grated Cheddar cheese
  Salt and pepper to taste

2 tablespoons bread or corn
  flake crumbs
1 tablespoon grated Parmesan
  cheese
  Paprika

1. Spread the fillets in a well-greased flat casserole.
2. In a small saucepan mix the soup, Cheddar, and salt and pepper to taste. Heat until the cheese is melted, and pour over the fish.
3. Mix the crumbs with the Parmesan cheese and sprinkle on top. Shake a little paprika over it.
4. Bake 35-45 minutes in a 375° oven, until the fish flakes readily and the surface is bubbly and golden. The exact time will depend upon the thickness of the fish. Serves 4.

*Serve with a rice casserole* (see Index) *and buttered baby Brussels sprouts.*


# FISH FILLET ROLLS WITH SESAME SEEDS

1½ pounds fillet of flounder
  1 teaspoon salt
  ⅛ teaspoon pepper
1½ cups milk
  3 tablespoons butter

3 tablespoons flour
¼ cup toasted sesame seeds*
¼ pound grated Cheddar cheese
3 tablespoons lemon juice
  Paprika

1. Roll up the fillets, fasten with toothpicks, and lay in a rather shallow greased casserole. Sprinkle them with salt and pepper and pour the milk over them.
2. Bake in a 350° oven, covered, 30-40 minutes, or until the fish flakes readily.

* See Index for how to toast sesame seeds.

3. Melt the butter in a saucepan, stir in flour and sesame seeds, and let cook a moment.

4. When the fish is cooked, pour off the milk and add it slowly to the flour mixture, stirring constantly over low heat until smooth and thickened.

5. Stir in the cheese and the lemon juice, and keep stirring until the cheese is melted.

6. Pour the sauce over the fish, sprinkle with paprika, and brown well under the broiler. Serves 6.

*Note:* If you wish, remove the toothpicks from the fish rolls after you pour off the milk.

*Serve with riced potatoes and any cooked greens: spinach, young beet greens, Swiss chard, or fiddlehead greens (now in wide distribution frozen).*

## NEW HAMPSHIRE FISH CASSEROLE

| | |
|---|---|
| 2½ cups cut-up white fish, any kind | ¼ cup flour |
| 3 cups milk | 2 egg yolks slightly beaten |
| Small onion sliced | Salt and pepper to taste |
| 1 sprig parsley | 2 tablespoons lemon juice |
| 1 blade mace (optional) | ⅔ cup buttered cracker crumbs |
| ¼ cup butter or margarine | |

1. Cook the fish 20-25 minutes in a double boiler with the milk, onion, parsley, and mace. Drain, reserving the liquid.

2. Break up the fish coarsely with a fork and spread it in a shallow casserole.

3. In a small saucepan melt the butter, blend in the flour, and slowly stir in the milk in which the fish was cooked. Season to taste.

4. Add a bit of the sauce to the egg yolks and stir back into the sauce. Add the lemon juice and pour over the fish in the casserole.

5. Top the casserole with the cracker crumbs and bake about 25 minutes in a 350° oven. Serves 4-5.

*Serve with fresh hot rice and buttered baby carrots.*

## BAKED HALIBUT

1½-pound halibut steak
  Salt and pepper
 ¼ cup butter or margarine
  softened

½ cup mushrooms sliced
1 cup light cream
1 tablespoon Angostura bitters

HALIBUT is one of our most flavorful fish, and the flavor here is enhanced by the bitters.
1. Wipe the steak, place in a greased shallow casserole, sprinkle with salt and pepper, and spread the butter on it.
2. Bake 15 minutes in a moderate oven, 375°.
3. Cover with the mushrooms and cream and bake 15 minutes longer.
4. Dribble the bitters into the sauce around the fish, stir it in as best you can, and bake 10 minutes longer, basting the fish twice with the pan juices. Serves 4-5.

*Serve with a rice casserole* (see Index) *and buttered lima beans.*


## BROILED HALIBUT

4 portions halibut cut 1 inch thick
6 tablespoons butter
1 cup dry vermouth
  Salt and pepper

1 tablespoon fine bread or
  corn flake crumbs
1 tablespoon grated Parmesan
  cheese

VERMOUTH adds wonderfully to the flavor of many foods. Here it performs its magic for halibut.
1. Lay the pieces of halibut in a flat casserole. Pour over them the butter and vermouth heated together in a small saucepan. Salt and pepper lightly.
2. Place the casserole about 6 inches under the broiler (preheated, of course) and baste frequently while it broils. It should take about 20 minutes to cook the halibut tender.

3. When it is about ready, remove the casserole from the broiler and sprinkle the fish with the crumbs and cheese mixed.

4. Return to the broiler for a minute or two, or until the topping browns. Serves 4.

*Serve with fluffy mashed potatoes and either corn on the cob or buttered cut corn.*

## DEVILED HALIBUT

1½ pounds halibut steak (one piece)
¼ cup chopped green pepper
¼ cup minced onion
1 tablespoon prepared mustard
1 teaspoon Worcestershire sauce
⅛ teaspoon Tabasco sauce

3½ tablespoons lemon juice
½ cup butter or margarine melted
2 cups fine bread or corn flake crumbs
2 tablespoons grated Parmesan cheese
Salt and pepper

THIS is an outstanding casserole, worth every minute of the time it takes to prepare.

1. Mix the green pepper, onion, mustard, Worcestershire sauce, Tabasco, and lemon juice.

2. Mix the butter and crumbs and combine both mixtures, blending well.

3. Spread half of this mixture on top of the steak, patting it down well.

4. Quickly turn it crumb-side-down in a shallow greased casserole. Season the top side and spread with the rest of the crumb mixture.

5. Bake the casserole 25-30 minutes in a 350° oven, or until the fish flakes easily with a fork.

6. Spread the cheese on top and brown 3-4 minutes under the broiler, watching carefully to see that it doesn't burn. Serves 4.

*Serve with creamed chopped spinach and little parsley-buttered potatoes.*

## SESAME HALIBUT STEAK

2 large halibut steaks 1¼ inches
   thick (about 2½ pounds)
   Salt and pepper
2 tablespoons butter or margarine
   softened
2 cups soft bread crumbs

3 tablespoons toasted sesame
   seeds*
½ teaspoon dried thyme or
   1½ teaspoons fresh, chopped
¼ cup melted butter
   Paprika

IN this recipe sesame seeds enhance the flavor of one of our best-liked fish.

1. Arrange the steaks in a shallow casserole that will hold them comfortably. Salt and pepper them lightly and spread the softened butter on them.

2. Mix the crumbs, ¾ teaspoon salt, ⅛ teaspoon fresh-ground pepper, toasted sesame seeds, thyme, and melted butter together and spread half on each steak.

3. Sprinkle lightly with paprika and bake 25-30 minutes in a moderate oven, 350°. The fish should then flake readily. Serves 6.

*Serve with buttered asparagus and riced potatoes.*


## BAKED SALMON STEAKS

3 pounds salmon steaks cut
   1 inch thick
¼ pound mushrooms minced
1 medium onion minced
2 tablespoons minced parsley

¼ cup butter or margarine
½ cup dry sherry
⅓ cup fine bread or corn
   flake crumbs

THIS is a French Canadian way of preparing their wonderful fresh salmon from the St. John's River.

1. Lay the steaks in a well-greased shallow casserole.

* See Index for how to toast sesame seeds.

2. Mix the mushrooms, onion, and parsley and spread over the fish.
3. Cut the butter into bits and dot over the top.
4. Pour the sherry in and bake in a moderate oven, 350°, 15 minutes.
5. Spread the steaks with the crumbs and continue baking another 10 or 15 minutes, or until fish flakes readily. Baste 2 or 3 times during the baking. Serves 6.

*Serve with parsley-butter potatoes and buttered green beans.*

## BAKED SALMON STEAKS ALMONDINE

| | |
|---|---|
| 4 salmon steaks 1 inch thick | 1 lemon sliced thin |
| 2 cups water | ¼ cup toasted slivered almonds |
| ¼ cup vinegar | ¼ cup whole white raisins |
| 1 small onion sliced | 2 egg yolks |
| Salt and pepper | 1 tablespoon chopped parsley |

1. Lay the steaks in a greased shallow casserole. Add the water and vinegar mixed, and the onion.
2. Season with salt and pepper, cover, and bake 30 minutes in a 350° oven.
3. Drain off the liquid from the casserole and measure 1 cup into a small saucepan.
4. Add the lemon, almonds, and raisins to the casserole, cover again, and cook 5 minutes more.
5. Beat the egg yolks well and stir in the cup of liquid from the salmon. Cook over low heat until it begins to thicken, stirring constantly. Season to taste, pour over the casserole, sprinkle with parsley, and serve.

Serves 4, though sometimes salmon steaks are large enough to make two servings each.

*Serve with purée of spinach and riced potatoes.*

# BAKED CANNED SALMON

1-pound can salmon
1 tablespoon butter or margarine
1 small onion chopped fine
½ medium green pepper chopped
1 can condensed cream of
  mushroom soup

¼ cup milk
½ cup coarse bread crumbs
  or tiny dice
1 tablespoon grated Parmesan
  cheese

EVEN canned salmon can make an appealing casserole.

1. Heat the butter in a small skillet and lightly sauté the onion and green pepper.

2. Add the soup and milk, blend well, and heat almost to boiling point.

3. Drain the can of salmon and remove skin and bones. Break it into good-sized chunks and lay in a small greased casserole.

4. Pour the soup mixture over, cover with crumbs, and sprinkle with cheese.

5. Bake in a hot oven, 400°, 20 minutes. Serves 4.

*Serve with a casserole of rice* (see Index) *and buttered baby Brussels sprouts.*


# SALMON TETRAZZINI

1-pound can salmon
½ cup butter or margarine
½ cup flour
2 cups hot chicken broth
½ teaspoon salt
⅛ teaspoon pepper
⅛ teaspoon nutmeg

¼ cup dry sherry
½ cup light cream
½ pound mushrooms sliced
½ pound spaghetti cooked
2 tablespoons butter or margarine
½ cup grated Parmesan cheese
½ cup bread or corn flake crumbs

THE name Tetrazzini has by now become a method, and can be used with chicken, turkey, various fish, and various meats. Whatever the main ingredient is, the dish is a wonderful concoction.

144

1. Make the cream sauce first. Melt the ½ cup butter, blend in the flour, and gradually add the hot chicken broth, stirring until the sauce is smooth and velvety. Season with salt and pepper, nutmeg, and sherry.
2. Drain the salmon and stir its liquid into the sauce also. Let it simmer 8-10 minutes, stirring occasionally. Add the cream and keep hot on an asbestos plate.
3. Sauté the mushrooms lightly in the 2 tablespoons butter and add them to the sauce.
4. Stir half of the sauce into the cooked spaghetti and spread it on a large flat casserole or deep oversize pie plate.
5. Flake the salmon coarsely and mix with the rest of the sauce. Carefully pour this over the spaghetti.
6. Sprinkle the top with the cheese and crumbs mixed and bake 15-20 minutes in a 350° oven, until well browned. If everything is hot when you put the casserole together you can merely brown the top well under the broiler. Serves 4.

*Serve with a mixed vegetable salad and warm garlic bread.*


## RED SNAPPER ALICANTE

1 pound red snapper fillets
1 medium onion sliced
½ teaspoon salt
  Dash pepper

2 tablespoons salad oil
1 tablespoon dry white wine
¼ cup chopped nuts

LAY onion slices on the bottom of a greased flat casserole. Arrange the fillets on top. Season them with salt and pepper. Pour the oil and wine over, sprinkle with nuts, and bake in a moderate oven, 350°, 15-20 minutes, or until the fish flakes readily. Serves 3.

*Serve with parsley-butter small potatoes and buttered green peas.*

# BAKED WHOLE RED SNAPPER

4-5-pound red snapper
dressed weight
1 tablespoon vinegar or
lemon juice
1 tablespoon salt
1 egg white slightly beaten

½ cup fine dry bread or corn
flake crumbs
1 teaspoon grated lemon peel
½ cup butter or margarine melted
(or more)

## Caper Stuffing

½ cup fine dry crumbs
½ cup capers
¼ cup minced onion
¼ cup minced parsley

½ teaspoon salt
2 well-beaten eggs
⅔ cup light cream

## Caper Sauce

2 tablespoons butter or
margarine
2 tablespoons flour
½ teaspoon salt

¼ teaspoon pepper
1½ cups heavy cream
1 tablespoon tomato paste
4 teaspoons capers

1. Rinse the fish inside and out and pat dry with paper towels.
2. Make the stuffing by mixing the crumbs, capers, onion, parsley, and salt together. Mix the eggs and cream and stir into the crumb mixture until well mixed.
3. Spoon this stuffing gently into the fish cavity and close the opening with skewers and twine or sew it together. Lay the fish in a long narrow casserole.
4. Brush the surface of the fish with the vinegar and salt mixed, and then with the egg white. Cut several deep gashes in the side, 1½-2 inches apart.
5. Mix the crumbs and lemon peel together and sprinkle on the fish.
6. Bake in a moderate oven, 350°, about 45 minutes, or until the fish flakes readily when tested with a fork. Drizzle melted butter over several times during the baking.
7. Remove skewers, garnish with lemon quarters, and serve with the sauce in a separate bowl. Serves 8-10.

*Sauce:* Heat the butter in a saucepan, stir in the flour, salt, and pepper, and slowly add the cream and tomato paste, stirring constantly. Bring to a boil, cook 1-2 minutes, and mix in capers.

*Serve with a rice casserole* (see Index) *and buttered broccoli.*


## BAKED FLOUNDER FLORENTINE

1½-2 pounds fillet of flounder
2 tablespoons butter or margarine
2 tablespoons minced onion
1 clove garlic minced
1 package frozen chopped spinach
¼ teaspoon salt
⅛ teaspoon fresh-ground pepper

⅛ teaspoon nutmeg
3 tablespoons lemon juice
1 teaspoon Worcestershire sauce
¼ cup melted butter or margarine
1 cup sliced mushrooms
2 tablespoons flour
1 cup dairy sour cream
3 tablespoons Parmesan cheese

1. Melt the 2 tablespoons butter in a heavy skillet and lightly sauté the onion and garlic. Lay in the block of frozen spinach, lower the heat to a bare simmer, cover, and cook until the spinach is thawed, turning the block 2 or 3 times. Press out excess moisture with a spatula and drain off.
2. Stir salt, pepper, and nutmeg into the spinach.
3. Wipe the fillets with paper towels or a damp cloth. Lay them out on a board or counter, and spread the spinach on them. Roll them up, fasten with toothpicks, and lay, seam side down, in a shallow greased casserole.
4. Mix the lemon juice, Worcestershire sauce, and melted butter and drizzle over the fish rolls.
5. Bake, covered, 20 minutes in a 400° oven, or until the fish flakes readily.
6. Remove casserole from the oven, drain off the liquid into a saucepan, and cook the mushrooms in it 5 or 6 minutes. Stir in the flour, blend in the sour cream, and pour back over the casserole.
7. Sprinkle with cheese and brown under the broiler. Serves 5-6.

*Serve with fluffy mashed potatoes and a tossed green salad.*

## FILLET OF SOLE WITH GRAPES

2½ pounds fillet of sole
  (or flounder)
2 cups milk
½ pound mushrooms sliced
¼ cup butter or margarine
2 cups white seedless grapes
3 tablespoons butter or margarine

4 tablespoons flour (scant)
  Salt and pepper
½ cup buttered bread or corn
  flake crumbs
2 tablespoons grated Parmesan
  cheese

THE grapes here add an unexpected and delightful flavor.

1. Put the milk in a large heavy skillet, heat to just below boiling, and poach the fillets in it 5 minutes, reducing the heat immediately so that the milk just simmers.

2. Sauté the mushrooms in the ¼ cup of butter about 3 minutes.

3. Combine mushrooms with grapes and spread in a large shallow casserole.

4. With a slotted spatula lift the fish fillets carefully from the milk and lay them on top of the grape-mushroom mixture.

5. Make a cream sauce with the 3 tablespoons of butter, the flour, and the milk in which the fillets were cooked. Season to taste and spread over the fish.

6. Top with the crumbs and cheese mixed together and bake in a hot oven, 400°, about 25 minutes, or until golden. Serves 6.

*Serve with little parsley-butter potatoes and buttered green peas.*


## SOLE AU GRATIN ON MUSHROOMS

8 fillets of sole (or flounder)
2 pounds mushrooms chopped fine
3 tablespoons wine vinegar
1 tablespoon Cointreau liqueur
3 ounces brandy
¾ cup salad oil
1 tablespoon minced parsley

1 medium onion sliced
  Few celery leaves
1 cup dry white wine
4 tablespoons butter or margarine
4 tablespoons flour
  Salt and pepper
2 egg yolks slightly beaten

148

| 1 tablespoon grated onion | ¼ pound Swiss cheese |
|---|---|
| 1 tablespoon minced chives | coarsely grated |
| 1 teaspoon dried tarragon or | 2 tablespoons grated |
| 1 tablespoon fresh, chopped | Parmesan cheese |

THIS is a real gourmet dish, obviously designed for a dinner party, and good for that because it can be prepared, up to the last step, early in the day.

1. Mix the vinegar, Cointreau, 1 tablespoon of the brandy, the oil, parsley, grated onion, chives, and tarragon, and stir in the chopped mushrooms to marinate.

2. In a large heavy skillet put the sliced onion, celery leaves, wine, the rest of the brandy, and a little water. Bring to a boil and lay in the fillets. If there is not enough liquid to barely cover them add a little more water. Lower the heat and just simmer the fillets 15 minutes.

3. Cook the mushrooms in their marinade in a saucepan, 2 minutes on high heat and 7 minutes on low. Drain through a fine sieve and spread mushrooms in a large shallow greased casserole.

4. With a slotted spatula lift out the fish fillets and lay on the mushrooms.

Up to this point the dish can be prepared hours ahead of time. If you do this, however, be sure to bring the casserole to room temperature (1 hour), and bake it 10 minutes in a 350° oven before you broil it.

5. Make a cream sauce with the butter, flour, and the stock the fish was cooked in, plus a little of the liquid drained from the mushrooms if needed. Discard remainder. Season to taste and stir in the Swiss cheese.

6. When the cheese is all melted, stir a little of the sauce into the egg yolks and quickly stir back into the sauce.

7. Pour over the fish, top with Parmesan cheese, and put under the broiler until golden brown. Serves 8.

*Serve with buttered noodles to which poppy seeds and slivered almonds have been added, buttered baby green peas, and a tossed green salad, with warm garlic bread.*

# FILLET OF SOLE ALMONDINE

4 fillets of sole (or flounder)
  Salt and pepper
¼ cup milk
¼ cup light cream

½ teaspoon dried rosemary or
  1½ teaspoons fresh, chopped
¼ cup blanched, slivered, and
  toasted almonds

1. Spread the fillets in a shallow greased casserole and season with salt and pepper.
2. Pour the milk and cream over, sprinkle with rosemary, and bake 20 minutes in a hot oven, 400°.
3. Sprinkle the almonds over the top and bake 10 minutes longer, or until the liquid is practically all absorbed.
4. If fish has not browned put under the broiler a minute or two. Serves 4.

*Serve with au gratin potatoes and buttered cut green beans.*


# FILLET OF SOLE CASSEROLE

2 pounds fillet of sole
  (or flounder)
  Salt and pepper
¼ cup dry white wine
2 tablespoons lemon juice
¼ cup flour
4 tablespoons butter or margarine
⅔ cup minced onion
½ cup chopped mushrooms

2 tablespoons chopped carrot
2 tablespoons chopped parsley
¼ teaspoon dried thyme or
  ¾ teaspoon fresh, chopped
4 small tomatoes peeled and
  sliced
½ cup bread or corn flake crumbs
2 tablespoons grated Parmesan
  cheese

1. Lay the fillets in a shallow greased casserole or oversize pie plate. Salt and pepper them lightly and pour in the wine and lemon juice mixed.
2. Cover and bake 10 minutes in a moderate oven, 350°—not long enough to completely cook the fish.
3. Put the flour in a shallow soup plate. Carefully lift out the fillets

with a slotted spatula and dredge them with flour on both sides.
4. Melt 2 tablespoons of the butter in a heavy skillet and when it is sizzling quickly brown the fillets on both sides.
5. Add the vegetables, except tomatoes, and herbs to the liquid in the casserole in which the fish was cooked. Gently lay the fillets on top as they are browned.
6. Cover with a closely fitted layer of tomato slices. Season with salt and pepper.
7. Melt the remaining 2 tablespoons of butter, and mix with the crumbs and cheese. Scatter on top of the tomatoes and bake an additional 20 minutes. Serves 5-6.

*Serve with fluffy mashed potatoes and buttered asparagus.*


## BAKED STRIPED BASS

| | |
|---|---|
| Whole bass weighing 3-5 pounds dressed | 1 medium can whole tomatoes drained |
| Salt and pepper | 1 small bay leaf |
| 2 tablespoons salad oil | ½ cup dry white wine |
| ½ cup melted butter or margarine | |

THIS fish will be easier to serve if you have the backbone removed, but keep the two halves together if you do.
1. Season the fish inside and out with salt and pepper and lay in a greased shallow casserole. Bake 10 minutes in a 350° oven.
2. Remove the casserole from the oven. Mix the oil and butter and drizzle over the fish.
3. Add to the casserole the tomatoes, broken into 2 or 3 pieces each, the bay leaf, and the wine. Season the tomatoes.
4. Return the casserole to the oven and bake until the fish flakes readily but is still moist. The total time should be about 10 minutes per pound. Serves 4-6, according to size.

*Serve with fluffy mashed potatoes and chopped spinach mixed with a little sour cream and a touch of nutmeg.*

## BAKED SWORDFISH

1¾ pounds swordfish, in 1 piece
¾ cup salad oil
½ clove garlic mashed
2 scallions minced (green onions)

½ teaspoon dried orégano or
1½ teaspoons fresh, chopped
Salt and pepper

MANY people consider swordfish the supreme "gift from the sea."
Now that it is available frozen, it can be enjoyed everywhere. It is
of course wonderful simply broiled, but the three casserole recipe
given here provide other delicious ways to fix it. This one is certainly
the easiest.

1. Mix all of the ingredients except the fish.
2. Lay the fish in a shallow casserole, pour the mixture over, and
let stand at room temperature at least 2 hours.
3. Bake 30-40 minutes in a 350° oven, or until it breaks up readily
Serves 4-5.

*Serve with a rice casserole* (see Index) *and corn on the cob if in
season, otherwise with buttered lima beans.*


## SWORDFISH PROVENÇALE

2-pound swordfish steak
   1 inch thick
   Salt and pepper
¼ cup salad oil
1 medium onion chopped
½ green pepper chopped
4 tomatoes peeled, seeded,
   and chopped

6-8 medium mushrooms sliced
   1 clove garlic minced
½ cup dry white wine
   3 sprigs parsley
¼ teaspoon dried thyme or
   ¾ teaspoon fresh, minced
   1 tablespoon flour
   2 tablespoons butter or margarine

1. Cut the swordfish into 6 portions, season, and brown quickly in
sizzling oil in a heavy skillet.
2. Arrange in a casserole and add all the remaining ingredients except

152

the last two, with enough water just to cover the fish. Cover and bake about 30 minutes in a 350° oven.

3. Drain the liquid from the casserole into a saucepan and boil hard until it is reduced to half its volume.

4. Knead the butter and flour together and stir in, continuing to stir until the sauce is thickened and smooth.

5. Pour over the fish and serve. Serves 6.

*Serve with buttered noodles and buttered baby carrots mixed with chopped parsley.*

## NEW ENGLAND BAKED SWORDFISH

1½-pound swordfish steak
  1 inch thick
  Top milk or half-and-half

Salt and pepper
2 tablespoons butter or
  margarine

LAY the fish in a shallow casserole. Add rich milk until it comes about halfway up the fish. Salt and pepper the fish and dot with bits of the butter. Bake 30 minutes in a 375° oven, basting several times. The milk should be absorbed then and the fish brown but moist. Serves 4.

*Serve with parsley-butter new potatoes and young green cabbage shredded and cooked not over 7 minutes in boiling salted water, drained, and buttered.*

## STUFFED FILLET OF SOLE ROLLS
## WITH MUSHROOM SAUCE

6 fillets of sole (or flounder)
7¾-ounce can of salmon, drained,
  boned, and flaked
2 tablespoons minced parsley
2 tablespoons chopped chives

½ teaspoon dried tarragon or
  1½ teaspoons fresh, chopped
½ teaspoon paprika
1 tablespoon lemon juice
1 tablespoon melted butter

*Mushroom Sauce*

1 shallot minced or 1 teaspoon
  minced onion
1 tablespoon butter or margarine

1 can condensed cream of
  mushroom soup
¼ cup light cream

1. Mix together the salmon, parsley, chives, tarragon, paprika, and lemon juice. Spread on the fillets, covering them to within ¼ inch of the edges. Beginning with the tail end, roll up and fasten with toothpicks.

2. Lay the rolls in a small shallow buttered casserole or pie plate, brush with melted butter, cover, and bake in a 350° oven 20 minutes, or until the fish flakes readily.

3. Drain the casserole and spread some of the mushroom sauce over the rolls. They can be served at this point, or you can sprinkle sauce-topped rolls with about 2 tablespoons buttered crumbs and broil 2-3 minutes, until golden. Serve with bowl of mushroom sauce. Serves 6.

*Mushroom Sauce:* Cook the shallot or onion 2-3 minutes in butter in a small saucepan, stir in soup and cream, and heat to boiling point.

*Serve with buttered new potatoes and buttered baby carrots.*


## CHINESE TUNA CASSEROLE

1 can tuna broken into
  small chunks

3-ounce can chow mein noodles
1 cup thin-sliced celery

1 can condensed cream of
　　mushroom soup
⅓ cup milk, chicken broth, or water

½ cup whole salted cashew nuts
¼ cup minced onion
Salt and pepper to taste

TUNA fish is certainly far more widely used in this country than any other fish—for salads, for sandwiches, and for main dishes. The remaining recipes in this section suggest some intriguing ways to use it in casseroles, beginning with this unusual Chinese recipe.

In a saucepan put the soup, the milk or broth, 1 cup of the noodles, the celery, cashews, onion, and salt and pepper. Heat and stir in the tuna. Pour into a quart casserole and bake 20 minutes in a 350° oven. Sprinkle the remaining noodles on top and bake 5 minutes more. Serves 4.

# CURRIED TUNA AND EGGS

7-ounce can tuna drained and
　　flaked
2 hard-cooked eggs quartered
6 tablespoons butter or margarine
¼ clove garlic mashed
½ teaspoon curry powder
⅓ cup chopped almonds

3 tablespoons flour
2 cups milk
¼ teaspoon Worcestershire sauce
½ teaspoon salt
1 tablespoon lemon juice
2 tablespoons buttered bread or
　　corn flake crumbs

1. Melt 2 tablespoons of the butter in a saucepan. Stir in the garlic, curry powder, and almonds and cook until slightly browned.
2. Melt the remaining 4 tablespoons butter in the top of a double boiler over simmering water, stir in the flour, and cook until bubbly. Blend in the milk and stir until smooth.
3. Add to this cream sauce the Worcestershire sauce, salt, lemon juice, tuna, eggs, and finally the curry-almond mixture. Stir gently until well mixed and pour into a smallish casserole.
4. Top with buttered crumbs and bake in a moderate oven, 350°, 25-30 minutes, or until nicely browned. Serves 4-5.

*Serve with fresh hot rice, as all curry is served, and buttered young summer squash. A tossed green salad is always a good idea with curry.*

## TUNA-BROCCOLI CASSEROLE

7-ounce can tuna fish drained
  and flaked
2 pounds fresh broccoli or
  2 packages frozen
4 tablespoons butter or margarine
4 tablespoons flour

1 cup light cream
1 cup chicken broth
  Salt and pepper to taste
1 tablespoon chopped parsley
2 hard-cooked eggs sliced
¼ cup grated Parmesan cheese

1. If the broccoli is fresh, trim off almost all of the stem part. (It can be cooked separately, chopped, buttered, and served as a separate vegetable another day.) Whether fresh or frozen, cook in boiling salted water until barely tender and arrange in a single layer in a shallow greased casserole.
2. Melt butter, blend in flour, and stir in the cream and broth to make a smooth sauce. Season to taste.
3. Stir in gently the parsley, tuna fish, and eggs. Pour carefully over the broccoli and top with the cheese.
4. Bake 15-20 minutes in a moderate oven, 350°, and then put under the broiler a minute or two to brown well. Serves 4-5.

*Serve with spaghetti cooked barely tender and mixed well with butter and grated Parmesan or Romano cheese, or a mixture of the two. A large tossed salad and warm garlic bread go well, too.*

## TUNA-CHEESE FONDUE

7-ounce can tuna fish drained
  and coarsely flaked
1 cup grated Swiss cheese
10 slices white bread,
  buttered, crusts removed
4 eggs well beaten

2 cups milk
1 teaspoon salt
¼ teaspoon paprika
½ teaspoon Worcestershire sauce
  Dash cayenne pepper

1. Cut 8 slices of the buttered bread into ½-inch cubes.

2. In a greased medium casserole make alternate layers of bread cubes, cheese, and tuna (3 layers of bread and cheese and 2 of tuna).
3. Blend the eggs, milk, salt, paprika, Worcestershire sauce, and cayenne and pour carefully over the casserole.
4. Cut the remaining 2 slices of buttered bread into triangles and stand them around the edge of the casserole, the broadest sides pushed into the fondue a little way.
5. Bake the fondue an hour in a 350° oven, or until well browned and firm in the center. Serves 6.

*Serve with a plate of sliced ripe tomatoes, topped with chopped chives and parsley mixed with French dressing, and cucumbers and carrot sticks.*

# TUNA-EGG CASSEROLE

7-ounce can tuna fish drained
  and coarsely broken up
4 hard-cooked eggs quartered
2 tablespoons butter or margarine
4 teaspoons flour
¾ teaspoon salt
1⅓ cups evaporated milk

⅔ cup water
⅛ teaspoon Tabasco sauce
2 tablespoons minced
  green pepper
2 tablespoons minced pimiento
1 cup buttered crumbs

1. Melt the butter in a saucepan, blend in flour and salt, and gradually stir in the milk and water. Cook until it thickens, stirring constantly.
2. Add the Tabasco, tuna, green pepper, and pimiento.
3. Arrange the quartered eggs on the bottom of a medium greased casserole and carefully pour the tuna mixture over them.
4. Top with a thick layer of crumbs.
5. Bake 20-25 minutes in a moderate oven, 375°. Serves 5-6.

*Serve with herbed rice and buttered Italian green beans.*

# TUNA-MACARONI CASSEROLE

7-ounce can tuna fish drained,
rinsed, and broken into chunks
2 cups elbow macaroni cooked
and drained
2 tablespoons butter, margarine,
or salad oil
2 tablespoons chopped onion

1 can condensed cream of
celery soup
1 cup milk
1 teaspoon salt
Dash pepper
¼ teaspoon whole celery seed
1 cup coarsely chopped
sharp Cheddar cheese

1. Sauté the onion lightly in hot fat. Gradually stir in the soup and the milk.

2. Fold in the tuna, season to taste, and add the celery seed and half of the cheese.

3. Mix the macaroni and the tuna mixture, put in a greased casserole, and top with the remaining cheese.

4. Bake 10-15 minutes in a moderate oven, 350°, or until the cheese is melted and the casserole bubbly. Serves 5-6.

*Serve with green peppers cut in 1-inch squares and slowly sautéed tender in butter or margarine, and cole slaw.*

# SHELLFISH

## DEVILED SEAFOOD

2 cups diced cooked shrimp,
  crabmeat, lobster, and fish,
  in any combination
5 tablespoons butter or margarine
2 tablespoons flour
2½ cups milk scalded
  Salt and pepper
1 teaspoon grated onion
2 tablespoons minced parsley
¼ teaspoon dried orégano or
  ¾ teaspoon fresh, chopped
½ teaspoon dry mustard
1 teaspoon Worcestershire sauce
2 tablespoons cocktail sauce
  or catsup
3 hard-cooked eggs chopped
⅓ cup bread or corn flake crumbs

1. Melt 3 tablespoons butter over medium heat and stir in flour and milk. Season to taste and stir until smooth and thickened.
2. Add the onion, parsley, orégano, mustard, Worcestershire sauce, and cocktail sauce. Blend well.
3. Gently fold in the chopped eggs and seafood.
4. Pour into a small greased casserole, top with crumbs, dot with remaining butter, and bake 15-20 minutes in a hot oven, 475°. Serves 4.

*Serve with hot fluffy rice and shredded green cabbage cooked until barely tender.*


## SEAFOOD SOUFFLÉ

½ pound crabmeat picked over
  and coarsely flaked (fresh,
  frozen, or canned)
1 pound shrimp cooked, shelled,
  deveined, and broken up
2 hard-cooked eggs chopped
¼ cup sweet pickle relish
2 tablespoons minced parsley
2 tablespoons lemon juice
  Salt and pepper
1 can lobster bisque
½ cup light cream
4 eggs separated

1. In a greased medium casserole or straight-sided soufflé dish mix

160

the crabmeat, shrimp, chopped eggs, relish, parsley, lemon juice, and salt and pepper to taste.

2. In a small saucepan heat the lobster bisque slowly and blend in the cream.

3. Remove from the heat and stir in the well-beaten yolks and the crab-shrimp mixture.

4. Beat the egg whites until stiff but not dry and gently fold into the seafood mixture.

5. Bake 40-50 minutes in a moderate oven, 350°, or until a knife inserted in the middle comes out clean. If you prefer a soufflé somewhat on the soft side bake it only until the knife comes out with a little egg on it. Serve at once. Serves 4-5.

*Serve with buttered lima beans and buttered baby carrots.*


## CLAM-CORN CASSEROLE

7½-ounce can minced clams, undrained
1 cup whole-kernel corn, canned, fresh, or frozen
2 eggs well beaten
1 cup milk
1¼ cups coarse soda cracker crumbs (12 large or 20 small)

3 tablespoons melted butter or margarine
2 tablespoons minced onion
1 tablespoon minced green pepper
½ teaspoon Worcestershire sauce
Salt and pepper
½ cup grated Cheddar cheese

HERE is a delicious combination of flavors, calling for the simplest possible preparation.

1. Combine the eggs, milk, and cracker crumbs and let them stand about 10 minutes.

2. Stir in all remaining ingredients except the cheese, seasoning to taste. Pour into a medium casserole and bake 50 minutes in a 350° oven, or until the center feels firm.

3. Spread the cheese on top and bake 5 minutes longer, or until the cheese is melted. Serves 4.

*Serve with buttered mixed vegetables and a tossed green salad.*

# SEAFOOD CASSEROLE

20 cooked small shrimp,
   shelled and deveined
½ pound crabmeat, fresh, frozen,
   or canned, picked over and
   coarsely flaked
½ pound cooked lobster meat
½ pound cooked scallops
   sliced thin crosswise
1 teaspoon chopped shallots or
   green onions
3 tablespoons butter or margarine
10 mushroom caps sliced thin
1 tablespoon flour

½ cup dry white wine
1 cup water
12 anchovy fillets, washed,
   dried, and cut up
   Juice of 1 lemon
1 teaspoon chopped chives
1 teaspoon Worcestershire sauce
1 tablespoon chili sauce (optional)
¼ cup heavy cream
   Salt and pepper
2 tablespoons buttered crumbs
2 tablespoons grated
   Parmesan cheese

A LOT of ingredients, perhaps, but the result is truly worth it!

1. Sauté the shallots in 1 tablespoon of the butter in a heavy skillet until golden.

2. Add the mushrooms and cook 3-4 minutes.

3. Sprinkle with flour and stir until flour is absorbed.

4. Blend in the wine and cook until very thick.

5. Add the water and simmer gently about 5 minutes, stirring occasionally, until the sauce is smooth and thick.

6. Stir in the seafood gently and simmer over very low heat 5 minutes or so, stirring frequently.

7. Add the anchovies, the remaining 2 tablespoons butter bit by bit, lemon juice, chives, Worcestershire sauce, chili sauce, and cream.

8. Season to taste, pour into a 2-quart casserole, top with crumbs, sprinkle with cheese, and brown under the broiler. Serves 8.

*Note:* If you prepare this casserole early in the day and refrigerate it, bring it to room temperature (1 hour) and bake it 20 minutes in a moderate oven, 375°, before broiling it.

*Serve with plenty of fluffy hot rice, mixed vegetables, and a tossed green salad. Warm garlic bread goes well, too.*

# SEAFOOD QUICHE

½ pound crabmeat or lobster lumps
½ pound cooked shrimp, shelled, deveined, and broken up if large
¼ pound scallops cooked (quartered if large)
Pastry for 9-inch pie shell
1 egg white
2 tablespoons butter or margarine
2 tablespoons minced shallots or scallions (green onions)
2 tablespoons cognac
1 teaspoon chopped chives
½ teaspoon dried tarragon or 1 teaspoon fresh, chopped
4 eggs well beaten
2 cups light cream
4 drops Tabasco
Salt and pepper
2 tablespoons grated Parmesan cheese

THIS is a real gourmet treat, an outstanding "company" dish.

1. Line a deep pie plate with the pastry, rolled out to ⅛-inch thickness, and crimp the edges. Brush with the egg white.

2. In a skillet melt the butter and cook the shallots 2-3 minutes.

3. Stir in the crabmeat, shrimp, and scallops and simmer long enough to heat well.

4. Remove the skillet from the heat and add the cognac, chives, and tarragon.

5. To the well-beaten eggs add the cream, Tabasco, and salt and pepper to taste. Stir in the seafood mixture and pour into the pie shell.

6. Sprinkle the top with Parmesan cheese and bake 15 minutes at 450°. Reduce heat to 350° and bake 20-25 minutes longer, or until the center is firm to the touch, or until a knife inserted in the center comes out clean. Serve at once. Serves 6.

*Serve with wilted cucumbers, sliced ripe tomatoes spread with chopped chives and chopped parsley mixed with French dressing, a tossed green salad with a sliced avocado stirred in, and warm garlic bread.*

## CLAMS AND SPAGHETTI

2 ten-ounce cans chopped clams
1 pound thin spaghetti broken
up and cooked
2 tablespoons butter or margarine
1 large onion chopped
1 small garlic clove mashed

1 cup sliced mushrooms
(canned will do)
Salt and pepper
3 eight-ounce cans tomato sauce
1 cup grated Parmesan cheese
½ cup buttered bread or
corn flake crumbs

1. Heat the butter in a heavy skillet and lightly sauté the onion, garlic, and mushrooms.
2. Stir in the clams, salt and pepper to taste, and tomato sauce.
3. In a good-sized casserole arrange layers of spaghetti and clam sauce, sprinkling a little cheese on each layer.
4. Top the casserole with remaining cheese and crumbs mixed and bake 30 minutes in a moderate oven, 375°, or until browned and bubbly. Serves 6 generously.

*Serve with buttered green beans, a tossed green salad, and warm garlic bread.*

## COLONIAL CLAM-AND-CHICKEN PIE

2 dozen clams chopped
(canned will do—2 cans)
1 cup diced cooked chicken
12 tiny white onions
(canned will do)
2 tablespoons butter, margarine,
or salad oil
2 hard-cooked eggs diced

1 cup diced cooked potatoes
½ cup chopped celery
¼ cup dry sherry
Salt and pepper
1 tablespoon flour
½ cup cream
Pastry for 1-crust pie

THIS is an old American recipe for a "solid" meat pie—one without gravy, in the English or Scottish style.
1. Sauté the onions in hot butter in a heavy skillet until they are somewhat soft. If you use canned onions, merely heat them.

2. Stir in the clams, chicken, eggs, potatoes, celery, and sherry. Season to taste and simmer about 5 minutes over very low heat.
3. Make a paste of the flour and cream and blend in well. Simmer another 5 minutes and pour into a small casserole that will be filled to within ¼ inch or so of the top.
4. Roll out the pastry to about ⅛ inch thickness and lay on top of the pie. Slash several times to permit steam to escape. Bake 15 minutes in a 400° oven and an additional 20 minutes with the heat reduced to 350°. Serves 6.

*Serve with sliced young zucchini (unpeeled) gently sautéed in butter in a covered skillet 10-15 minutes.*

## CRABMEAT ALMONDINE

1 cup fresh or frozen or
  canned crabmeat
¼ cup butter
⅓ cup flour
1 cup evaporated milk
⅓ cup water
¾ cup chopped celery
¼ cup chopped green pepper

1 pimiento chopped
2 hard-cooked eggs chopped
¼ cup slivered and toasted almonds
1 teaspoon salt
½ cup shredded or grated
  sharp Cheddar
Buttered crumbs
Paprika

As always, the almonds here add flavor to an already pleasing combination of ingredients.
1. Pick over the crabmeat carefully and flake it coarsely.
2. Melt butter in saucepan, blend in flour, and gradually stir in the milk and water mixed. Simmer until smooth and thickened, stirring constantly.
3. Add to the sauce the crabmeat, celery, green pepper, pimiento, eggs, and almonds. Season and pour into a small greased casserole.
4. Top with a mixture of cheese and crumbs, dust with paprika, and bake 30-35 minutes in a 350° oven. Serves 4.

*Serve with herbed rice and buttered green peas.*

# CRABMEAT AU GRATIN

1 cup crabmeat picked over and
  flaked (canned, fresh, or frozen)
3 tablespoons butter
3 tablespoons flour
⅛ teaspoon pepper
½ teaspoon salt
¼ teaspoon paprika

1½ cups thin cream
½ cup grated Cheddar cheese
1 tablespoon Worcestershire
  sauce
2 tablespoons dry sherry
⅓ cup bread or corn flake crumbs

1. Melt the butter in a saucepan, stir in the flour, pepper, salt, and paprika, and gradually blend in the cream, stirring constantly until the sauce is smooth and velvety.
2. Add to the sauce the cheese, Worcestershire sauce, and crabmeat, stirring until the cheese is melted.
3. Add the sherry and pour into a buttered casserole.
4. Top with crumbs and bake 15-20 minutes in a hot oven, 400°, or until golden brown. Serves 4.

*Serve with buttered noodles and buttered baby carrots.*


# CRAB-CORN CASSEROLE

1 cup crabmeat picked over and
  flaked (canned, fresh, or frozen)
1 package frozen cut corn
  cooked or 1½ cups canned
3 hard-cooked eggs, minced
1 tablespoon chopped parsley
2 teaspoons lemon juice
3 tablespoons butter or margarine
1 tablespoon minced onion
2 tablespoons flour

1 teaspoon dry mustard
1 cup milk
½ teaspoon salt
½ teaspoon Worcestershire sauce
1 tablespoon melted butter or
  margarine
½ cup bread crumbs or corn
  flake crumbs
¼ cup grated Parmesan cheese

THIS is an interesting combination of flavors, with just enough lemon juice, mustard, etc., to keep it from being bland.

1. Mix the crabmeat lightly with the corn, eggs, parsley, and lemon juice.
2. Put the 3 tablespoons butter in a saucepan and cook the onion until it is transparent.
3. Stir in the flour, mustard, and milk, stirring until the sauce is smooth and thickened. Add salt and Worcestershire sauce.
4. Combine the crabmeat mixture and sauce and pour into a medium casserole.
5. Top with a mixture of the melted butter, crumbs, and cheese.
6. Bake 20-25 minutes in a 375° oven, or until golden brown and bubbly. Serves 6.

*Serve with creamed chopped spinach and cole slaw.*

## NEW ENGLAND CRABMEAT CASSEROLE

6-ounce can crabmeat flaked
6 ounces broad noodles
  broken up and cooked
1 tablespoon butter or margarine
14-ounce can white asparagus
  tips drained

4-ounce can sliced mushrooms
  drained
1 small green pepper chopped
½ teaspoon salt
¼ teaspoon fresh-ground pepper
1 cup seasoned white sauce
1 cup grated Cheddar cheese

1. Drain the noodles well, stir in the butter, and pour into a medium casserole, well buttered.
2. Arrange in layers over the noodles first the crabmeat, and then the asparagus tips, mushrooms, and green pepper. Salt and pepper lightly.
3. Make the cream sauce with 2 tablespoons butter or margarine, 2 tablespoons flour, and 1 cup milk. Season to taste and pour over the casserole.
4. Top with grated cheese and bake in a moderate oven, 350°, about 35 minutes, or until golden brown and bubbly. Serves 4.

*Serve with buttered green peas and a tossed green salad.*

# CRABMEAT CRÊPES

*Crêpes*

3 eggs
1 cup milk
½ teaspoon salt

⅔ cup flour
3 tablespoons melted butter

*Filling*

1½ cups flaked crabmeat
1½ cups rich white sauce
¼ cup dry sherry
¼ teaspoon grated lemon peel

¼ teaspoon grated nutmeg
1 teaspoon curry powder
Salt and pepper
2 tablespoons minced parsley

*Topping*

6 ounces Hollandaise
(¾ cup—canned will do)

½ cup dairy sour cream
¼ cup toasted sliced almonds

STUFFED pancakes can be one of the most delicate dishes imaginable. Stuffings vary greatly, but none can top crabmeat.

*Crêpes:* Mix the ingredients in order and beat until just blended. Make the crêpes one at a time. Pour 2 tablespoons of the batter into a hot buttered skillet not over 6 or 7 inches in diameter, and rotate it quickly to cover the bottom. Cook until brown on both sides. Keep warm in the oven if you are going to serve right away, but they can be made well in advance and reheated without loss of flavor.

*Filling:* Make the white sauce with 3 tablespoons butter or margarine, 3 tablespoons flour, and 1½ cups top milk or half-and-half. Season to taste. Stir in the remaining ingredients.

Put ¼ cup of this filling on each crêpe, roll it up, and lay in a buttered shallow casserole, seam side down.

*Topping:* Blend Hollandaise and sour cream and spread over the top of the crêpes. Scatter almonds on top and bake in a hot oven, 475°, 10-15 minutes, until heated through. Serves 6.

*Note:* If you make this casserole early in the day, bring it to room temperature (1 hour) before baking, and add the topping then. Instead of the almonds you can use 2 tablespoons grated Parmesan cheese, for a different flavor.

*Serve with buttered asparagus and a tossed green salad.*

## CRAB-STUFFED MUSHROOMS

1 pound crabmeat, fresh,
  frozen, or canned
12 very large mushroom caps
¼ cup + 3 tablespoons butter or
  margarine
2 tablespoons chopped shallots or
  1 tablespoon chopped onion
2 tablespoons dry sherry

1 cup medium cream sauce
1 teaspoon dry mustard
1 teaspoon dried marjoram or
  1 tablespoon fresh, chopped
  Salt and pepper
¾ cup Hollandaise (canned will do)
½ cup heavy cream whipped

1. Soak the mushroom caps in cold water 2 hours to keep them from shrinking. Dry, and sauté 7-8 minutes in the ¼ cup of butter.
2. Heat the 3 tablespoons butter in a saucepan and sauté the shallots (or onions) just until they look wilted.
3. Add the crabmeat, carefully picked over and flaked, and sauté over very low heat 5 minutes. Add the sherry.
4. Make the cream sauce with 2 tablespoons butter, 2 tablespoons flour, and 1 cup milk. Stir in the mustard and marjoram, season to taste, and mix well with the crabmeat mixture.
5. Use this mixture to fill the mushroom caps and lay them in a shallow greased casserole, close together.
6. Mix the Hollandaise sauce and the whipped cream and spread over the mushrooms.
7. Put under the broiler, at least 5 inches from the heat, until they are bubbly and brown. Serves 6.

*If serving for lunch serve with shoestring potatoes, a tossed green salad, and hot sesame seed rolls. For Sunday-night supper serve with a rice casserole (see Index), sliced ripe tomatoes, and a tossed green salad.*

# CRABMEAT CASSEROLE WITH EGGS

6-ounce can crabmeat flaked
2 hard-cooked eggs sliced
3 tablespoons butter or margarine
3 tablespoons flour
1 cup milk
  Salt and pepper

½ cup chopped celery
¼ cup chopped green pepper
1 teaspoon Worcestershire sauce
  Grated Parmesan cheese
  Dash paprika

1. Make a cream sauce of the butter, flour, and milk, seasoning to taste.
2. Blend in the crabmeat, celery, and green pepper.
3. Remove the saucepan from the heat and gently stir in the eggs and Worcestershire sauce.
4. Spread in a small shallow casserole, sprinkle with grated cheese and paprika, and brown under the broiler 3-4 minutes, until golden and bubbly. Serves 4.

*Serve with buttered green peas to which you have added 2 or 3 coarsely chopped mushrooms lightly sautéed in butter, French fried potatoes, and a tossed green salad.*

# CRAB GOURMET

2 cups canned crabmeat or frozen
  crabmeat thawed, picked over,
  and flaked
½ cup toasted walnuts
  broken up coarsely
2 hard-cooked eggs chopped
½ cup mayonnaise
2 teaspoons lemon juice

1 teaspoon Worcestershire sauce
¼ teaspoon dry mustard
¼ teaspoon salt
  Dash cayenne pepper
1 cup soft bread crumbs
¼ cup melted butter or margarine
  Chopped parsley

THIS delectable dish is true gourmet fare.
1. Mix the crabmeat lightly with the walnuts and eggs.
2. Mix the mayonnaise with lemon juice, Worcestershire sauce, mustard, salt, and cayenne. Stir into the crab mixture.

170

3. Pour gently into a small shallow casserole.

4. Top with the fresh bread crumbs mixed with melted butter and parsley, and bake in a hot oven, 400°, about 20 minutes, or until the top is well browned. Serves 4.

*Serve with asparagus Hollandaise and a tossed green salad to which is added grated carrot, sliced cucumber (unpeeled), and thin tomato wedges.*

## CRAB IMPERIAL

3 six-ounce packages frozen king crab or 1½ pounds canned or fresh crab
2 tablespoons butter or margarine
2 tablespoons minced green pepper
2 tablespoons flour
½ teaspoon dry mustard
½ teaspoon salt

⅛ teaspoon paprika
½ cup rich milk
½ cup mayonnaise
1 tablespoon dry sherry
2 tablespoons minced green pepper
2 tablespoons minced pimiento

CRAB Imperial is a noted dish, and, as with many other famous dishes, there are many ways of making it. This recipe is a delectable one.

1. Melt butter in saucepan and lightly cook the green pepper, just for 2-3 minutes.

2. Blend in flour, mustard, salt, and paprika. Cook for a moment and stir in the milk.

3. Remove from the heat and stir in the mayonnaise.

4. Pick over the crabmeat carefully, keeping it in quite large chunks. Stir gently into the cream sauce with the sherry and pimiento.

5. Spread out in a shallow casserole or in 6 crab shells or ramekins and bake in a 375° oven, 25 minutes for the single casserole, 15 minutes for the individual ones. Serves 6.

*Serve with a rice casserole (see Index) and a tossed green salad with frozen cooked hearts of artichokes (or canned) added, together with wedges of ripe tomatoes.*

## CRAB QUICHE

1½ cups crabmeat, fresh,
    frozen, or canned
  4 eggs lightly beaten
    9-inch pie shell, unbaked
  2 cups light cream
  ¾ teaspoon salt

¼ teaspoon nutmeg
    Dash of pepper
1 tablespoon chopped celery
1 tablespoon chopped parsley
1 tablespoon chopped onion
2 tablespoons dry sherry

1. Beat the eggs and use a little to brush the pie shell. Chill it while you prepare the filling.
2. Pick over the crabmeat carefully to remove bits of shell, cartilage, etc. Break it into rather coarse chunks.
3. Mix the eggs, cream, and seasoning.
4. Mix the celery, parsley, onion, and sherry with the crabmeat and spread this in the chilled pie shell. Pour the egg mixture over.
5. Bake 35-40 minutes in a hot oven, 425°, reducing the heat to 375° the last 15 minutes. When the quiche is done a knife inserted in the center should come out clean. Serves 6.

*Serve with sliced ripe tomatoes and a tossed green salad for luncheon. For supper add asparagus with lemon-butter-crumb sauce.*

## CRABMEAT ORIENTAL

6-ounce package frozen
    crabmeat or 6½-ounce can
1 can chow mein noodles
1 can condensed cream of
    celery soup
½ cup thin cream

½ cup sliced mushrooms
    lightly sautéed
¼ cup whole cashew nuts or
    whole salted almonds
1 tablespoon minced onion
    Salt and pepper

1. Pick over the crabmeat carefully, to remove bits of shell and cartilage. Flake coarsely.
2. Set aside half of the noodles, and combine the remainder with all the other ingredients, mixing gently.

3. Place in a small greased casserole and bake 30 minutes in a moderate oven, 350°.
4. After 15 minutes top the casserole with the remaining noodles. Serves 4.

*Serve with buttered Italian green beans and cole slaw.*

## CRAB SARDI

3 cups crabmeat, fresh, frozen,
   or canned
½ cup warmed dry sherry

2 packages frozen asparagus
   (jumbo size), or 24 stalks fresh,
   cooked barely tender
2 cups sauce
¼ cup grated Parmesan cheese

*Sauce*

½ cup dry sherry
1½ cups cream sauce made with
   chicken broth instead of milk
   (Velouté sauce)

4 tablespoons light cream
½ cup Hollandaise sauce
   (canned will do)
½ cup cream whipped

THIS is a mouth-watering dish, though sinfully rich.
1. Pick over the crabmeat carefully, to get out bits of shell and cartilage.
2. Pour over the warmed sherry and let stand 10 minutes.
3. Spread out in a buttered shallow casserole, with the sherry.
4. Lay the asparagus stalks over the crabmeat, cover with the sauce, top with Parmesan cheese, and brown under the broiler. Serves 4-5.

*Sauce:* Reduce the sherry to half its volume by boiling rapidly in a small saucepan. Make the Velouté sauce with 3 tablespoons butter, 3 tablespoons flour, and 1½ cups chicken broth. Season to taste. Add the thin cream and reduced sherry to it and cool somewhat. Fold in the Hollandaise and whipped cream blended together.

*Serve with tiny French peas, potato puffs (obtainable frozen), tossed green salad, and sesame seed rolls.*

# CRABMEAT WITH SPAGHETTI

3 cups crabmeat picked over
and flaked coarsely
2½ cups thin spaghetti
broken up and cooked
1 can condensed cream of
mushroom soup
1 tall can evaporated milk
1 cup grated American cheese
¼ cup minced green pepper
1 tablespoon minced onion
½ teaspoon salt
¼ teaspoon dried thyme or
¾ teaspoon fresh
1 teaspoon chopped parsley
1 tablespoon butter or margarine
½ cup soft bread crumbs

1. Stir together the drained spaghetti, crabmeat, soup, milk, cheese, green pepper, onion, salt, and herbs. Pour into a greased 2-quart casserole.

2. Melt the butter, stir in the crumbs, and spread on top of the casserole.

3. Bake 45 minutes in a moderate oven, 350°, or until golden and bubbly. Serves 8.

*Serve with sliced ripe tomatoes, mixed vegetables, and a tossed green salad.*

# DEVILED CRAB

1 pound crabmeat,
preferably fresh or frozen
2 tablespoons chopped onion
1 tablespoon chopped green
pepper
1 tablespoon butter or margarine
½ teaspoon salt
Dash cayenne
2 cups cream sauce
1 teaspoon prepared mustard
2 egg yolks
¼ cup light cream
1 tablespoon chopped chives
1 tablespoon chopped parsley
½ teaspoon Worcestershire sauce
Buttered crumbs

1. Pick over the crabmeat to remove bits of shell and cartilage, but leave in fairly good-sized chunks.

2. Cook the onion and green pepper in butter until the onion is transparent. Add salt and cayenne.

3. Make the cream sauce with 3½ tablespoons butter or margarine, 3½ tablespoons flour, and 2 cups milk. Season to taste and stir in the mustard.

4. Add the egg yolks beaten with the cream, the chives, parsley, and Worcestershire sauce, then the onions and green pepper, and finally the crabmeat.

5. Spread in a shallow casserole and top with crumbs.

6. Bake in a moderate oven, 350°, 35 minutes, or until golden brown and bubbly. Serves 4.

*Serve with thin spaghetti tossed with Parmesan or Romano cheese and butter and a tossed green salad with grated carrot, sliced cucumbers (unpeeled), and tomato wedges added. Warm garlic bread goes well, too.*

## DEVILED CRAB WITH ALMONDS

1 cup crabmeat (fresh, frozen, or canned) picked over and coarsely flaked
3 tablespoons butter or margarine
1 tablespoon chopped onion
¾ cup thinly sliced celery
3 tablespoons flour
1⅓ cups milk
¾ teaspoon salt
⅛ teaspoon fresh-ground pepper
Dash cayenne pepper
½ teaspoon prepared mustard
¼ teaspoon Worcestershire sauce
2 hard-cooked eggs diced
3 tablespoons chopped parsley
3 tablespoons diced pimiento
⅓ cup blanched and slivered almonds
¼ cup buttered crumbs

1. Melt the butter in a heavy skillet, stir in the onion and celery, cover, and cook over very low heat about 5 minutes.

2. Stir in the flour, milk, salt and pepper, cayenne, mustard, and Worcestershire sauce, stirring until the sauce is smooth and thick.

3. Gently mix into the sauce the crabmeat, eggs, parsley, pimiento, and almonds.

4. Spread out in a shallow buttered casserole, top with crumbs, and bake 15 minutes in a 375° oven. Serves 4.

*Serve with herbed rice and succotash.*

# CHINESE LOBSTER OR CRABMEAT CASSEROLE

2 pounds lobster or crabmeat
  (fresh, frozen, or canned)
¼ cup butter or margarine
1 egg lightly beaten
3 tablespoons minced onion
1 tablespoon soy sauce
1 tablespoon cornstarch
⅓ cup water

2 cups hot cooked rice
1 cup bean sprouts
  (canned) drained
1 tablespoon minced candied or
  preserved ginger
1 tablespoon grated orange rind
Salt

1. Heat the butter in a medium casserole in a 300° oven. When it is melted stir in the lobster or crab, picked over and broken into good-sized lumps. Return to the oven.

2. Blend the egg, onion, soy sauce, and the cornstarch mixed with the water. Stir into the lobster and continue to bake about 10 minutes, stirring 2 or 3 times.

3. Remove the casserole from the oven and push the lobster mixture into the middle. Mix the rice and bean sprouts and arrange around the lobster.

4. Top the rice with ginger and orange rind, cover, and bake 20 minutes. Serves 4.

*Serve with buttered baby Brussels sprouts and a green salad.*


# LOBSTER PIE

2 two-pound boiled lobsters or
  2 pounds lobster meat diced
6 tablespoons butter or
  margarine (¾ bar)
2 tablespoons flour
2 cups top milk or half-and-half

½ cup Madeira or dry sherry
2 egg yolks
⅓ cup light cream
  Salt and pepper
½ recipe biscuit dough or
  pastry for 1-crust pie

1. Melt the butter in a saucepan and blend in the flour. Gradually blend in the milk and cook, stirring, until the sauce is smooth and thickened.

2. Add the wine and the egg yolks beaten with the cream. Season to taste and remove from the heat.

3. Remove lobster meat from shells if boiled lobsters are used. Arrange the lobster meat in a medium casserole and pour the sauce over it.

4. Pat the biscuit dough to ½-inch thickness on a lightly floured board and cut out small biscuits. Lay them gently, close together, on top of the casserole.

5. Brush with melted butter and bake 20-25 minutes in a hot oven, 425°, or until golden brown. If you prefer, make the topping of pastry, slashing it well to permit steam to escape. Serves 6.

*Serve with fluffy mashed potatoes and cut green beans.*

## LOBSTER QUICHE

1 pound lobster meat in
　good-sized chunks
3 tablespoons butter or margarine
　Salt and pepper
3 tablespoons dry sherry or
　Madeira
　Pastry for 9-inch pie
4 eggs

1 tablespoon flour
½ teaspoon salt
　Dash cayenne
2 cups light cream
2 tablespoons grated Parmesan
　cheese
1 tablespoon melted butter or
　margarine

1. Melt the 3 tablespoons butter in a heavy skillet and sauté the lobster meat lightly in it 2-3 minutes.

2. Season with a very little salt and pepper, stir in the sherry or Madeira, cover, and simmer over very low heat 3-4 minutes.

3. Roll out the pastry to ⅛-inch thickness, line a shallow casserole or pie plate with it, and pour in the lobster, with juice.

4. Beat together the eggs, flour, salt, and cayenne. Stir in the cream and pour over the lobster in the pie shell.

5. Sprinkle with the Parmesan cheese and drizzle the melted butter over. Bake in a moderate oven, 375°, about 40 minutes, or until the custard is firm to the touch and the crust brown. Serves 6.

*Serve with steamed cauliflower flowerets with lemon-butter-crumb sauce and a tossed green salad with slices of ripe tomato.*

## DEVILED OYSTERS

1 quart shucked oysters with
  their juice
2 tablespoons salad oil
¼ cup minced onion
1 cup cracker crumbs
2 tablespoons Worcestershire sauce
2 tablespoons catsup

4 dashes Tabasco sauce
  Juice of ½ lemon
2 tablespoons minced parsley
2 tablespoons fine bread or
  corn flake crumbs
1 tablespoon butter

THIS tangy dish will please those who like their food hot.
1. Heat the oysters in their own liquor until the edges curl.
2. Heat the oil in a skillet and sauté the onion lightly.
3. Stir in the cracker crumbs, Worcestershire sauce, catsup, Tabasco, lemon juice, and parsley.
4. Stir the oysters and their juice into this mixture and turn into a greased shallow casserole.
5. Top with crumbs, dot with bits of butter, and bake 15 minutes in a hot oven, 425°, or until sizzling. Serves 4-5.

*Serve with cole slaw, buttered green peas, and a green salad.*


## OYSTERS BAKED IN WINE SAUCE

3 dozen oysters shucked
1½ cups dry white wine
4 tablespoons butter
3 tablespoons flour

¾ cup heavy cream
Salt and pepper
Dash of cayenne
3 tablespoons buttered crumbs

HERE is a wonderful way to prepare cooked oysters, and simple, too.
1. Heat the wine in a large heavy skillet. When it is just under boiling lay in the oysters and poach them 1 minute. Lift them out with a slotted spoon or spatula and arrange in a large shallow casserole.
2. Strain the wine through a fine sieve.
3. Melt the butter in a saucepan, stir in the flour, and cook briefly.

Gradually blend in the wine in which the oysters were poached, stirring until the sauce is smooth and thick.

4. Stir in the cream, season to taste with salt, pepper, and cayenne, and pour the sauce over the oysters.

5. Top with crumbs and bake in a hot oven, 450°, 10 minutes, or until golden brown. Serves 5-6.

*Serve with buttered baby beets and buttered baby carrots.*

## OYSTERS FLORENTINE

| | |
|---|---|
| 1 quart shelled oysters with their liquor | 3 tablespoons flour |
| | 1 cup clam juice (canned) |
| 6 tablespoons butter or margarine | ¼ cup cream |
| 2 cups chopped spinach (1 package frozen, thawed and well drained) | ½ teaspoon garlic salt |
| | 1 tablespoon lemon juice |
| ¼ cup chopped onion | ½ cup buttered bread or corn flake crumbs |
| ⅛ teaspoon nutmeg Salt and pepper | 2 tablespoons grated Parmesan cheese |
| 2 tablespoons chopped parsley | |

HERE is a pleasant combination of flavors, especially useful because it can be completely prepared early in the morning and refrigerated until an hour before baking.

1. Melt 2 tablespoons of the butter in a skillet and simmer in it the spinach and onion. Season to taste and add the nutmeg and parsley.

2. In a saucepan melt the remaining 4 tablespoons of butter and make a cream sauce with the flour, clam juice, liquor drained from the oysters, and cream. Stir until smooth and thick. Season with garlic salt and lemon juice.

3. Spread the spinach on the bottom of a large flat greased casserole. Lay oysters on top in one layer and cover with the sauce.

4. Top with the crumbs and cheese mixed. Bake in a hot oven, 400°, 15-20 minutes, or until bubbly and golden. Serves 5-6.

*Serve with fluffy mashed potatoes, sliced ripe tomatoes, and a plain tossed green salad.*

# BAKED OYSTERS WITH POTATO TOPPING

1 pint shucked oysters with
  their liquor
2 cups hot mashed potatoes
¼ cup butter or margarine melted
4-ounce can sliced mushrooms
1 tablespoon chopped onion
2 tablespoons minced
  green pepper

Light cream
2 tablespoons cornstarch
½ teaspoon salt
⅛ teaspoon pepper
¼ cup chopped pimiento
2 tablespoons dry sherry
1 egg beaten

1. Simmer the oysters in their own liquor 5 minutes. Drain, saving the liquid.

2. In a saucepan heat the butter and lightly sauté the mushrooms, onion, and green pepper 5 minutes.

3. Add enough cream to the oyster liquid to make 1¼ cups. Mix a little of this with the cornstarch. Add the rest to the saucepan and when it is hot stir in the cornstarch mixture, continuing to stir until thick and smooth. Season to taste.

4. Add the oysters, pimiento, and sherry to the sauce and pour into a medium casserole or 9-inch pie plate.

5. Beat the egg into the mashed potatoes and make a border around the top of the casserole.

6. Broil 5 minutes, or until golden brown, about 4 inches from the heat. Serves 4.

*Serve with thin-sliced zucchini gently sautéed in butter, covered, about 15 minutes.*

# OYSTER SOUFFLÉ

1 pint shucked oysters with
  their liquor
  Milk
¼ cup butter or margarine
¼ cup flour

Dash grated nutmeg
1 teaspoon salt
Fresh-ground pepper
4 eggs separated
2 tablespoons brandy

1. Simmer the oysters in their liquor 5 minutes. Drain them, reserving the liquid. Add enough milk to the liquid to make ¾ cup.
2. Chop the oysters quite fine.
3. Melt the butter in a saucepan, stir in the flour, nutmeg, salt, and pepper. Gradually blend in the milk mixture, stirring until the sauce is smooth and thick.
4. Blend a little of it into the beaten egg yolks and quickly stir back into the sauce.
5. Stir in the oysters and brandy. Cool somewhat and blend in the egg whites beaten until stiff.
6. Pour into a deep quart casserole or soufflé dish, well greased, and bake in a moderate oven, 350°, 30 minutes, or until firm in the center. Serve at once. Serves 4.

## OYSTERS TETRAZZINI

| | |
|---|---|
| 3 dozen oysters, shucked, with their liquor | 2½ teaspoons salt |
| ½ pound fine noodles cooked | ¼ teaspoon fresh-ground pepper |
| ½ cup butter or margarine melted | 2 teaspoons Worcestershire sauce |
| 1 cup soft bread crumbs | 3 cups milk |
| ¼ cup grated Parmesan cheese | ¼ cup dry sherry |
| ¼ cup flour | ½ teaspoon paprika |

1. Drain the oysters, reserving ½ cup of their liquor.
2. Drain the noodles well and arrange them in a shallow greased casserole or deep pie plate.
3. Mix 3 tablespoons of the melted butter with the fresh bread crumbs and cheese.
4. Use the rest of the butter to make a cream sauce, blending in the flour, 2 teaspoons salt and ⅛ teaspoon pepper, Worcestershire sauce, and finally the milk and the oyster liquor. Cook until it is smooth and thick, stirring constantly. Add the sherry.
5. Spread the oysters on top of the noodles, sprinkle with ½ teaspoon of salt and ⅛ teaspoon pepper. Carefully pour over the sauce.
6. Top with the crumb mixture and sprinkle with paprika. Bake 30-35 minutes in a 400° oven, or until bubbly and golden. Serves 6.

# SCALLOPS DUXELLES

2 pounds scallops
7 tablespoons butter
2 tablespoons minced onion
¾ pound minced mushrooms
1 cup dry white wine
1 tablespoon lemon juice
2 teaspoons chopped parsley
½ teaspoon salt
¼ teaspoon pepper
¼ teaspoon nutmeg

½ cup water
¼ teaspoon dried thyme or
  ¾ teaspoon fresh, chopped
1 sprig parsley
1 small bay leaf
4 tablespoons flour
1 cup light cream
6 tablespoons grated
  Parmesan cheese
Pinch cayenne

1. Melt 3 tablespoons of the butter in a heavy skillet and sauté the onion until it is barely soft.

2. Add the mushrooms and continue to cook until the liquid evaporates.

3. Stir in ½ the wine, the lemon juice, chopped parsley, salt, pepper, and nutmeg. Cook until the wine evaporates, and set aside.

4. In a saucepan heat the rest of the wine, the water, thyme, sprig of parsley, and bay leaf. Bring to a boil and add the scallops. Poach them gently 5-6 minutes, or until they turn white and are tender. Strain them, reserving the broth.

5. In a skillet melt the remaining 4 tablespoons butter, blend in the flour, and stir in the cream and 1 cup of the scallop broth. Keep stirring until the sauce is thick and smooth. Correct the seasoning.

6. Combine ½ cup of the sauce with the mushroom mixture and spread on the bottom of a medium casserole. Arrange the scallops on top.

7. Add to the rest of the sauce 4 tablespoons of the cheese and the cayenne and pour over the scallops. Sprinkle with the remaining cheese and bake 10 minutes in a hot oven, 425°, or brown under the broiler. Serves 6.

*Serve with parsley-butter potatoes and buttered baby beets.*

182

# SCALLOPS MÉNAGÈRE

1 pound scallops
8 large mushrooms sliced and
   lightly sautéed
½ cup dry white wine
1 cup water
1-inch piece of celery
   Small sprig parsley
2 peppercorns bruised
   Pinch of thyme
1 teaspoon chopped onion
¼ teaspoon salt

Bones of any white fish
4 tablespoons butter or margarine
4 tablespoons flour
2 cups milk
   Salt and pepper
   Pinch nutmeg
2 tablespoons bread or
   corn flake crumbs
4 tablespoons grated
   Parmesan cheese
2 tablespoons melted butter

1. Make a court bouillon by boiling in a saucepan about 15 minutes the wine, water, celery, parsley, peppercorns, thyme, onion, ¼ teaspoon salt, and fish bones. Drain the bouillon, discard the bones and vegetables, and reheat the broth. Drop in the scallops, bring to a boil again, and simmer about 8 minutes. Drain and cut each one crosswise in three slices.

2. Make a cream sauce with the 4 tablespoons butter, the flour, and milk. Season to taste and add the nutmeg.

3. Stir the mushrooms and scallops into the sauce and pour into a medium casserole.

4. Top with crumbs and cheese mixed and drizzle the melted butter over.

5. Put under the broiler, about 5 inches from the heat, and brown well. Serves 4.

*Serve with riced potatoes and cut green beans.*

G

## CAPE COD BAKED SCALLOPS

1 quart scallops
1 green pepper chopped very fine
1½ cups fine bread or
    corn flake crumbs
½ teaspoon dry mustard

Salt and pepper
1 teaspoon Worcestershire sauce
Dash Tabasco
¼ cup melted butter or margarine
¼ cup solid butter or margarine

1. Mix together the green pepper, crumbs, mustard, a little salt and pepper, Worcestershire sauce, and Tabasco. Spread in a soup plate.
2. Put the melted butter in another soup plate, warmed.
3. Have ready a medium casserole, preferably rather wide and shallow. Roll the scallops first in the melted butter, then in the crumb mixture, and lay in the casserole.
4. Dot with butter and bake in a moderate oven, 350°, about 3 minutes.
5. Garnish with parsley and serve with lemon wedges. Serves 6.

*Serve with buttered noodles, to which poppy seeds and slivered toasted almonds are added, and succotash.*


## CHINESE SHRIMP CASSEROLE

¾ pound cooked and cleaned
    small shrimp
½ cup chopped celery
1 cup chopped onion
½ cup water
4-ounce can sliced mushrooms
2 tablespoons butter or margarine
¾ cup chopped green pepper
6-ounce can cashew nuts
    chopped

4-ounce can pimiento drained
    and chopped
5-ounce can water chestnuts
    sliced
2½ cups medium cream sauce
    Salt and pepper
2 three-ounce cans Chinese
    noodles

1. Simmer the celery and onion in the water in a covered saucepan until the onion is soft, 5-7 minutes. Drain.
2. Sauté the mushrooms lightly in the butter. Stir in the celery-onion

mixture, green pepper, cashews, pimiento, water chestnuts, and shrimp.

3. Make the cream sauce with 3½ tablespoons butter or margarine, 3½ tablespoons flour, 2½ cups milk, and salt and pepper to taste.

4. Combine the cream sauce and the shrimp mixture and mix well.

5. Spread 1 can of the noodles on the bottom of a casserole.

6. Pour the shrimp mixture over, and top with the other can of noodles.

7. Bake 30 minutes in a moderate oven, 350°. Serves 8-10.

*Serve with Italian green beans and a tossed green salad with additions of grated carrot, sliced unpeeled cucumbers, and thin wedges of tomato.*

# CHINESE SHRIMP WITH BAMBOO SHOOTS AND HAM

1 pound small shrimp shelled
   and deveined
1 egg white
2 tablespoons dry sherry
1 teaspoon cornstarch
3 tablespoons salad oil
1 teaspoon sugar

½ teaspoon salt
2 tablespoons diced cooked ham
2 tablespoons chopped
   bamboo shoots
½ cup partly cooked green peas
   Chicken stock, white wine, or
   water

1. Whip the egg white lightly with a fork and combine with half of the sherry and the cornstarch.

2. Heat the oil to sizzling in a heavy skillet.

3. Roll the shrimp in the egg white mixture and cook in the oil, lowering the heat as soon as the shrimp are added. Stir frequently until tender, or until they are all pink.

4. Stir in the sugar, salt, remaining sherry, ham, bamboo shoots, and peas.

5. Put in a casserole and add a little liquid—chicken stock, white wine, or water—not more than ½ cup.

6. Cover and bake in a hot oven, 400°, 10 minutes. Serves 4.

*Serve with buttered narrow noodles and buttered Brussels sprouts.*

## QUICK SHRIMP CURRY

2 pounds shrimp shelled
  and deveined
2 tablespoons salad oil
1 medium onion chopped
2 tablespoons flour
2 tablespoons curry powder,
  or to taste

8½-ounce can pineapple chunks
  (or frozen or spiced)
2 cups light cream
½ cup chopped chutney
Salt and pepper
½ cup salted peanuts

LIKE all curries, this one improves on standing, and it is a good idea to make it in the morning and merely reheat at serving time. If you do this do not add the peanuts until you are ready to serve.

1. Heat the oil in a heavy casserole on top of the stove and sauté the shrimp and onion until the onion becomes transparent and the shrimp begin to turn pink.

2. Blend the flour and curry powder into the shrimp mixture and gradually add the pineapple (with its juice) and cream. Bring just to a boil.

3. Stir in the chutney and season to taste. Turn down the heat and simmer, covered, 15-20 minutes.

4. Stir in the peanuts just before serving. Serves 4-6.

*Serve with the usual curry condiments, as listed in the recipe for Special Chicken Curry (see Index). A large green salad is needed, too.*

## SHRIMP FIESTA PIE

¾ pound cooked shrimp cut up
2 tablespoons butter, margarine,
  or salad oil
¼ cup chopped onion
3 tablespoons chopped
  green pepper
2 cans condensed cream of
  mushroom soup

3 tablespoons milk
2 tablespoons chopped pimiento
1 teaspoon Worcestershire sauce
1½ cups biscuit mix
½ cup grated sharp
  Cheddar cheese

186

1. Heat the butter in a saucepan and sauté the onion and green pepper until tender.
2. Stir in soup, milk, shrimp, pimiento, and Worcestershire sauce and heat almost to boiling. Pour into a small casserole.
3. Roll out the biscuit dough (prepared according to package directions) into a rectangle 7" x 12" x ¼" and sprinkle the cheese evenly over it. Since this is to be rolled up, it will expedite the rolling if you roll out the dough on a lightly floured piece of waxed paper.
4. Roll the dough lengthwise, lifting the waxed paper as you roll.
5. With a sharp knife cut into 1-inch slices, laying them close together on top of the shrimp mixture as you cut. Bake 25 minutes in a 400° oven. Serves 6.

*Serve with fluffy mashed potatoes and green peppers, cut in 1½-inch squares and gently sautéed in butter.*


## WESTERN SHRIMP AND NOODLE CASSEROLE

| | |
|---|---|
| 2 cups small shrimp cooked, shelled, and deveined | 2 cups sharp Cheddar grated (½ pound) |
| 8 ounces narrow noodles cooked | 2 cups whole-kernel corn cooked (canned or frozen) |
| ⅓ cup butter or margarine | ⅔ cup sliced mushrooms (or 6-ounce can) |
| ⅓ cup flour | 2 tablespoons buttered crumbs |
| 2 cups milk | |
| Salt and pepper | |

1. Make a cream sauce with the butter, flour, and milk, adding salt and pepper to taste.
2. Stir in the cheese, continuing to stir until it is melted.
3. Add the noodles, shrimp, corn, and mushrooms to the sauce. Blend well and pour into a greased medium casserole.
4. Top with crumbs and bake about 30 minutes in a hot oven, 400°, or until browned and bubbly. Serves 5-6.

*Serve with young zucchini sliced (unpeeled) and gently sautéed, covered, in butter or margarine.*

# SHRIMP FLORENTINE

3 cups cooked and deveined
  shrimp
3 cups cooked chopped spinach
9 tablespoons butter or margarine
6 tablespoons flour
2¾ cups milk scalded
  Salt and pepper
½-¾ cups heavy cream

Few drops lemon juice
⅛ teaspoon nutmeg
2 tablespoons shallots or
  green onions minced
½ cup dry white wine
1½ tablespoons grated
  Parmesan cheese

1. Melt 4 tablespoons of the butter in the top of a double boiler over direct heat.

2. Blend in the flour and cook a minute or two, but don't let it color. Beat in the hot milk vigorously. Season to taste and let cook over low heat about 2 minutes.

3. Thin out with cream until the sauce just coats the spoon.

4. Stir in lemon juice to taste and keep hot over hot water.

5. Melt 2 tablespoons of the butter in a heavy skillet and heat the spinach until the liquid is all evaporated, stirring frequently.

6. Stir in ½ cup of the cream sauce and season to taste with salt, pepper, and nutmeg. Spread evenly in a large greased casserole.

7. Heat 2 tablespoons of the butter to sizzling in a heavy skillet and add the shrimp and shallots. Season lightly with salt and pepper and sauté over medium heat 2-3 minutes, stirring often. Add the wine and increase the heat to evaporate most of the liquid.

8. Stir half the remaining cream sauce in and spread over the spinach.

9. Pour over the rest of the sauce, top with cheese, and dot with the remaining tablespoon of butter.

10. Bake 15 minutes in a 400° oven, or until bubbly and golden. Serves 8.

*Serve with shoestring potatoes and a tossed green salad.*

# SHRIMP AND RICE ALMONDINE

½ pounds shrimp cooked,
   shelled, and deveined
¾ cup raw rice cooked
1 tablespoon lemon juice
3 tablespoons salad oil
2 tablespoons butter or margarine
¼ cup minced green pepper
¼ cup minced onion

1 teaspoon salt
⅛ teaspoon pepper
   Dash cayenne
1 can condensed tomato soup
1 cup heavy cream
½ cup dry sherry
¾ cup slivered blanched almonds

IF you like shrimp this is a delicious dish, and one that can be prepared completely early in the day, ready to bake when needed.

1. Spread the cooked rice in a good-sized greased casserole. Arrange the shrimp on top and sprinkle with lemon juice and salad oil.

2. Heat the butter in a saucepan and cook the green pepper and onion over low heat about 5 minutes, or until soft but not brown.

3. Stir in salt and pepper, cayenne, soup, cream, sherry, and half the almonds. Pour over the shrimp in the casserole and stir gently to mix.

4. Bake 35 minutes, uncovered, in a moderate oven, 350°.

5. Sprinkle the remaining almonds on top and continue to bake 20 minutes longer, or until bubbly and golden. Serves 6-8.

*Serve with buttered green peas and a large green salad. Warm garlic bread goes well, too.*

# ORIENTAL SHRIMP CASSEROLE

2 cups cooked small shrimp
  (or large ones cut up)
2 tablespoons butter or margarine
2 cups diagonally sliced celery
1 cup chopped onions
1 cup sliced mushrooms
  (or 4-ounce can)
5-ounce can water chestnuts
  sliced coarsely

½ cup toasted slivered
  blanched almonds
2 three-ounce cans Chinese
  noodles
10-ounce can condensed cream
  of mushroom or cream of
  chicken soup
¾ cup top milk
2 teaspoons soy sauce
  Paprika

1. Sauté the shrimp lightly in butter 2-3 minutes.

2. Add the celery, onion, mushrooms, water chestnuts, almonds, and half the noodles. Pour into a medium casserole and cover with the remaining noodles.

3. Mix the soup, milk, and soy sauce and pour over the noodles.

4. Sprinkle with paprika and bake in a moderate oven, 350°, 40 minutes. Serves 6.

*Note:* This recipe can also be made with leftover roast pork cut in ¾-inch dice.

*Serve with chopped spinach mixed with a little dairy sour cream and a tossed green salad.*

# ONE-DISH MEALS

# BEEF AND CABBAGE WITH RICE

1 pound lean chuck ground
1 small cabbage shredded fine
1 cup cooked rice
1 medium onion chopped
6 tablespoons butter or margarine
2 hard-cooked eggs chopped
2 tablespoons flour
2 small cloves garlic mashed

2 tablespoons catsup
1 cup canned tomatoes
1 cup water
3- or 4-ounce can chopped
  mushrooms with liquid
1 tablespoon chopped parsley
Salt and pepper

1. Sauté the onion in 2 tablespoons butter until soft. Add the beef and cook 3-4 minutes, stirring.
2. Add the rice and eggs and heat well. Pour into a fairly shallow but wide casserole.
3. Spread the cabbage on top of the meat mixture.
4. Melt the remaining 4 tablespoons butter in a saucepan and blend in the flour. Cook 2-3 minutes and then stir in the garlic, catsup, tomatoes, water, mushrooms, parsley, and salt and pepper to taste. Simmer about 5 minutes and pour on top of the cabbage.
5. Cover the casserole and bake about 30 minutes in a moderate oven, 350°. Uncover for the last 10 minutes. Serves 6-8.

# BEEF CACCIATORE

3 pounds lean beef cut in
  1-inch cubes
  Olive oil or salad oil
2 medium onions chopped
  Flour
2 medium cloves garlic
  minced or mashed
2 teaspoons salt

½ teaspoon orégano
½ teaspoon crushed red pepper
  or dash cayenne
1 cup condensed consommé
½ cup red wine
1-pound can whole tomatoes
2 green peppers cut in strips
12 ounces noodles cooked

1. Heat oil in heavy skillet and lightly brown onions. Remove them to a bowl for the moment.

2. Dredge the beef with flour and brown it well on all sides in the same oil.

3. Transfer to a large casserole and add to it the onions, garlic, salt, orégano, red pepper or cayenne, and consommé.

4. Cover and simmer over very low heat or bake in a 300° oven 2 hours, or until the beef is *almost* tender. Look at it occasionally and add a little consommé if it seems dry.

5. Add the wine and tomatoes, cover, and simmer or bake 10 minutes more.

6. Stir in the green peppers and cook, uncovered, 15 minutes more.

7. Stir in the cooked noodles. Serves 8.


## BEEF, CORN, AND NOODLES

1 pound lean beef ground
12-ounce can whole kernel corn
8-ounce package wide noodles
3 tablespoons salad oil
1 medium onion chopped
1 medium green pepper chopped
1 clove garlic minced

1 teaspoon minced parsley
1 teaspoon salt
¼ teaspoon fresh-ground pepper
1-pound can tomatoes
1 cup pitted ripe olives
1 cup Cheddar cheese cut in small pieces

1. Heat the oil in a large skillet and sauté the onion, green pepper, and garlic until they are somewhat soft, and then add the meat. Continue cooking until the beef is browned.

2. Stir in the parsley, salt and pepper, tomatoes, corn, olives, and the uncooked noodles, broken up into fairly small pieces.

3. Pour all this into a casserole and bake, covered, about an hour in a 350° oven. Stir the mixture a couple of times while baking.

4. About 10 minutes before you are ready to serve stir in the cheese and continue cooking about 10 minutes, uncovered. Serves 6.

## BEEF, RICE, AND EGGPLANT

1 pound lean beef ground
1 medium eggplant cut in
  1-inch cubes (unpeeled)
2 cups cooked rice
5 tablespoons salad oil
½ cup minced onion
¼ cup chopped green pepper

1 tablespoon chopped parsley
1 teaspoon salt
¼ teaspoon pepper
½ cup bread or corn flake crumbs
2 tablespoons grated
  Parmesan cheese

1. Cook the eggplant cubes in boiling salted water until tender, about 10 minutes. Drain well and mash.

2. Brown the beef in 3 tablespoons of the oil.

3. Add onion and green pepper and cook over low heat until onions are transparent.

4. Stir together the eggplant, meat mixture, parsley, salt, pepper, and rice. Turn into a medium casserole.

5. Stir the crumbs into the remaining 2 tablespoons oil and spread on top of the casserole.

6. Top with cheese and bake in a moderate oven, 375°, 20-25 minutes, or until brown and bubbling. Serves 4-5.


## BRAISED SHORT RIBS OF BEEF

4 pounds lean short ribs
  Flour, salt, and pepper
4 tablespoons beef fat or salad oil
1 bay leaf
2 small cloves of garlic
1 onion stuck with 4 cloves
1 teaspoon dried rosemary or
  1 tablespoon fresh, chopped

4 small carrots scraped and
  split both ways
1 cup red wine
1 cup cut green beans
4 medium potatoes cut in half
  (optional)

1. Dredge ribs with seasoned flour and lay them in a large heavy casserole. Add beef fat or oil and brown them well. (Or brown them in a skillet.)

194

2. Add bay leaf, garlic cloves, onion, rosemary, carrots, and enough water barely to cover.

3. Bring to a boil on top of the stove, cover, and move to a 300° oven.

4. Bake one hour and add the wine and beans. If you use potatoes add them also at this time. Bake another hour.

5. If you prefer a sauce with more body, drain off the liquid into a saucepan and thicken it somewhat, using either flour-and-water paste or flour and butter kneaded together. Check the seasoning and pour sauce back in the casserole. Serves 4.

## BEEF AND VEGETABLE CASSEROLE I

1½ pounds lean beef ground
   Salt and pepper
  4 tablespoons salad oil
  1 pound fresh string beans
   cut in 1-inch diagonals
  3 large tomatoes peeled
   and sliced

2 medium onions sliced
3 green peppers seeded
  and sliced
½ cup chopped parsley
½ teaspoon marjoram or orégano

1. Season the meat to taste with salt and pepper and shape into balls the size of a walnut.

2. Heat half the oil in a heavy skillet and brown the meat balls on all sides. Set aside.

3. Combine beans, tomatoes, onions, peppers, and parsley in a large casserole, salt to taste, stir in the rest of the oil, cover, and bake in a slow oven, 250°, for an hour.

4. Stir in the meat balls and any fat left in the skillet, add the marjoram, re-cover, and continue to bake another hour. Serves 6.

*Note:* If you want to enlarge the casserole, add 3 slender zucchini sliced thin, 6 large mushrooms sliced, and 2 cups thin diagonal celery slices. Two or 3 potatoes, cut as for French fries, can also be added. However, this would call for another ¾ pound of meat and additional seasoning.

# BEEF AND VEGETABLE CASSEROLE II

2 pounds top round of beef
   cut in 1-inch cubes
3 tablespoons butter or margarine
¼ cup brandy slightly warmed
12 small white onions or
   1-pound can cooked onions
6 small carrots scraped, split
   lengthwise, and cut in
   3 or 4 pieces each
6 small white turnips
   peeled and quartered

1 celery heart sliced thin
6 large mushrooms quartered
½ teaspoon tomato paste
1 teaspoon meat glaze
3 tablespoons flour
1½ cups condensed consommé
¼ cup dry red wine
   Salt and pepper
1 small bay leaf

1. Heat 1 tablespoon of the butter in a heavy skillet and quickly brown the meat in it.

2. Light the brandy and pour it flaming over the meat. When the flames die down transfer the meat to a good-sized casserole.

3. Add the remaining butter to the skillet and in it brown lightly the onions, carrots, turnips, and celery. [If you use canned onions, add them later.] Add the mushrooms and cook another minute or two. Lift all of these vegetables out with a slotted spoon and arrange them on top of the meat in the casserole.

4. Reduce the heat to a simmer and blend into the fat in the skillet the tomato paste, meat glaze, and flour. Add the consommé slowly, bring up the heat a little, and stir until the mixture thickens.

5. Stir in the wine, season to taste, and add the bay leaf. Pour over the casserole.

6. Cover and bake 1-1¼ hours, or until the meat is tender. Serves 5-6.


# SPANISH STEW

2 pounds boneless chuck
   cut in 1½-inch cubes

2 tablespoons chopped parsley
1 large can tomatoes

196

¼ cup salad oil
3 small onions chopped
1 clove garlic
2 teaspoons salt
3 green peppers cut in strips

½ teaspoon dried sweet basil or
  1 teaspoon fresh, chopped
4 medium potatoes cut in wedges
Flour-and-water paste

1. In a heavy medium-size casserole heat the oil and lightly sauté onions and garlic. Remove the garlic as soon as it begins to brown and sauté the meat with the onions.
2. Add salt, green peppers, parsley, basil, and tomatoes.
3. Cover the casserole and bake in a slow oven, 300°, an hour.
4. Stir in the potatoes and continue baking until the potatoes are tender—15-20 minutes.
5. Thicken the sauce slightly with flour-and-water paste. Serves 4-5.

## JOHNNY MAZETTE

1 pound lean ground beef
1 pound lean ground pork
½ cup butter, margarine, or
  salad oil
2 cups chopped green pepper
1 cup chopped celery
2 cups chopped onion
  Salt and pepper
⅓ cup chopped stuffed olives

4-ounce can sliced mushrooms
  and liquid
1 can condensed tomato soup
8-ounce can tomato sauce
8-ounce can meatless tomato-
  mushroom sauce
1 pound broad noodles cooked
2 cups grated Parmesan cheese

1. In a large skillet or Dutch oven melt the butter and lightly sauté the pepper, celery, and onion.
2. Add both meats and continue to cook until the red disappears.
3. Season to taste and stir in the olives, mushrooms, soup, and both sauces.
4. Turn the well-drained noodles into a large greased casserole. Pour the meat mixture on top and gently stir into the noodles. When well mixed spread the cheese on top.
5. Bake about 35 minutes in a 350° oven. Serves 10-12.

# DOROTHEA'S LASAGNE

I.  3 tablespoons salad oil
    2 pounds ground beef
    1½ teaspoons mixed herbs
        (orégano, basil, thyme)
    1 clove garlic mashed
    2 medium onions chopped

    4-ounce can button
        mushrooms
    1 can tomato sauce
    1½ cups water
    Salt to taste

II. 1½ cups cooked chopped
        spinach or 1 package
        frozen, cooked
    1 cup bread or corn
        flake crumbs
    ½ cup salad oil

    ½ cup grated Parmesan cheese
    4 eggs beaten
    ½ teaspoon mixed herbs
        (orégano, basil, thyme)
    Salt to taste

½ pound lasagne cooked until
    just tender

4-ounce can button mushrooms
Grated Parmesan cheese

1. Mix the ingredients in group I and simmer 15-20 minutes.
2. Mix the ingredients in II.
3. Arrange in a large shallow casserole, well oiled, beginning with a layer of lasagne noodles laid side by side and close together on the bottom. Cover with a layer of mixture II, and then with a layer of mixture I.
4. Spread another layer of lasagne noodles, this time going crosswise of the casserole, and close together. Cover with the same layers as before.
5. Top with a layer of mixture II, the other can of button mushrooms, drained, and a generous sprinkling of grated Parmesan.
6. Bake 45 minutes in a 350° oven.
7. Add more cheese and bake 5 minutes more. Serves 8.

# PARTY SPAGHETTI WITH BEEF

1 pound linguine (a form of
spaghetti) cooked
2 pounds lean beef ground
3 tablespoons salad oil
½ pound mushrooms sliced thin
or 2 four-ounce cans
2 medium onions chopped
¼ cup chopped parsley
2 eight-ounce cans tomato sauce
1 can tomato paste

1 teaspoon dried orégano or
1 tablespoon fresh, chopped
1 teaspoon garlic powder
Salt and pepper
8-ounce package cream cheese
softened
2 cups cottage cheese
½ cup dairy sour cream
½ cup chopped chives
½ cup buttered crumbs

HERE is a delightfully flavored hearty casserole for a party, especially
for a buffet supper.

1. Heat the oil in a heavy skillet and cook the meat until it begins
to brown.

2. Stir in mushrooms (and their juice if canned), onions, parsley,
tomato sauce, tomato paste, orégano, and garlic powder. Season to
taste and simmer 15 minutes.

3. Combine cream cheese, cottage cheese, sour cream, chives, and
salt to taste. Blend well.

4. Pour half the linguine, well drained, in a larg  buttered casserole.
Cover with all of the cheese mixture. Add the rest of the linguine.
Top with the meat mixture.

5. Cover with buttered crumbs and bake 30-40 minutes in a moderate
oven, 350°, or until browned and bubbly. Serves 12.

# NASI GORENG

½ pound lean beef ground
2 tablespoons bread or
  corn flake crumbs
1 egg
1¼ cup chopped onions
½ teaspoon salt
⅛ teaspoon pepper
½ cup margarine or salad oil

1 cup diced celery
½ pound cooked crabmeat
½ pound shelled and
  deveined shrimp
2 cups chicken broth
2 cups cooked rice
1-2 tablespoons curry powder

THIS famous Javanese dish is fine for a buffet supper.

1. Mix the beef, crumbs, egg, ¼ cup of the onions, and salt and pepper and shape into small balls, the size of a walnut. Let stand 30-40 minutes.

2. Heat 2 tablespoons of the fat in a saucepan and lightly sauté the remaining onions and the celery. Spread them out in a large casserole.

3. In the same skillet melt ¼ cup of the fat and sauté the carefully picked-over crabmeat and shrimp 2-3 minutes, or until the shrimp begin to turn pink. Add them to the onion mixture.

4. Brown the meat balls in the same skillet, stirring constantly to prevent sticking. Add these to the casserole.

5. Still in the same skillet heat the chicken broth, rice, curry powder, and the balance of the fat. Bring to a boil and pour over the casserole. Stir the contents of the casserole gently but thoroughly, cover, and bake 20-25 minutes in a moderate oven, 350°. Serves 6.


# SWISS STEAK CASSEROLE DINNER

3½-pound slice of round steak
½ cup flour
1½ teaspoons salt
½ teaspoon fresh-ground pepper
¼ cup salad oil
2 cans condensed
  onion soup undiluted

8 or more scrubbed new
  potatoes, unpeeled
6 scraped carrots, quartered
1 package frozen peas
1 package frozen cut green beans

1. Cut the meat into 8 serving portions. Mix the flour with the salt and pepper and cut or pound into the meat with the blunt side of a heavy butcher knife, edge of a saucer, etc.

2. In a large casserole heat the oil and brown the meat well on both sides.

3. Add the soup, cover, and bake in a moderate oven, 350°, 40 minutes, or until the meat begins to be tender. Or bake in a slow oven, 275°, 2 hours, or until tender.

4. Stir in the potatoes and carrots and bake 25 minutes more. Add more salt if needed.

5. Break up the frozen vegetables in chunks and poke down in the casserole. Cover again and bake 20 minutes longer. Serves 8.

## MEAT BALL SUPPER

| | |
|---|---|
| 1 pound lean beef ground | 1 teaspoon salt |
| 1 egg | ¼ teaspoon dried marjoram or |
| 1 cup soft bread crumbs | ¾ teaspoon fresh, chopped |
| 1 tablespoon chopped parsley | 1 tablespoon salad oil |

*Sauce*

| | |
|---|---|
| 2 tablespoons butter or margarine | ½ teaspoon salt |
| 1 medium onion chopped | 2 cups wide noodles broken up |
| 2¼ cups tomato juice | 2 cups cooked green peas or |
| 1¼ cups condensed consommé | cut green beans |
| 1 teaspoon sugar | |

1. Mix the beef, egg, crumbs, parsley, salt, and marjoram lightly and shape into balls about the size of a walnut.

2. Heat the oil in a heavy skillet, brown the meat balls on all sides, and arrange in a medium casserole.

3. Melt the butter in a saucepan and sauté the onion until transparent but not brown.

4. Add the tomato juice, consommé, sugar, and salt. Pour over the meat balls.

5. Stir in the noodles, cover, and bake in a slow oven, 325°, 20-25 minutes, or until the noodles are tender and the liquid mostly absorbed.

6. Five minutes before serving stir in the peas or beans. Serves 6.

## BURGER-RICE CASSEROLE

2 pounds lean beef ground
1 tablespoon salad oil
1 large onion chopped (1 cup)
1 cup chopped celery
1 clove garlic mashed
1 large can or 4 twelve-ounce cans V-8 juice
1 tablespoon sugar

1 teaspoon dried sweet basil or
 1 tablespoon fresh, chopped
1 teaspoon dried orégano or
 1 tablespoon fresh, chopped
1 tablespoon chopped parsley
2 teaspoons salt
⅛ teaspoon fresh-ground pepper
1 small bay leaf crushed
1½ cups raw rice

1. Heat the oil in a heavy skillet—an electric fry pan is fine—until it is sizzling.

2. Shape the meat into one large patty about 1 inch thick and sauté it about 5 minutes on each side, reducing the heat to medium. Break it up carefully into pieces about the size of a large olive, and lay them in a large casserole.

3. To the fat left in the skillet add the onion, celery, and garlic and sauté lightly, adding a bit more oil if necessary. Spread over the meat in the casserole.

4. Now add to the skillet the V-8 juice, the sugar, all the herbs, the salt, pepper, and bay leaf. Heat just to boiling.

5. Sprinkle the rice over the casserole and pour on the boiling liquid. Cover and bake about 45 minutes in a 350° oven, or until the rice is tender and the liquid absorbed.

6. Check about 15 minutes ahead of time and if there seems to be too much liquid for the rice, remove the cover of the casserole. Stir lightly with a long-tined fork before serving. Serves 8.

## HAM CASSEROLE WITH VEGETABLES

1¾ cups cooked ham diced small or julienned
1 cup cooked green beans

1 can condensed cream of mushroom soup
½ cup milk

1 cup cooked whole-kernel corn  ½ cup buttered crumbs
2 cups cooked little white onions
   or No. 2 can

MIX all ingredients except crumbs in a medium casserole. Top with the buttered crumbs and bake 20-25 minutes in a 375° oven, or until golden and bubbly. (If you prepare it early bring it to room temperature before baking, or allow an extra 10 minutes.) Serves 4.

## HAM AND TURKEY SANDWICH CASSEROLE

2 three-and-one-fourth-ounce  2 cups grated sharp
   cans deviled ham                  Cheddar (½ pound)
8 slices cooked turkey         ½ teaspoon dry mustard
4 slices bread, crusts removed  1 teaspoon salt
   Butter or margarine          2 eggs well beaten
¼ cup flour                    ½ cup toasted slivered almonds
2 cups milk

THIS is an easy and delicious luncheon dish. Select a casserole for it just the size to fit the 4 slices of bread, or use a deep Pyrex pie plate and cut the bread to fit.
1. Toast the bread on one side (under the broiler) and spread the other side generously with butter. Fit them so as to make a fairly solid layer in the casserole, buttered side up.
2. Spread the deviled ham lavishly on the bread and arrange the turkey slices on top.
3. Make a cheese sauce by melting ¼ cup butter, blending in the flour, and gradually adding the milk. Stir constantly until thick and smooth. Add the cheese and mustard and stir until the cheese is melted. Season to taste. Stir in the eggs.
4. Pour the sauce over the sandwiches, sprinkle with almonds, and bake in a hot oven, 450°, 15-20 minutes, until bubbly and well browned.
   If you have had to cut the bread to fit a round casserole, cut across both ways with a sharp knife to divide the turkey neatly before taking to the table. Serves 4.

# HAM AND EGG PIE

2 cups cooked ham cut in
½-inch dice
2 hard-cooked eggs sliced
1 tablespoon vegetable oil
2 tomatoes peeled and chopped
1 clove garlic mashed
1 teaspoon sugar
½ teaspoon cinnamon
½ pound garlic sausage sliced

2 cups cooked peas,
fresh or frozen
4 canned artichoke bottoms
diced small
Salt and pepper
Boiling water
Biscuit dough (1 cup
flour or mix)
1 tablespoon melted butter

1. Heat the oil in a medium casserole on top of the stove and brown the pieces of ham lightly in it. Skim out the ham and reserve.

2. In the fat remaining in the casserole cook the tomatoes and garlic. Stir in the sugar, cinnamon, sausage, eggs, peas, artichokes, and seasoning to taste. Add boiling water barely to cover and simmer gently 20 minutes.

3. Stir in the reserved ham.

4. Roll out the biscuit dough rather thin. Cut out biscuits and lay them carefully on top of the mixture in the casserole, as close together as possible.

5. Brush with the melted butter and bake 15-20 minutes at 400°, or until the biscuits are a deep golden brown. Serves 4.


# LAMB, RICE, AND EGGPLANT CASSEROLE

3 pounds boned lamb shoulder
cut in 1-inch dice
1 cup raw rice cooked
2 smallish eggplants cut in
1-inch dice
½ cup salad oil
1 cup minced onions
½ cup minced green peppers

Boiling salted water
2½ cups Italian tomatoes
(No. 2 can)
1 cup dry red wine
1 cup grated Parmesan cheese
2 teaspoons salt
½ teaspoon garlic salt

1. Brown the lamb well in the oil, adding the onions and green peppers as the lamb begins to brown.
2. Transfer to a good-sized casserole, cover, and bake 30 minutes in a slow oven, 325°.
3. Cook the eggplant 5 minutes in boiling salted water, stirring it a couple of times. Drain.
4. Stir the eggplant, cooked rice, tomatoes, wine, ½ cup of the cheese, salt and garlic salt into the casserole with the lamb.
5. Top with the rest of the cheese and bake another hour uncovered, or until brown and bubbly. Serves 8.

## LAMB SHANKS DINNER IN A CASSEROLE

6 lamb shanks
1 clove garlic
¼ cup flour
2 teaspoons salt
1 teaspoon paprika
2 tablespoons salad oil
½ cup lemon juice
½ cup dry white wine

½ cup chicken broth
2 tablespoons grated lemon rind
1 small bay leaf
4 peppercorns
12-16 small new potatoes
1 package cut green beans thawed (2 packages if no other vegetable)

1. Trim the fat from the shanks and rub well all over with the garlic clove cut in two. Roll in a mixture of the flour, salt, and paprika spread on a piece of waxed paper.
2. Brown all over in sizzling oil in a heavy skillet and lay in a large casserole.
3. Stir the lemon juice into the skillet, loosening all the browned particles. Add wine and chicken broth. Pour over the lamb.
4. Sprinkle the lemon rind over and add the bay leaf and peppercorns.
5. Cover and bake 1 hour in a moderate oven, 350°.
6. Add the potatoes and beans and bake 45 minutes longer, covered.
7. Ten minutes before serving, fish out the lamb shanks and cut the meat off, leaving it in quite large chunks. Return to casserole. (Whole shanks are difficult to manage on one's plate.) Serves 6.

# CASSOULET

2 cups dried white beans
8 slices bacon
¼ cup diced salt pork
1½ pounds pork loin cut in
    ¾-inch cubes
1 pound lamb shoulder cut in
    ¾-inch cubes
1 garlic sausage sliced
1 carrot cut in ¼-inch slices

1 onion stuck with 2 cloves
3 cloves garlic cut in two
    Salt and pepper
¾ cup butter, margarine, or
    salad oil
2 large onions chopped
2 tablespoons tomato paste
3 cups beef bouillon
3 cups crumbs

ONE of the most delightful dishes of the French provinces is the cassoulet, and of course there are endless versions of it. The true cassoulet, though, is essentially a combination of white beans (haricot beans), sausage, pork, mutton, and preserved goose, cooked for a long time and served with a golden crust. The recipe given here is typical of this peasant dish.

1. Soak the beans in water to cover overnight, or at least 4 hours, and drain.

2. Line a large casserole or a large beanpot with the bacon.

3. In a bowl mix the beans, carrot, whole onion, 1 clove garlic, and salt and pepper to taste.

4. Pour this mixture into the pot, cover with water, and bake in a slow oven, 275°, 2 hours.

5. While the beans are cooking, brown the meats in ¼ cup of the butter. Stir in the chopped onions, the 2 remaining garlic cloves, the tomato paste, and the bouillon. Simmer over very low heat 1½ hours, stirring occasionally.

6. Turn the meat mixture into the bean pot, stir well, and top with one cup of the crumbs. Dot with ¼ cup of butter, increase the heat to 375°, and bake until the crumbs are brown, about 15 minutes.

7. Stir the crumbs into the cassoulet and repeat this twice more, with the remaining crumbs. Serve when brown the third time. Serves 6.

*Note:* A duck or a chicken can be cut up, browned, and added if desired.

# SWEDISH LAMB WITH DILL

3 pounds lamb from leg or
   shoulder, cut in 1½-inch cubes
2 tablespoons salad oil
12 small white onions
2 tablespoons flour
1-pound can tomatoes

1 tablespoon fresh dill or
   1 teaspoon dried or dill weed
1 cup chicken broth
Salt to taste
4 medium potatoes peeled and
   quartered

THE dill flavor here makes this an unusual and delightful meal.

1. Brown the meat well in hot oil.

2. Add the onions and brown lightly, stirring almost constantly. Arrange in a large casserole.

3. Sprinkle with flour and stir well.

4. Add tomatoes, dill, and chicken broth.

5. Season to taste, cover, and bake 1½ hours in a 325° oven.

6. Add potatoes 20 minutes before you are ready to serve. Serves 8.


# LAMB CHOP CASSEROLE DINNER

8 rib lamb chops
2 tablespoons butter
1 teaspoon salt
¼ teaspoon fresh-ground pepper
4 tomatoes peeled and cut in
   thick slices

4 small white onions
4 apples cored and pared
   and sliced thick
4 potatoes peeled and sliced
   rather thick
1 cup tomato juice

1. Brown the chops delicately in butter, sprinkle with salt and pepper, and set aside.

2. In a good-sized greased casserole arrange the vegetables and apples in the order listed above, salting each lightly. Lay the chops on top. Pour the tomato juice over.

3. Cover the casserole and bake in a slow oven, 325°, 45 minutes, or until the chops are tender. Uncover the last 10 minutes. Serves 4.

## LAMB RAGOUT

3 pounds spring lamb cut in
  1½-inch cubes
1 tablespoon salt
⅓ cup salad oil
1 stalk of celery with top,
  sliced thin
2 medium onions quartered
4 tablespoons flour
  Consommé and dry red or
  white wine, half-and-half,
  or half water
1 small clove garlic mashed

½ bay leaf
1 cup tomatoes skinned and
  chopped
¾ cup string beans partly cooked
  and buttered
¾ cup carrots diced, partly
  cooked and buttered
¾ cup green peas, slightly
  cooked and buttered
2 cups potato balls, lightly
  sautéed in butter

1. Salt the lamb, heat the oil in a large heavy skillet, and brown the lamb on all sides.

2. With a slotted spoon remove to a large casserole, cover, and put in 325° oven for 45 minutes. Stir occasionally.

3. To the fat in the pan add the celery and onions and brown lightly. Stir in the flour and continue to cook until lightly browned, stirring frequently.

4. Blend in the consommé and wine (or water)—enough almost to cover the meat in the casserole—and stir until smooth and thickened.

5. To the meat in the casserole add the sauce, garlic, bay leaf, tomatoes, and all the buttered vegetables. Mix thoroughly. Continue to bake another hour, or slightly longer if lamb is not fork tender by that time.

If there is too much or too thin sauce at this time, drain it off into a saucepan and boil hard to reduce. Serves 6-8.

## LAMB STEW WITH SPRING VEGETABLES

2 pounds shoulder lamb cut in
  1½-inch cubes
6 tablespoons salad oil
  Salt and pepper

Bouquet of thyme and parsley,
  2 sprigs each
1 small bay leaf
  Hot water

½ teaspoon sugar
2 tablespoons flour
½ cup tomato purée
1 clove garlic crushed

8-12 small new potatoes
1 dozen baby carrots
1 cup green peas

1. Sear the lamb cubes well in hot oil, season with salt and pepper, and sprinkle with sugar to caramelize the meat a bit. Pour off most of the fat.

2. Sprinkle the meat with flour and cook 2-3 minutes.

3. Stir in the tomato purée, garlic, herb bouquet, and bay leaf. Cover with hot water and bring to a boil. Let it cook a few minutes, removing any scum that develops. Remove to a medium casserole, cover, and bake in a 350° oven an hour.

4. Carefully drain the liquid from the casserole into a small saucepan and boil hard to reduce it about a third. Strain it back into the casserole.

5. Stir in the vegetables, cover again, and continue to bake about 45 minutes, or until lamb is fork tender and the potatoes done. Serves 4-5.

## YORKSHIRE HOTCHPOT

4 shoulder lamb chops
1 clove garlic mashed
4 small white onions
4 medium potatoes pared and
  cut in half
1 package frozen cut green beans
2 teaspoons salt

⅛ teaspoon pepper
1 can condensed cream of
  mushroom soup
½ can water
Paprika
1 tablespoon chopped parsley

1. Cut off bits of fat from the chops, try them out in a heavy skillet, and brown the chops on both sides. Arrange in a casserole large enough to take them without overlapping.

2. Add garlic, onions, and potatoes to the casserole, and the beans, thawed just enough to break up. Season with salt and pepper.

3. Stir the water into the soup and pour over.

4. Cover and bake 1 hour in a 375° oven, or simmer gently on top of the stove 45-50 minutes.

5. Sprinkle with paprika and parsley before serving. Serves 4.

## LUNCHEON MEAT WITH SWEET POTATOES AND PINEAPPLE

12-ounce can luncheon meat
  cut in 4 pieces lengthwise
4 medium sweet potatoes cooked
  and halved (or 1 can)
4 pineapple slices, drained
1 cup pineapple syrup

¼ cup brown sugar (packed)
1 tablespoon cornstarch
¼ teaspoon salt
¼ cup dry sherry
2 tablespoons butter or margarine

1. In a greased shallow casserole arrange the pineapple. Lay the meat slices on top and the potatoes over that.
2. Heat the pineapple syrup to boiling. Stir in the brown sugar, cornstarch, and salt, stirring until the syrup is clear and thickened.
3. Stir the sherry and butter into the hot syrup and pour over the casserole.
4. Bake at 375°, uncovered, about 40 minutes. Serves 4.


## PORK AND MACARONI CASSEROLE WITH CORN

4 pork chops cut ¾-inch thick
1 cup thin macaroni
  broken up and cooked
1 can cream-style corn (17 ounces)
  Salt and pepper
1 tablespoon salad oil
2 tablespoons minced onion

¼ cup chopped green pepper
2 tablespoons flour
1 tablespoon brown sugar
½ cup water
½ cup chili sauce or catsup
1 tablespoon vinegar

1. Trim excess fat from the chops, season with salt and pepper, and brown well in sizzling oil in a heavy skillet. (If you prefer, try out the fat scraps and brown the chops in that fat.) Remove the chops to a plate until the other ingredients are prepared.
2. In the fat remaining in the skillet lightly brown the onion and green pepper. Stir in the flour, brown sugar, water, chili sauce, and vinegar.

210

Stir until the sauce is thick and smooth. Season to taste.

3. Mix the cooked macaroni and corn with the sauce, season to taste, and pour into a medium casserole.

4. Arrange the chops on top and bake, covered, about 1 hour, or until the chops are very tender. Remove the cover during the last 15 minutes. (If you prepare the casserole in the morning and refrigerate it, bring it to room temperature before baking and allow 1½ hours for baking.) Serves 4.

## PORK AND RICE CASSEROLE

4 loin pork chops cut ¾-inch thick
   Seasoned salt
¾ cup rice
1 can condensed consommé

4 medium onions quartered
2 large carrots sliced
   diagonally in 1-inch pieces

1. Trim excess fat from chops and try out in a heavy skillet.

2. Skim out the fat pieces when they are brown and brown the chops well in the fat, on both sides. Remove to a medium casserole that will hold them in one layer. Salt them lightly.

3. In the fat remaining in the skillet brown the raw rice, stirring constantly until it is colored.

4. Stir in the consommé.

5. Arrange the onions and carrots around the chops in the casserole, salt lightly, and pour the rice-consommé mixture over.

6. Cover the casserole and bake 1 hour in a 350° oven. Serves 4.

## VEAL CASSEROLE MEAL

3 pounds boneless veal
    cut in 1½-inch cubes
6 slices bacon cut in thin strips
6 medium onions sliced
    Salt and pepper
6 medium potatoes peeled and
    cut in wedges

3 large tomatoes skinned and
    quartered
2 tablespoons tomato paste
¾ cup chicken broth
2 packages cut green beans
½ cup grated Parmesan cheese

1. Cook bacon in a heavy skillet. When it begins to sizzle add the veal and onions, cooking until lightly browned. Arrange in a large casserole. Season to taste.

2. In the fat remaining in the skillet brown the potato wedges lightly and add to the casserole. Salt them lightly.

3. Put in the skillet the tomatoes, tomato paste, and chicken broth. When it boils stir in the frozen beans. When they are well broken up add to the casserole, with the liquid.

4. Cover the casserole and bake an hour at 350°.

5. Sprinkle the cheese on top and brown under the broiler. Serves 6.


## VEAL PARTY CASSEROLE

5 pounds boneless veal cut in
    1½-inch cubes
⅓ cup salad oil
2 onions chopped or sliced thin
1 pound-4-ounce can tomatoes
1 can tomato purée
1 can tomato sauce
1 can chicken broth
½ cup dry sherry
1 cup dry white or rosé wine
1½ teaspoons salt
1 teaspoon Tabasco

1 teaspoon thyme or orégano
2 small bay leaves
1 cup sliced celery
⅓ cup flour
½ cup water
½ pound mushrooms sliced or
    2 four-ounce cans
2 one-pound cans small
    white onions drained
1 package frozen peas thawed
1 package frozen cut green
    beans thawed

1. Brown the veal in small batches in sizzling oil, transferring the pieces to a large casserole or 2 medium-to-large ones.
2. In the remaining fat cook the onions lightly. Stir in the tomatoes, tomato purée, tomato sauce, chicken broth, sherry, white wine, salt, Tabasco, thyme, bay leaves, and celery. Simmer 5 minutes.
3. Stir in the flour and water mixed to a paste, stirring constantly until thick and smooth. Pour this mixture over the veal.
4. Cover and bake at 325° 1¼ hours.
5. Stir in the mushrooms and whole onions. Bake 10 minutes more, uncovered.
6. Stir in the peas and beans and bake 15 minutes longer. Serve on buttered wide noodles. Serves 12-14.

## QUICK SUPPER CASSEROLE

2 cups chopped cooked meat
  (any kind), coarsely flaked
  tuna, or sliced hard-cooked eggs
2 cups soft bread crumbs
½ cup grated sharp cheese
2 tablespoons melted butter
  or margarine
1 cup cooked peas, cut beans,
  or cut asparagus

3 tablespoons butter
2 tablespoons minced onion
3 tablespoons flour
1½ cups milk
  Salt and pepper
1 large tomato skinned and
  cut in ¼-inch slices

1. Mix together the bread crumbs, cheese, and melted butter. Spread half in a rather wide shallow casserole and arrange the peas on top.
2. In a saucepan melt the 3 tablespoons butter, sauté the onion lightly in it, blend in flour, and gradually add the milk. Stir until smooth and thick and season to taste.
3. Stir into the cream sauce the meat, fish, or eggs, and pour over the peas.
4. Lay the tomato slices on top of the sauce and cover with the remaining crumbs.
5. Bake 25 minutes in a moderate oven, 350°. Serves 4.

# CHICKEN HOTCH POTCH

1½ pounds chicken legs
6 cups well-salted water
Salt
1 cup green peas
1 cup lima beans
2 carrots diced

1 onion sliced
1 small cauliflower broken
into flowerets
1 small head lettuce shredded
2 tablespoons chopped parsley

1. Bring the chicken legs to a boil in the water, skimming the froth off as it forms. Put in a large casserole both the chicken legs and the broth. Add the peas, beans, carrots, and onion. Cover and bake 1½ hours in a slow oven, 325°.

2. Add the cauliflower and lettuce and bake 35-40 minutes longer.

3. Fish out the chicken legs, skin and bone them, and cut the meat into fair-sized chunks. Return to the "soup," add the parsley, and cook 10 minutes more. Check and correct seasoning.

4. If you prefer this slightly thickened, stir in a flour-and-water paste. For a little extra flavor stir in ½ cup dairy sour cream too.

Reheat and serve in large soup plates. Serves 6.

# CHINESE CHICKEN CASSEROLE

1½ cups cooked chicken diced
2 tablespoons salad oil
½ cup thinly sliced onion
½ cup sliced mushrooms
1 cup thinly sliced celery
1 can (5 ounce) water
chestnuts sliced
1 cup chicken broth

1 teaspoon cornstarch
¼ teaspoon salt
2 tablespoons water
1 tablespoon soy sauce
1-pound can bean sprouts
½ cup toasted blanched
slivered almonds

1. Heat the oil in a large skillet or electric fry pan and lightly sauté the onion, mushrooms, celery, and water chestnuts 5 minutes or so. Put in a medium casserole.

2. Add the chicken and the broth, cover, and bake about 15 minutes in a 350° oven.

3. Blend together the cornstarch, salt, water, and soy sauce and stir into the casserole. Bake another 10 minutes.

4. Stir in the bean sprouts and almonds, heat well (about 5 minutes) and serve on hot fluffy rice. Serves 5-6.

## PAELLA

4½-5-pound chicken cut up
  ½ cup olive oil (or salad oil)
  5 cloves garlic bruised
    but not peeled
  1 medium onion minced
  1 cup green beans cut up
  1 cup cauliflower flowerets
1½ cups lobster coarsely diced

1½ cups shrimp shelled and
    deveined
  2 medium tomatoes chopped
1½ teaspoons paprika
  3 cups dry rice (preferably
    wild, but then 2 cups)
  1 cup chopped parsley
    Salt
    Boiling water

PAELLA is certainly one of the most popular Spanish dishes, made in a slightly different way in each province of Spain. This recipe is a relatively simple one, and the following one is a little more elaborate. Both are delicious.

1. Heat the oil in a large heavy skillet and brown the garlic in it. Remove the garlic and brown the chicken pieces well. Arrange in a large casserole or Dutch oven.

2. Sauté the onion lightly in the skillet for 5 minutes.

3. At 5-minute intervals add the following, in order: beans, cauliflower, lobster and shrimp together, tomatoes, paprika, rice, parsley.

4. When the parsley has been in 5 minutes turn the whole mixture into the casserole or Dutch oven. Pour over boiling water barely to cover and bake, covered, 40 minutes in a slow oven, 300°. Or simmer over very low heat 20-30 minutes, stirring occasionally. Check seasoning. Serves 6-8.

*Note:* If you use converted rice add it dry—do not rinse. But if you use wild rice wash it well in several waters.

## PAELLA VALENCIANA

4 chicken breasts (8 halves)
8 chicken legs
⅓ cup salad oil
3 Spanish sausages (or
    Portuguese or Italian)
    sliced ½-inch thick
1½ pounds shelled and
    deveined shrimp
12 littleneck clams or
    mussels or both
1 cup chopped onion
1 clove garlic mashed

4 cups chicken broth
3½ teaspoons salt
½ teaspoon pepper
¾ teaspoon dried tarragon or
    1½ teaspoons fresh, chopped
½ teaspoon paprika
1 teaspoon saffron crumbled
2 cups raw rice
2 cups canned tomatoes
1 package frozen peas
7-ounce can artichoke hearts
    (or frozen, cooked)

1. In a Dutch oven heat the oil and brown the chicken pieces we
Remove and set aside.

2. In the same oil sauté the onion and garlic until soft.

3. Add the chicken broth, salt and pepper, tarragon, paprika, a
saffron.

4. Bring to a boil, add rice, and simmer over medium heat until abo
half of the liquid has been absorbed—about 20 minutes.

5. Stir in the tomatoes, sausage, shrimp, and chicken. Cover, tu
down the heat to a simmer, and cook until rice is almost dry—20-2
minutes.

6. Put the clams or mussels in a kettle with a bit of water over hig
heat until the shells open—2-3 minutes. Cool enough to handle a
break off the tops of the shells. Add to the pot.

7. Add the peas and artichoke hearts, stir lightly, and continue
cook until hot.

Serve in the pot if it is a modern one with porcelain jacket; othe
wise pour the paella into a large casserole. Serves 8.

# PARTY CHICKEN-NOODLE CASSEROLE

5-pound fowl cut up
¾ pound medium noodles
  broken up
⅓ cup minced onion
⅓ cup green pepper minced
3-ounce can sliced mushrooms
1 cup pitted ripe olives
1 can condensed cream of
  mushroom soup

1½ cups grated sharp
  Cheddar cheese
¼ cup minced pimientos
1 tablespoon minced parsley
½ teaspoon celery salt
  Salt and pepper
½ cup buttered bread or
  corn flake crumbs

THIS is a good hearty dish for a buffet supper. It can be enlarged by adding canned boned chicken and increasing all remaining ingredients a little.

1. Put the chicken in a large kettle with barely enough water to cover and the usual items to give it flavor: 2 teaspoons salt, ½ onion cut in pieces, stalk of celery cut up, 1 carrot cut up, 2 sprigs parsley, a bay leaf, etc. Cover and simmer until well done—1½-2 hours.

2. Remove the chicken pieces from the broth, cool them, skin, and cut up the meat in rather large chunks.

3. Strain the broth and chill it so that you can skim off the fat. Save the fat. The chicken can be cooked the day before you need it.

4. Measure the chicken broth you have and add enough canned chicken broth, or boiling water and chicken stock base, or bouillon cubes, to make 6 cups of broth. Include the juice from the mushrooms.

5. Bring to a boil and cook the noodles in it about 7 minutes.

6. In 2 tablespoons of the skimmed-off chicken fat lightly sauté the onion, green pepper, and mushrooms. Stir in the chicken and olives.

7. Partially drain the cooked noodles, leaving them just a little soppy.

8. Stir in the soup, cheese, pimientos, parsley, celery salt, and salt and pepper to taste.

9. In a large casserole make alternate layers of the chicken mixture and the noodle mixture. Top with a fairly thick layer of buttered crumbs and bake about 1 hours at 325°, or until bubbly and golden. Serves 10.

## RICE CASSEROLE DINNER

1½ cups raw rice
5 or 6 chicken livers cut in
  3-4 pieces each
5 slices prosciutto or
  boiled ham, shredded
1 small sweetbread cooked
  and diced
⅔ cup butter or margarine
¼ cup minced onion

¼ pound mushrooms sliced
½ cup dry white wine
½ cup marsala wine or sherry
1 truffle chopped (optional)
1 tablespoon meat glaze
2 cups condensed consommé
1 cup cooked peas
Salt and pepper
¼ cup grated Parmesan cheese

1. Heat half the butter in a large casserole or Dutch oven. Stir in the onion, chicken livers, prosciutto, sweetbread, and mushrooms. Brown lightly, stirring often.
2. Stir in the two wines, the rice, and the truffle, cooking over very low heat until the wines have been evaporated.
3. Stir the meat glaze into the consommé and add to the pot, with the peas. Season to taste.
4. Cover and simmer until the rice is tender, about 20 minutes. Check occasionally and add a bit more water or consommé if needed, but the dish should be quite dry.
5. Stir in the remaining butter and the cheese before serving. Serves 6.


## RICE AND SAUSAGE WITH VEGETABLES

3 cups cooked rice
¾ pound sweet Italian sausages
  cut in ¼-inch slices
¼ cup butter or margarine
1 medium onion minced
15-ounce can artichoke hearts
  drained and quartered

1 package frozen peas
  partly thawed
3-ounce can boiled chopped
  mushrooms, drained
1 can condensed consommé
½ cup grated Parmesan cheese

1. Heat the butter in a large heavy skillet and lightly brown the onion and sausage.

2. Stir in the artichokes, peas, mushrooms, and ½ cup of the consommé. Simmer 10 minutes or so.

3. Stir in the rice and remaining consommé and pour into a greased medium casserole.

4. Sprinkle with cheese and bake 15 or 20 minutes in a moderate oven, 375°, or until cheese is well browned. Serves 6.

## RICE HAWAIIAN

2½ cups cooked rice
3 tablespoons butter or margarine
1 cup diced cooked ham, chicken, or tongue
¾ cup diced pineapple, canned, fresh, or frozen

¼ cup pine nuts or slivered almonds
Salt and pepper
½ cup chopped watercress, stems removed

HEAT the butter in a small casserole and lightly brown the ham. Add the pineapple, rice, nuts, and seasoning to taste. Cover and bake in a moderate oven, 350°, 15 minutes, or until piping hot. Sprinkle with watercress before serving. Serves 4.

## SPAGHETTI CASSEROLE MEAL

1 cup thin spaghetti broken up and cooked
1 cup cooked turkey, chicken, or diced roast meat
1 cup julienned cooked ham
1 cup diced sharp Cheddar
3 tablespoons butter or margarine

2 tablespoons flour
1 cup top milk
Salt and pepper
1 cup heavy cream
1 Bermuda onion sliced thin
Paprika

1. Make a cream sauce with the butter, flour, and milk, seasoning it to taste.

2. Stir into the sauce the meat and cheese, the well-drained spaghetti, and the cream. Pour into a medium casserole.

3. Top with layers of onion carefully arranged.

4. Sprinkle with paprika and bake 20 minutes in a slow oven, 325°. Serves 6.

# TURKEY ALMONDINE

2 cups cooked turkey
(or chicken) cut up
2 tablespoons butter or margarine
2 tablespoons flour
1 teaspoon salt
¼ teaspoon fresh-ground pepper
¼ teaspoon prepared mustard

2 cups milk
1 cup grated sharp Cheddar
(¼ pound)
1 package frozen broccoli cooked
2 cups medium noodles
(¼ pound) cooked
⅓ cup slivered, toasted almonds

1. In a saucepan over low heat make a cream sauce by melting th
butter, blending in the flour, salt, pepper, and mustard, and graduall
adding the milk. Stir constantly until smooth and thick.
2. Add the cheese and stir until melted.
3. Cut off the broccoli stems and chop them small. Spread the stem
in a shallow greased casserole, cover with noodles, and then wit
turkey.
4. Pour the cheese sauce over the casserole and scatter the brocco
flowerets on top, pressing them lightly into the sauce.
5. Sprinkle the almonds over all.
6. Bake in a moderate oven, 350°, 15 minutes, or until bubblin
Serves 4-5.


# TURKEY CASSEROLE FOR A PARTY

1 quart cooked turkey cut in
julienne strips
½ cup butter, margarine, or
salad oil
¾ cup cooked ham cut in
julienne strips
½ pound mushrooms sliced
1 pound thin spaghetti cooked
½ cup Parmesan cheese
2 tablespoons heavy cream

2 tablespoons sherry
1½ cups heavy cream whipped
2 teaspoons paprika
3 cups rich cream sauce
(4 tablespoons butter,
4 tablespoons flour, 3 cups
top milk, and seasoning to taste
3 eggs yolks beaten a little
⅜ cup dry sherry
3 tablespoons melted butter

1. Heat ¼ cup of the butter in a large skillet and sauté the ham and mushrooms until the mushrooms are tender, about 5 minutes. Stir often.

2. Drain the cooked spaghetti and toss it with the remaining ¼ cup of butter, half of the grated Parmesan cheese, the 2 tablespoons cream, and the 2 tablespoons sherry. Spread the spaghetti on the bottom of a large greased casserole.

3. Stir the whipped cream and paprika into the cream sauce and heat almost to boiling.

4. Stir ½ cup or so of the sauce into the egg yolks and stir quickly back into the sauce.

5. Stir in the ham and mushroom mixture and the turkey. Heat well.

6. Stir in the ⅜ cup of sherry. Correct the seasoning and pour the mixture over the spaghetti, being careful not to disturb it.

7. Dribble the 3 tablespoons melted butter on top and sprinkle with the rest of the cheese.

8. Bake 25-30 minutes in a slow oven, 275°, and brown quickly under the broiler. Serves 12.

*Note:* If you prepare the casserole early in the day, bring it to room temperature—2 hours—before baking.

## TUNA CASSEROLE SUPPER

2 cans tuna fish rinsed in cold water
1 can condensed cream of mushroom soup
1-pound can of peas
4-ounce can pimiento diced small

1 small onion chopped
1 tablespoon Worcestershire sauce
1 cup grated sharp Cheddar
½ can French-fried onions (3½ ounces)

1. Mix the soup, peas (with their liquid), pimiento, onion, and Worcestershire sauce.

2. Fold in the tuna, broken in medium lumps, and the cheese. Pour into a medium casserole.

3. Arrange the French-fried onions around the outside edge, leaving the center uncovered.

4. Bake in a moderate oven, 375°, about 25 minutes, or until the onions are crisp and the tuna mixture bubbly. Serves 6.

# QUICK TUNA LUNCHEON CASSEROLE

2 cans tuna (6½-7 ounces)
  drained and broken into chunks
1 small onion chopped
½ cup diced green pepper
2 tablespoons butter or margarine
2 tablespoons flour
1 teaspoon salt
¼ teaspoon pepper

¼ teaspoon dried thyme or
  ½ teaspoon fresh, chopped
3-ounce can button mushrooms
1 cup evaporated milk
1 tablespoon Worcestershire sauce
4-ounce can whole kernel corn
  or ½ cup frozen or fresh
4-ounce can potato sticks

1. In a saucepan sauté the onion and green pepper lightly in the butter. Blend in the flour, salt, pepper, and thyme. Add gradually the liquid drained from the mushrooms and the milk. Stir until the sauce is smooth and thick.

2. Add the Worcestershire sauce, corn, mushrooms, and tuna to the sauce.

3. Turn into a medium casserole and top with potato sticks.

4. Bake 20 minutes in a moderate oven, 375°, or until bubbly. Serves 4-6.

# VEGETABLES

## CASSEROLE OF FROZEN VEGETABLES

HERE is an easy way to cook frozen vegetables in the oven when you are already using it for another casserole.

Put in a casserole a frozen block of any vegetable, with 2 tablespoons butter or margarine, ½ teaspoon salt, ⅛ teaspoon pepper, and 2 tablespoons water except in the case of squash. Cover and bake 35-60 minutes, depending upon the temperature you are using for the main casserole.

An alternative method is to wrap the frozen block of vegetables in heavy-duty foil, double-sealing the package by folds. Lay the block in an open casserole. You can put 2 or 3 such blocks in one casserole.


## RATATOUILLE (Mixed Vegetables)

3 large onions chopped fine
3 large peppers seeded and
    coarsely chopped
6 small zucchini sliced thin
    (unpeeled)
1 medium eggplant diced
    (unpeeled)

6 large tomatoes peeled,
    seeded, and coarsely chopped
Salad oil
1 cup chopped parsley
3 cloves garlic minced
Salt and pepper
Grated Parmesan cheese

1. Cover the bottom of a large heavy skillet with oil and sauté the onions until they begin to color.
2. Add the green peppers and cook about 2 minutes more.
3. Stir in zucchini and eggplant and cook about 5 minutes, or until they begin to look transparent.
4. Turn these vegetables into a large casserole and stir in the tomatoes.
5. Cover and bake in a very slow oven, 250°, 1½ hours.
6. Stir in the parsley and garlic, season to taste, cover again, and bake 20 minutes longer.
7. Sprinkle with cheese before serving. Or chill the casserole well and serve cold. Serves 8.

# VEGETABLES WITH RICE

¼ cup chopped green pepper
1 small onion chopped
¼ cup butter or margarine
1 cup raw rice
1 cup canned tomatoes undrained
8-ounce can small onions and juice

1-pound can cream-style corn or
  1 package frozen thawed
2 tablespoons catsup
½ teaspoon salt
⅛ teaspoon pepper
1 cup chicken broth

1. Cook green pepper and chopped onion in butter until tender.
2. Stir in rice and cook until rice is yellow, stirring constantly.
3. Add remaining ingredients and turn into medium casserole.
4. Bake 40 minutes at 350°, or until rice is tender and liquid all absorbed. Serves 6.


# TIAN (Cold Vegetable Casserole)

1 pound raw spinach chopped
1 pound raw Swiss chard chopped
3-4 small zucchini diced
  small (unpeeled)
1 medium onion chopped fine
  Salad oil (preferably olive oil)
2 cloves garlic mashed (small)

¼ cup fresh sweet basil chopped
  fine or 1 tablespoon dried
¾ teaspoon salt
¼ teaspoon fresh-ground pepper
4 eggs slightly beaten
½-¾ cup grated Parmesan cheese
  Bread or corn flake crumbs

1. Heat enough oil in a large skillet to cover the bottom. Cook the spinach and Swiss chard in it until barely wilted. Remove and drain well.
2. Add more oil to the skillet and cook the zucchini, onion, and garlic until the onion begins to be transparent.
3. Mix all the vegetables and stir in the basil, salt, and pepper. Arrange in a lightly greased casserole.
4. Pour over the eggs and top with cheese and crumbs mixed.
5. Bake in a 350° oven 25-30 minutes, or until the eggs are set. Chill and serve cold. Serves 6.

## MIXED VEGETABLE CASSEROLE

8 small new potatoes scraped
8 baby carrots scraped
1 small cauliflower broken
   into flowerets

1 cup fresh peas (or frozen)
2 cups medium cream sauce
¾ cup coarsely grated Cheddar
   Chopped parsley

1. Cook the vegetables in a minimum of boiling salted water until tender but still crisp—just short of done: potatoes alone, carrots and cauliflower together, peas alone. Arrange in a casserole.
2. Make a smooth cream sauce of 3 tablespoons butter or margarine, 3 tablespoons flour, 2 cups whole milk, and seasoning to taste. When thick, stir in cheese until melted.
3. Pour over vegetables in the casserole and bake 15 minutes in a moderate oven, 350°, or until bubbly.
4. Sprinkle parsley on top before serving. Serves 4.


## VEGETABLE GHIVETCHI (Rumanian Casserole)

½ bunch baby carrots scraped
   and sliced
2 potatoes diced
½ eggplant diced (unpeeled)
8-ounce can small white onions
½ cup each peas, limas,
   and cut green beans
½ green pepper cut in strips
½ small cabbage shredded
   Small cauliflower broken
   into flowerets

½ summer squash diced
½ celery root diced
5 small tomatoes quartered
2 onions sliced thin
2 cloves garlic mashed
¼ cup butter or margarine
1 cup chicken stock or consommé
½ cup salad oil
   (preferably olive oil)
1 tablespoon salt
   Fresh-ground pepper

THIS is as good a casserole as you are likely to find in a long search. For a "company" dinner or for a special buffet party it is sure to make a hit. Best of all, it can be completely put together early in the day and refrigerated until 2 hours before needed.

1. Arrange all the vegetables except the sliced onions in a large casserole, in the order given.
2. Sauté the onions and garlic in butter until golden.
3. Add the stock and bring to a boil.
4. Stir in the oil, salt, and pepper, pour over the casserole, cover, and bake in a 325° oven 30-40 minutes, or until tender but still crisp. Serves 10-12.


## BLACK BEANS IN RED WINE

2 cups black beans
1½ quarts water
2 teaspoons salt
⅛ pound salt pork
  Boiling water
2 tablespoons butter or margarine
1 small onion chopped

1 clove garlic mashed
½ cup dry red wine
1 medium carrot diced
  Bouquet of parsley, bay leaf, and thyme
Chopped parsley

1. Combine the beans, water, and salt and let stand overnight. Or boil 2 minutes and let soak an hour. Do not drain.
2. Cover the salt pork with boiling water, let stand an hour, drain, and then dice pork rather fine.
3. Melt the butter in a saucepan and sauté the onion and garlic until tender but not brown.
4. Add the wine and bring to a boil. Reduce the heat at once and simmer a few minutes.
5. Add the salt pork to the beans and bring to a boil.
6. Stir in the carrot, bouquet of herbs tied in a bit of cheesecloth, and the wine mixture.
7. Pour into a casserole, cover, and bake 2-3 hours in a slow oven, 300°. Uncover the last half hour.
8. Sprinkle with parsley before serving. Serves 6-8.

## ASPARAGUS-CHEESE PUDDING

1½ pounds fresh asparagus
  3 slices white bread,
    crusts removed
  1 cup shredded sharp Cheddar
  2 eggs lightly beaten

2 cups milk scalded
1 teaspoon salt
½ teaspoon pepper
1 tablespoon melted butter
  or margarine

1. Clean the asparagus well and cut off 2-inch tips to be used later. Cut the crisp part of remaining stalks into 1-inch pieces.

2. Toast the bread and cut in 1-inch squares.

3. In a shallow casserole or a rectangular baking dish 10″ x 6″ x 2″ arrange alternate layers of bread squares, asparagus, and cheese.

4. Combine the eggs, milk, salt, pepper, and butter.

5. Pour over the casserole and bake in a 325° oven 45 minutes to an hour, or until the custard is set.

6. At the same time salt the reserved tips and wrap them in a square of aluminum foil. Fold the edges to seal and put them in the oven with the casserole. Unwrap and arrange on the top of the pudding before serving. Serves 8.


## ASPARAGUS-BACON PIE

3 cups cooked asparagus cut in
  1-inch pieces, or frozen
  asparagus cuts
6 slices crisply cooked bacon
3 eggs lightly beaten
1 tablespoon chopped scallions
  (green onions)

1 teaspoon sugar
1 teaspoon salt or to taste
¼ teaspoon pepper
  Pinch nutmeg
1½ cups light cream
1 cup grated Parmesan cheese
  Pastry for 9-inch pie shell

1. Line a deep pie plate with the pastry.

2. Crumble the bacon and spread it on the bottom.

3. Arrange the asparagus over the bacon.

4. Mix the eggs, scallions, sugar, salt, pepper, nutmeg, cream, and half the cheese. Pour gently over the asparagus.

5. Spread the remaining cheese on top and bake 10 minutes in a 400° oven.

6. Reduce the heat to 350° and continue to bake 25-30 minutes longer, or until a knife inserted in the center comes out clean. Serves 6.

## QUICK GREEN BEAN CASSEROLE

2 ten-ounce packages frozen
   French-style string beans
¾ cup boiling salted water
7-ounce package frozen French-
   fried onion rings

2 cans condensed cream of
   mushroom soup
½ cup top milk

1. Cook the beans in the water, but not more than 3-4 minutes after they come to a boil, and that over very low heat. Drain well.

2. Alternate layers of beans and onions in a casserole.

3. Heat the soup and mix with the milk. Pour over the casserole and bake 25 minutes in a 350° oven. Serves 6-7.

## BRUSSELS SPROUTS DE LUXE

1 quart Brussels sprouts, or 3
   packages frozen, cooked barely
   tender
½ cup chopped carrots
¼ cup chopped onion
¼ cup chopped celery

½ cup cooked chestnuts broken up
1½ cups condensed consommé
3 tablespoons butter or margarine
   Salt and pepper
2 thin slices lemon quartered

1. Arrange the sprouts in a greased casserole.

2. Put in a saucepan the carrots, onion, celery, chestnuts, and consommé. Bring to a boil, reduce the heat, and simmer about 10 minutes.

3. Add the butter, seasoning to taste, and lemon pieces.

4. Pour over the sprouts and bake in a moderate oven, 350°, 30 minutes. Cover the casserole for the first 20 minutes. Serves 6.

# LIMA BEAN SOUFFLÉ

1 cup cooked Fordhook limas
3 tablespoons butter or margarine
3 tablespoons flour
1 cup rich milk

Salt and pepper to taste
4 eggs separated
1 tablespoon brandy

*Spanish Sauce*

½ cup chopped onion
3 tablespoons salad oil
1 cup peeled and seeded tomatoes
  chopped
½ cup ripe or green olives coarsely
  chopped

½ teaspoon celery salt
2 teaspoons Worcestershire sauce
½ teaspoon garlic salt
1 tablespoon meat glaze
2 tablespoons brandy

1. Make a cream sauce with the butter, flour, and milk.
2. Season to taste and put in blender with the lima beans. Blend 30 seconds.
3. Add the egg yolks and brandy and blend 20 seconds more.
4. Beat the egg whites until stiff but not dry and fold into the lima bean mixture. Pour into a greased medium casserole or soufflé dish and bake in a slow oven, 325°, 35-40 minutes, or until a knife inserted in the center comes out clean. Serve with Spanish Sauce. Serves 6.

*Spanish Sauce:* Sauté the onion lightly in oil. Add the tomatoes and simmer 10 minutes. Stir in the olives and remaining ingredients except the brandy, which should be added just before serving.

If desired, the sauce may be thickened a little with flour-and-water paste.


# BROCCOLI CASSEROLE

1 large bunch fresh broccoli or
  2 packages frozen

⅔ cup evaporated milk (1 small
  can)

Boiling salted water
1 cup grated Cheddar
1 can condensed cream of
  mushroom soup

3½-ounce can French-fried
  onion rings

1. If the broccoli is fresh, trim off all of the thick part of the stems and slit the untrimmed part. Split large pieces. (Stems can be cut up, cooked in boiling salted water, drained, chopped quite fine, and mixed with salt, pepper, and butter to make another vegetable for another day.) Cook in boiling salted water until stems are barely tender. Drain.
2. If broccoli is frozen cook it barely 4 minutes after it comes to a boil, and drain.
3. Arrange the broccoli in a casserole and sprinkle with the cheese. Mix the soup and milk and pour over.
4. Bake 25 minutes in a moderate oven, 350°.
5. Top with onion rings and bake 8-10 minutes more, or until onions are crisp. Serves 6.


## CAULIFLOWER WITH GREEN BEANS

1 medium cauliflower
½ cup finely slivered string beans
1½ cups hot milk
2 tablespoons butter or margarine

2 tablespoons flour
Salt and pepper
½ cup corn flake crumbs

1. Trim the cauliflower and break into flowerets. Steam for 10 minutes, or until just tender.
2. Cook beans in milk, keeping them just simmering. The beans should be crisp, not soft. Drain, reserving the milk.
3. Melt the butter in a saucepan, blend in the flour, and gradually add the milk the beans were cooked in. Season to taste and stir in the beans.
4. Arrange the cauliflower in a medium casserole, pour the sauce over, top with crumbs, and bake about 20 minutes in a hot oven, 400°, or until brown. Serves 4.

## ALSATIAN SAUERKRAUT

3 pounds sauerkraut, well rinsed
½ teaspoon caraway seeds
12 peppercorns
2 carrots scraped and quartered
lengthwise
8 small shoulder pork chops or 4
large, bone removed

1 pound boneless smoked pork
tenderloin or pork butt trimmed
and sliced thick
1 cup dry white wine
Salt to taste
½ pound knackwurst sliced

THIS is practically a classic way of preparing sauerkraut. To be at its best, however, it should be prepared a day ahead, as it improves greatly on standing.

1. In a large heavy casserole mix the well-drained kraut with the caraway seeds, peppercorns, and carrots. Cover with slices of pork tenderloin and the chops (cut in two if large).

2. Stir in the wine, sprinkle with salt, cover tightly, and simmer, on top of the stove, over the lowest possible heat. If it tends to boil put an asbestos plate underneath. Cook 2-3 hours, cool, and refrigerate.

3. Next day allow the casserole to come to room temperature (1-2 hours), stir in the knackwurst, and correct seasoning.

4. Reheat over very low heat just long enough to heat thoroughly—20-30 minutes. Serve with boiled new potatoes. Serves 8.


## CHOUCROUTE GARNIE (Garnished Kraut)

3 pounds sauerkraut well rinsed
1 tablespoon butter or margarine
¾ pound bacon diced
1 large onion with 3 cloves
stuck in
1 Polish sausage cut in 2-inch
pieces
1 pound smoked pork shoulder

6 peppercorns tied in cheesecloth
2 small bay leaves
¼ teaspoon dried thyme
Salt to taste
2 cups dry white wine
2 cups water
12 medium potatoes peeled and
boiled

¼ cup brandy                12 frankfurters
1 carrot sliced

CHOUCROUTE Garnie is almost as well-known as Alsatian sauerkraut —better known in many places. And it is equally delicious if you like sauerkraut.

1. Melt the butter in a Dutch oven or large heavy kettle. Add the bacon and onion and cook until browned. Add the sausage and pork shoulder and brown. Remove the meat and set aside.

2. Squeeze the kraut as dry as possible and add it to the kettle. Stir until slightly browned.

3. Add the brandy and stir.

4. Add the carrot, peppercorns, bay leaves, thyme, salt, wine, and water. Bring to a boil, stir in the meat, cover, and simmer over the lowest possible heat 3 hours. Use an asbestos mat, or 2 mats, under the pot if the kraut tends to boil.

5. At this point the dish can be cooled and refrigerated. Next day bring it to room temperature, stir in the potatoes and franks, and simmer 30 minutes. Slice the pork shoulder before serving. Serves 6-8.

## SWEET-SOUR RED CABBAGE

1 medium head red cabbage      ½ cup water
    shredded fine                  2 tablespoons sugar
    Boiling salted water         2 tablespoons vinegar
¼ cup pork or bacon drippings    1 onion stuck with 6-8 cloves
1 large apple peeled and chopped   1 tablespoon flour

1. Cover the cabbage with boiling salted water and simmer 10 minutes. Drain thoroughly. Put in a large casserole.

2. Stir into the cabbage the drippings, apple, water, sugar, and vinegar. Push the onion well down in the middle. Cover and bake 1½ hours in a slow oven, 300°. Or simmer over the lowest possible heat on top of the stove.

3. Just before serving sprinkle the flour over and stir it in. Remove the onion. Serves 6.

# CAULIFLOWER À LA MOUSSELINE

1 large head cauliflower
2 eggs separated
2 tablespoons cream
½ teaspoon salt

½ teaspoon sugar
¼ teaspoon paprika
2½ tablespoons lemon juice
¼ cup butter

1. Break the cauliflower into flowerets, trim off excess stems, and steam about 10 minutes. Or cook 8-10 minutes in barely enough boiling salted water to cover. Watch carefully to see that cauliflower does not become soft. Drain.
2. In the top of a small double boiler beat the egg yolks and cream hard. Blend in the salt, sugar, and paprika. Set over hot but not boiling water.
3. When this mixture is hot pour in slowly, beating constantly, the lemon juice. Keep beating until it has the consistency of thick cream.
4. Remove the whole double boiler from the heat and beat in the butter in small pieces. Remove the top part from the double boiler.
5. Beat the egg whites until stiff but not dry and fold into the sauce.
6. Arrange the cauliflower in a shallow casserole, pour the sauce over, and brown briefly under the broiler. Serves 6.


# CAULIFLOWER ALMONDINE

1 package frozen cauliflower
¼ cup boiling salted water
1 can cream of mushroom soup, undiluted

¼ cup blanched and slivered almonds
1 tablespoon butter melted
2 tablespoons bread or corn flake crumbs

1. Cook cauliflower in the water until barely tender. Drain and arrange in a small casserole.
2. Heat the soup and stir in the almonds. Pour over the cauliflower.
3. Top with butter and crumbs mixed. Bake 10 minutes in a 325° oven. Serves 4.

# CELERY ALMONDINE

4 cups celery sliced in thin diagonals
Boiling water
3 tablespoons butter or margarine
3 tablespoons flour
1½ cups chicken broth
½ cup cream
Salt and pepper
½ cup chopped blanched almonds
2 tablespoons grated Parmesan cheese
2 tablespoons bread or corn flake crumbs

SLIVERED, sliced, or chopped almonds can be used with a number of vegetables, but they seem to do more for celery than for any other one.
1. Parboil the celery; that is, barely cover it with boiling water and let it come to a boil again. Drain.
2. Make a cream sauce by melting the butter, blending in the flour, and gradually adding the chicken broth and cream.
3. Season to taste, stir in the almonds, and pour over the celery in a medium casserole.
4. Combine the cheese and crumbs to make a topping.
5. Bake 20 minutes in a moderate oven, 375°, or until browned and bubbling. Serves 4-6.


# COGNAC CARROTS

4 cups carrots sliced diagonally very thin
2 tablespoons butter
4 tablespoons good cognac
4 tablespoons water
Salt and pepper
1 tablespoon minced parsley

MELT butter in medium casserole. Stir in remaining ingredients, except parsley, keeping salt and pepper on the light side. Cover tightly and bake in a slow oven, 300°, 20 minutes, or until carrots are tender and liquid absorbed. Sprinkle with parsley before serving. Serves 5-6.

# CALIFORNIA CARROTS

4 cups shredded or coarsely grated
  carrots
2 tablespoons butter or margarine

1 medium onion minced
Salt and pepper
½ cup dry white wine

MELT the butter in a medium casserole and stir in the carrots and onion. Sprinkle lightly with salt and pepper and pour the wine over. Cover the casserole and bake in a moderate oven, 350°, 25-30 minutes. Uncover the last 5 minutes. Serves 4.


# CARROTS ALMONDINE

2½ cups grated raw carrots
1½ tablespoons butter or margarine
2 eggs well beaten
1 cup evaporated milk

½ teaspoon salt
½ teaspoon sugar
½ cup coarsely chopped almonds

MELT the butter in a small casserole. Mix the remaining ingredients and stir into the casserole. Bake 30-40 minutes in a moderate oven, 350°. Serves 4.


# CARROT SOUFFLÉ

2 cups mashed cooked carrots
2 tablespoons butter or margarine
2 tablespoons flour
½ cup warm milk

½ teaspoon salt
½ cup grated almonds
4 eggs separated

1. Melt the butter in a saucepan, blend in the flour, gradually add the milk, season, and simmer 5 minutes or so.
2. Stir in the carrots and almonds.
3. Remove from the heat and stir in the well-beaten yolks. Cool to lukewarm.

4. Fold in the egg whites beaten until stiff but not dry.
5. Pour gently into a small greased soufflé dish or casserole and bake in a moderate oven, 350°, 50-60 minutes, until soufflé feels firm at the center, or until a knife inserted in the center comes out clean. Serves 6-8.

## BACON-CORN PUDDING

2 packages frozen cut corn,
   cooked, or 2 medium cans whole-
   kernel corn
3 eggs well beaten
¼ cup light cream
1 teaspoon salt

Dash pepper
2 tablespoons minced onions
¼ teaspoon baking powder
Thinly sliced sharp Cheddar
3 slices bacon cut in 1-inch squares

Mix the corn, eggs, cream, seasonings, onions, and baking powder. Pour into a greased medium casserole. Cover with cheese, cut to fit, and then with bacon squares. Bake 40-45 minutes in a moderate oven, 350°, or until firm. Serves 6.

## BAKED CORN OMELET

1 cup drained canned or cooked
   fresh or frozen whole-kernel corn
3 eggs separated

½ teaspoon salt
¼ teaspoon paprika
3 tablespoons butter or margarine

1. Beat egg yolks until thick. Stir in corn, salt, and paprika.
2. Beat the egg whites until stiff but not dry and fold into the corn mixture.
3. Melt the butter in a small casserole and pour in the corn mixture.
4. Bake in a moderate oven, 350°, 25 minutes, or until knife inserted in the center comes out clean.

    Serve with a cheese sauce (a cream sauce in which ½-¾ cup grated sharp Cheddar or American cheese is melted). Serves 4.

## CORN-CHEESE TART

1½ cups cooked corn cut from cob,
frozen cooked, or canned whole-
kernel
¼ cup grated Swiss cheese
(packed)
Pastry for deep 9-inch pie

6 slices crisply cooked bacon
Salt and pepper
5 eggs lightly beaten
1½ cups light cream
2 tablespoons grated Parmesan
cheese

THIS "pie" is hearty enough to serve as the main dish for a luncheon party or Sunday-night supper.

1. Roll out the pastry ⅛ inch thick and fit it into a deep pie plate. Crumble the bacon and spread on it.

2. Mix the corn, Swiss cheese, and salt and pepper to taste. Spread over the bacon.

3. Blend the eggs and cream and pour gently over the corn-cheese mixture.

4. Top with Parmesan cheese and bake in a hot oven, 400°, 15 minutes.

5. Reduce the heat to 350° and continue to bake 20-30 minutes longer, or until tart is firm in the center, or until a knife inserted in the center comes out clean. Serves 6.

## DEVILED CORN PUDDING

2 cups whole-kernel corn cooked,
canned, fresh, or frozen
5 tablespoons butter or margarine
½ cup chopped onions
1 cup diced cooked ham
1 teaspoon prepared mustard
3 tablespoons flour
1 teaspoon salt

½ teaspoon dry mustard
2 cups milk
2 eggs lightly beaten
1 tablespoon Worcestershire sauce
1 cup soft bread crumbs
2 tablespoons melted butter or
margarine

238

1. In a medium casserole melt 2 tablespoons of the butter and sauté the onions and ham. Stir in the prepared mustard.
2. In a saucepan melt the remaining 3 tablespoons butter, blend in the flour, salt, and dry mustard, and gradually add the milk. Stir constantly until thickened and smooth.
3. Add to the sauce the eggs, corn, and Worcestershire sauce. Pour over the ham in the casserole.
4. Mix the soft crumbs with the melted butter and spread over the pudding.
5. Bake in a moderate oven, 375°, about an hour, or until the center is firm to the touch. Serves 4-6.

## PLANTATION CORN PUDDING

| | |
|---|---|
| 1-pound can cream-style corn | 2 tablespoons chopped green |
| 1¾ cups milk | pepper |
| 1 tablespoon butter or margarine | 2 tablespoons grated onion |
| 4 eggs slightly beaten | 1 tablespoon sugar |
| 2 tablespoons chopped pimiento | 1 teaspoon salt |

SCALD milk and melt butter in it. Combine eggs, pimiento, green pepper, onion, sugar, and salt. Stir hot milk in gradually, blending thoroughly. Turn into greased medium casserole and bake in slow oven, 300°, 45-60 minutes, or until knife inserted in center comes out clean. Serves 6.

## CORN CASSEROLE WITH MUSHROOMS

| | |
|---|---|
| 1½ cups drained canned or cooked fresh or frozen whole-kernel corn | ⅔ cup sliced mushrooms |
| | ½ cup light cream |
| | Salt and pepper |
| 2 tablespoons butter or margarine | 1 tablespoon chopped parsley |
| 2 tablespoons chopped onion | |

HEAT butter in a medium casserole and lightly sauté onion and mushrooms. Stir in corn, cream, and seasonings. Cover and bake in slow oven, 325°, 20-25 minutes. Remove cover the last 5 minutes. Sprinkle with parsley before serving. Serves 6.

# CORN AND ASPARAGUS CASSEROLE

1 package frozen cut corn, cooked, or No. 2 can whole-kernel corn
1 package frozen asparagus cuts or No. 300 can all-green asparagus, cut up
½ cup milk
2 tablespoons butter or margarine
2 tablespoons flour
¼ teaspoon celery salt
1 tablespoon bread or corn flake crumbs
1 tablespoon grated Parmesan cheese
1 tablespoon chopped parsley

1. If you use frozen corn and asparagus, cook them separately in a scant ¼ cup boiling water, until barely tender. If you use canned vegetables, drain them; in either case save the liquid.
2. Combine these liquids and measure out ½ cup. Add the milk.
3. Melt butter in a saucepan, blend in the flour, cook briefly, and gradually add the liquid. Stir constantly until thick and smooth. Add the celery salt.
4. Spread the corn in a shallow casserole and cover with the cut-up asparagus. Pour the cream sauce over and top with mixed crumbs and cheese.
5. Bake in a moderate oven, 350°, 20 minutes, or until golden and bubbly.
6. Sprinkle with parsley before serving. Serves 6-8.

# CUCUMBERS IN CREAM

6 medium cucumbers
   Boiling salted water
3 tablespoons butter or margarine
½ teaspoon sweet basil
⅛ teaspoon pepper
3 tablespoons minced scallions (green onions)
1 cup heavy cream
   Salt to taste
2 teaspoons chopped parsley

Most people think of cucumbers as either a vegetable to be eaten raw or as the makings of pickles. However, cooked cucumbers have a delicate flavor and should be more widely served.

1. Peel the cucumbers, cut in quarters lengthwise, and scrape out the seeds, unless the cucumbers are really young. Cut them into 1-inch pieces. Cover with boiling salted water and simmer three minutes. Drain well.

2. Melt butter in a shallow casserole. Stir in the basil, scallions, and pepper. Add the cucumbers and stir until they are well coated.

3. Bake in a moderate oven, 375°, 15 minutes, stirring two or three times.

4. Put the cream in a saucepan and boil it quite hard, reducing the cup to ½ cup. Season to taste. Stir it into the cucumber casserole, continue baking 4-5 minutes more, and sprinkle with parsley. Serves 4.


## BAKED EGGPLANT

| | |
|---|---|
| 1 medium eggplant | ½ teaspoon dried basil or |
| Boiling water | 1 teaspoon fresh, chopped |
| 1½ tablespoons salt | ½ teaspoon dried orégano or |
| ¼ cup salad oil or olive oil | 1 teaspoon fresh, chopped |
| 1 onion chopped | ⅛ teaspoon pepper |
| 1 medium green pepper cut in | ½ cup bread or corn flake crumbs |
| ¼-inch cubes | 2 tablespoons butter |
| 1 tomato skinned and chopped | |

1. Wash eggplant and cover with boiling water. Add 1 tablespoon of the salt and boil 20 minutes. Turn it several times to cook evenly, since it will ride on top of the water. Drain and rinse it in cold water.

2. Peel the eggplant and cut in ¾-inch cubes.

3. Heat the oil in a skillet and lightly sauté the onion. Stir in the eggplant, green pepper, tomato, basil, orégano, remaining ½ tablespoon salt, and pepper.

4. Place in a greased medium casserole, cover with crumbs, and dot with butter.

5. Bake in a 350° oven about 30 minutes, or until well browned. Serves 4-5.

## EGGPLANT SPECIAL

1 eggplant sliced ½ inch thick,
   unpeeled
¼ cup French dressing
1 medium onion sliced

2 tablespoons flour
½ teaspoon salt
1½ cups milk
¾ cup grated sharp Cheddar

1. Arrange the eggplant slices in a shallow casserole (cut them in half if very large). Cover them with French dressing and onion, using about half of the dressing. Let stand an hour and drain off any French dressing that has not been absorbed.
2. Bake about 15 minutes in a hot oven, 450°, or until the skin is black.
3. Heat the remaining French dressing in a saucepan, stir in flour and salt, and blend in milk. Stir until thick and smooth.
4. Add cheese and stir until cheese is melted.
5. Pour the cheese sauce over the eggplant and continue baking about 10 minutes longer, or until bubbly. Serves 4-6, depending upon size of eggplant.

## EGGPLANT SOUFFLÉ WITH ALMONDS

1 medium eggplant peeled and
   cut in 1-inch cubes
   Boiling salted water
½ cup bread or corn flake crumbs
½ cup milk
2 tablespoons butter or margarine
   Salt and pepper

1 tablespoon onion juice or
   scraped onion
¼ teaspoon nutmeg (scant)
3 eggs separated
2 tablespoons buttered crumbs,
   bread or corn flake
2 tablespoons sliced or slivered
   toasted almonds

1. Cover the eggplant with boiling salted water and simmer until soft —8-10 minutes at most. Drain well and mash.
2. Cover the ½ cup crumbs with the milk and let stand 2-3 minutes.

242

3. Mix the crumbs, butter, salt and pepper, onion juice, and nutmeg.

4. Stir in the eggplant and the well-beaten egg yolks. Cool to luke-warm.

5. Beat the egg whites until stiff but not dry and fold into the eggplant mixture.

6. Pour into a well-greased medium soufflé dish, sprinkle with the 2 tablespoons crumbs and almonds, and bake in a hot oven, 400°, 30 minutes, or until firm to the touch, or until a knife inserted in the center comes out clean. Serves 4-6.

## CREOLE EGGPLANT

1 medium eggplant cut in ½-inch slices, unpeeled
Salt and pepper
Boiling water
2 tablespoons salad oil or olive oil
1 small bay leaf
¼ teaspoon dried sweet marjoram or ¾ teaspoon fresh, chopped
3-4 scallions cut up fine, both tops and ends
1 tablespoon chopped parsley
1 can condensed tomato soup

1. Salt the eggplant slices and pile them up in the original shape. Let stand 15-20 minutes to draw out the bitterness eggplant sometimes has. Wipe off the slices and cook them in boiling water 6-8 minutes, or until they begin to look transparent. Drain and arrange in a medium casserole.

2. Heat the oil in a small saucepan and cook the scallions, marjoram, and bay leaf in it. Add the parsley.

3. Stir in the soup and simmer 3-4 minutes.

4. Pour over the eggplant and bake, covered, in a moderate oven, 350°, 10-15 minutes. Serves 4-6, depending on size of eggplant.

# EGGPLANT WITH ANCHOVIES

1 large eggplant cut in ¾-inch
  cubes, unpeeled
  Boiling salted water
3 strips bacon diced and cooked
  crisp
¾ cup chopped onion
½ cup chopped celery
6 anchovy fillets chopped

1 cup peeled and diced tomatoes
  or small can Italian tomatoes,
  drained
¼ cup chopped parsley
1 cup bread or corn flake crumbs
1 egg
  Salt and pepper to taste
½ cup grated Parmesan cheese

1. Cook the cubed eggplant in boiling salted water 4-5 minutes, or steam over boiling water about 10 minutes, until tender. Drain well.
2. When the bacon is crisp add the onion and celery to the skillet in which it is cooked, and cook until the onion becomes transparent but not brown.
3. Stir in the eggplant, anchovies, tomatoes, parsley, and half the crumbs. Mix lightly and add the egg.
4. Season with care—you may not need salt because of the anchovies.
5. Pour into a well-greased casserole and top with the cheese mixed with the rest of the crumbs.
6. Bake in a slow oven, 325°, 30 minutes. Serves 6.


# EGGPLANT ARLÉSIENNE

1 eggplant, about 1½ pounds, cut
  in ½-inch cubes, unpeeled
¾ cup minced onion
2 small green peppers seeded
  and julienned
2 tablespoons salad oil or olive oil
2 medium tomatoes skinned and
  coarsely chopped

1 large clove garlic mashed
1½ teaspoons salt
¾ teaspoon dried orégano or
  1 tablespoon fresh, chopped
⅛ teaspoon fresh-ground pepper
1 tablespoon drained capers
¼ cup coarsely chopped walnuts
  Strips pimiento

1. Sauté the onion and peppers in hot oil 6 or 7 minutes.

2. Stir in the eggplant and sauté 3 or 4 minutes.

3. Add tomatoes, garlic, salt, orégano, and pepper. Blend well and arrange in a medium casserole, well greased.

4. Bake, covered, in a medium oven, 350°, 35-40 minutes, or until eggplant is tender.

5. Uncover, stir in capers and walnuts, and bake 15-20 minutes longer, uncovered, or until quite dry.

6. Lay several strips of pimiento on top before serving. Serves 6.

## EGGPLANT, ZUCCHINI, AND TOMATOES

1 medium eggplant cut into ½-inch slices, not peeled
2 thin zucchini cut in thin slices, unpeeled
2 large tomatoes skinned and sliced ¼ inch thick
2 medium onions sliced
¼ cup salad oil
½ teaspoon dried basil or 1 teaspoon fresh, chopped
½ teaspoon dried thyme or 1 teaspoon fresh, chopped
½ teaspoon dried rosemary or 1 teaspoon fresh, chopped
2 tablespoons chopped parsley
Salt and pepper
¼ cup grated Parmesan cheese or sliced mozzarella cheese

1. Salt the eggplant slices and pile them up. Let stand about 30 minutes and wipe the slices with paper towels.

2. In a good-sized casserole arrange alternate layers of eggplant (cut to fit), onions, zucchini, and tomatoes.

3. Drizzle a little oil on each layer and sprinkle each with a bit of each herb. Lightly salt and pepper all the layers except eggplant.

4. Sprinkle the top with Parmesan cheese or cover with slices of mozzarella cheese.

5. Bake 45 minutes in a moderate oven, 350°, or until the top is browned and bubbly. Serves 6.

# EGGPLANT AU GRATIN

1 large or 2 medium eggplants
    sliced ¼ inch thick
    Boiling salted water
¼ pound butter or margarine

¼-½ pound thinly sliced Swiss
    cheese
Fresh-ground pepper

1. Soak the eggplant slices in cold water 20 minutes. Drain and cover with boiling salted water. Drain again and dry the slices on paper towels.
2. Melt the butter in a skillet and sauté the eggplant slices on both sides until delicately brown.
3. Arrange the slices of eggplant in a large shallow casserole, laying a slice of cheese over each slice of eggplant. Sprinkle each layer with a bit of pepper.
4. Bake the casserole in a moderate oven, 350°, 30 minutes, or until the cheese is bubbling. Serves 6.

# EGGPLANT NIÇOISE

1 medium eggplant peeled and
    cut in 1-inch cubes
4 tablespoons olive oil or salad oil
1 clove garlic mashed
¼ cup minced onion
1 stalk celery chopped
2 small green peppers cut in 1-inch
    squares

12 pitted green olives
3 medium tomatoes peeled,
    seeded, and chopped
1 teaspoon capers
    Salt and pepper
3 tablespoons buttered bread or
    corn flake crumbs

1. Heat the oil in a large heavy skillet and sauté the garlic and onion lightly.
2. Add the eggplant, celery, peppers, and olives and simmer 10 minutes, stirring frequently.
3. Stir in the tomatoes and capers, and season to taste.
4. Spread in a medium casserole, sprinkle with crumbs, and bake in

a moderate oven, 350°, 30 minutes, or until brown and bubbly. Serves 6.

## CONTINENTAL CASSEROLE OF ENDIVE

3 whole Belgian endive
2 cups chopped Belgian endive
3 tablespoons butter or margarine
½ cup minced green pepper
Salt
½ teaspoon sugar
2-3 outside leaves of lettuce
1 tablespoon lemon juice
¼ cup water

1 can condensed cream of mushroom soup
½ cup milk
½ cup bread or corn flake crumbs
2 tablespoons grated Parmesan cheese
2 tablespoons melted butter or margarine

THIS is a rather fussy recipe, but it makes a wonderful vegetable casserole to serve with a plain meat.

1. Melt 2 tablespoons of the butter in a saucepan and stir in the chopped endive, green pepper, ½ teaspoon salt, and sugar.

2. Lay enough lettuce leaves over just to cover. Cover the saucepan and cook over very low heat, without stirring, 15 minutes. Remove the lettuce leaves and discard.

3. At the same time, put the whole endive heads in a saucepan with the lemon juice, the remaining tablespoon of butter, water, and salt to taste. Bring to a boil and simmer, covered, over the lowest possible heat until tender—25-30 minutes on each side. Drain.

4. Mix the soup and milk. Stir in the chopped endive mixture. Spread in a greased shallow casserole and top with a mixture of the crumbs, cheese, and melted butter. Bake 20 minutes in a 350° oven.

5. Slit the whole endives lengthwise and arrange the halves, cut side down, around the edge of the casserole. Bake 10 minutes longer. Serves 6.

# BRAISED BELGIAN ENDIVE WITH WALNUTS

4 large heads of Belgian endive
¼ cup butter or margarine
¼ teaspoon dried basil or ¾
teaspoon fresh, chopped

Salt and pepper
1 cup condensed consommé
2 tablespoons chopped walnuts
1 tablespoon butter or margarine

BELGIAN endive makes a delicious cooked vegetable, though few
Americans ever think of cooking it.
1. Cut the endive heads (or spears) in half lengthwise and let stand
in ice water 15 minutes to crisp. Dry with paper towels.
2. Melt the ¼ cup butter in a shallow casserole and stir in the basil
Brown the endive halves lightly on both sides and season very lightly
3. Pour over about half of the consommé and bake the endive in a
moderate oven, 350°, 25-30 minutes, turning the pieces occasionally
and adding a little consommé as the endive becomes dry.
4. Brown the walnuts in the remaining tablespoon of butter and pour
over the endive before serving. Serves 4.


# INDIAN LENTILS

1 pound dried lentils
2 onions chopped
Piece of ginger root the size of a
small walnut
3 tablespoons butter or margarine

1 teaspoon turmeric
½ teaspoon chili powder
Salt
4 cups water

1. Soak the lentils overnight in water to cover. In the morning drain
them, rinse, and drain again.
2. Sauté the onions and ginger root in butter until the onions are
golden, stirring frequently.
3. Add the lentils, turmeric, and chili powder, and cook until most
of the butter is absorbed. Fish out the ginger root and discard.
4. Pour the lentil mixture into a medium casserole with salt to taste
and water.

248

5. Cover and bake in a slow oven, 300°, 1-1¼ hours, or until the lentils are tender and most of the water absorbed. Check once or twice, and add a bit more water if the lentils seem dry.

6. Uncover the last 10 minutes of the cooking time. Serve with wedges of lemon. Serves 4-5.

## MUSHROOM PIE

| | |
|---|---|
| 2 pounds mushrooms, washed, and trimmed if stems are long | 3 tablespoons flour |
| | 1½ cups chicken broth |
| 6 tablespoons butter or margarine | ⅛ teaspoon dried marjoram |
| 1 teaspoon salt | ½ cup dry sherry |
| ½ teaspoon fresh-ground pepper | ½ cup heavy cream |
| 2 tablespoons lemon juice | Pastry for 1-crust pie |

1. If the mushrooms are large quarter or halve them.

2. Melt 4 tablespoons of the butter in a skillet and add the mushrooms, salt, pepper, and lemon juice. Cover and simmer 10 minutes over low heat, stirring occasionally. Skim the mushrooms out and arrange them in a shallow casserole.

3. To the juices remaining in the pan add the remaining butter, blend in the flour, and gradually stir in the chicken broth. Add the marjoram, correct seasoning, and cook until thickened, stirring constantly.

4. Remove the skillet from the heat, stir in the sherry and cream, and pour over the mushrooms.

5. Roll out the pastry to ⅛-inch thickness and place over the mushrooms. If casserole is small enough to be filled by the mushrooms, seal the pastry to the edge and slit several times to allow steam to escape. However, if casserole is not filled, cut the pastry to size and lay on top of the mushrooms.

6. Bake in a hot oven, 425°, 10-12 minutes. Reduce heat to 350° and bake 10-15 minutes longer, or until pastry is golden. Serves 6-8.

## MUSHROOM CASSEROLE

1 pound mushrooms, halved or
    quartered if large
½ cup melted butter
1 teaspoon dried marjoram or
    2 teaspoons fresh, chopped

½ teaspoon salt
1 tablespoon chopped chives
4 tablespoons chicken broth
2 tablespoons heavy cream

1. Wash the mushrooms and cut off part of the stems where they are quite long. Arrange in a small shallow casserole.
2. Combine the melted butter, marjoram, salt, and chives and pour over the mushrooms. Stir well to be sure the mushrooms are all coated.
3. Mix the chicken broth and cream and pour over the mushrooms.
4. Cover the casserole and bake 20 minutes in a 375° oven. Uncover the last 5 minutes. Serves 4-5.


## STUFFED MUSHROOMS TARRAGON

1 pound large mushrooms
5 tablespoons butter or margarine
2 tablespoons chopped shallots or
    1 tablespoon chopped onion
1 tablespoon chopped fresh
    tarragon or 1 teaspoon dried

1 egg beaten
2 tablespoons brandy
½ cup bread or corn flake crumbs
    Salt and pepper

1. Remove the stems from the mushrooms and chop fine. Sauté in 2 tablespoons of the butter with the shallots.
2. Add the tarragon, egg, brandy, crumbs, and salt and pepper to taste.
3. Sauté the mushroom caps in the remaining 3 tablespoons butter until golden.
4. Arrange cap side down in a shallow casserole, stuff them with the stems-crumb mixture, and broil them 4 inches from the heat 6-8 minutes, or until well browned. Serves 4.

# STUFFED MUSHROOMS VERNON

1 pound large mushrooms
4 tablespoons bread or corn flake
  crumbs
2 tablespoons minced parsley
¼ pound melted butter

3 tablespoons minced shallots or
  2 tablespoons minced onion
1 teaspoon lemon juice
Salt
Paprika

REMOVE the stems from the mushrooms and chop fine. Mix with the crumbs, parsley, shallots, melted butter, lemon juice, and salt to taste. Fill the caps with this mixture and arrange in a greased shallow casserole. Sprinkle with paprika and bake 5 minutes in a hot oven, 450°. Put under the broiler for an additional 3-4 minutes. Serves 4.

# ONIONS DE LUXE

3 pounds small white onions
  peeled or 3 one-pound cans,
  drained
Boiling salted water
1½ cups thick cream sauce
  Salt and pepper
1 teaspoon dry mustard

¼ teaspoon nutmeg
1 cup chopped salted almonds or
  salted peanuts
1 small can deviled ham
  (optional)
¼ cup buttered bread or corn
  flake crumbs

1. If raw onions are used cook them in rapidly boiling salted water until tender. Drain, and arrange half of them in a greased casserole.
2. Make the cream sauce with 2½ tablespoons butter or margarine, 2½ tablespoons flour, and 1½ cups milk, stirring until smooth and thick. Season to taste and add mustard and nutmeg.
3. Sprinkle half of the nuts on the onions and cover with half of the cream sauce. Repeat the layers of onions, nuts, and cream sauce.
4. Mix the bread or corn flake crumbs with the deviled ham and spread over the top.
5. Bake in a hot oven, 425°, about 25 minutes, or until brown and bubbly. Serves 6-8.

# BAKED ONIONS WITH CREAM AND SHERRY

12 medium onions sliced
  Boiling salted water
¾ cup light cream
3 tablespoons dry sherry

½ teaspoon salt
  Fresh-ground pepper
3 tablespoons butter or margarine

1. Cover the onions with boiling salted water and cook until they are tender but still crisp—about 10 minutes. Drain and spread in a medium casserole.
2. Mix the cream, sherry, salt and pepper and pour over the onions.
3. Dot with butter, cover, and bake in a moderate oven, 325°, until tender, about 30 minutes. Remove cover the last 5 minutes. Serves 6.

# BERMUDA ONION CASSEROLE

2 Bermuda onions sliced quite thin
  Salt and pepper
1 cup dairy sour cream

3 tablespoons buttered bread or
  corn flake crumbs
  Paprika

SPREAD the onions evenly in a shallow greased casserole or pie plate. Season to taste, spread sour cream over evenly, top with crumbs, and sprinkle with paprika. Bake 35-40 minutes in a 375° oven. (The exact time will depend on the thickness of the onion slices.) Serves 4.

*Note:* You can substitute sweet cream, a thin cream sauce, or consommé for the sour cream. If either of the last two, do not cover, and baste occasionally, adding more liquid if dry.

# ONION CUSTARD

1 pound small white onions peeled
  or 1-pound can
¼ cup butter or margarine
3 eggs well beaten

¼ cup heavy cream
½ teaspoon nutmeg
  Salt and pepper
1 strip bacon shredded

1. Let the onions (if raw) stand in cold salted water an hour or so.
2. Slice them and sauté them lightly in sizzling butter, until they are soft but not colored. Let them cool.
3. Combine the eggs, cream, nutmeg, salt and pepper. Stir in the onions and pour into a small greased casserole.
4. Scatter the bacon shreds on top and bake about 20 minutes in a moderate oven, 350°—until the custard is set and firm to the touch. Serves 4.


## SCALLOPED ONIONS ALMONDINE

2 one-pound cans tiny whole onions drained

1 can condensed cream of mushroom soup

½ cup grated sharp American cheese

¼ cup chopped or slivered toasted almonds

MIX the onions with the soup and pour into a small greased casserole. Top with the cheese and sprinkle with almonds. Bake in a 375° oven 30 minutes. Serves 6.


## PEAS AND PASTA SHELLS

No. 2 can tiny peas
8-ounce package pasta shells cooked
¼ cup salad oil
4 tablespoons butter or margarine

1 cup onion chopped fine
2 small cloves garlic mashed
¼ cup chopped parsley
½ teaspoon salt
Grind of pepper

HEAT the oil and butter and lightly sauté the onion and garlic. Heat the peas in their liquid and drain well. Put them into a small casserole and stir in the pasta, onion and garlic, parsley, and seasonings. Bake 15 minutes in a moderate oven, 350°, just long enough to heat it well. Serves 4.

# BAKED POTATO PUDDING

6-8 large Maine or Idaho potatoes
   peeled and grated
¼ cup onion grated

3 eggs well beaten
1 cup hot milk
6 tablespoons melted butter

MIX all the ingredients and pour into a well-greased medium casserole. Bake in a moderate oven, 350°, 1¼ hours, or until firm. Exact time will depend on depth of potatoes in casserole. Serves 8-10.


# BAKED SLICED POTATOES

1. Peel medium Idahos. Hold them firmly and slice them medium thick, keeping the shape of the potato. Transfer potatoes when sliced to a well-buttered shallow casserole and press so that the slices fan out, overlapping slightly. Sprinkle with salt.
2. Mix grated Parmesan and grated Romano cheese and spread over the potatoes rather thickly.
3. Drizzle over a generous amount of melted butter or margarine.
4. Bake the casserole 20 minutes in a hot oven, 500°, or 30 minutes in a 450° oven. Two potatoes will serve 3 people.


# CREAMY SCALLOPED POTATOES

5 cups sliced raw potatoes
1 can condensed cream of
   mushroom soup

½ cup milk
1 medium onion minced

MIX the soup with the milk and onion. In a buttered medium casserole arrange alternate layers of potatoes and soup. Cover and bake 1 hour in a 375° oven. Uncover and bake an additional 15 minutes. Serves 6.

# DEVILED POTATO PIE

*Crumb Part*

¼ cup butter or margarine
1 teaspoon salt

2 teaspoons onion powder
4 cups corn flake crumbs

*Pie Part*

1½ cups corn flake crumbs
2 tablespoons soft butter or
   margarine
2 cups whipped cottage cheese

2 cups hot mashed potatoes
2½-ounce can deviled ham
Salt and pepper
2 eggs slightly beaten

1. Mix the ingredients for the crumb part well and press two-thirds of the mixture on the bottom and sides of a buttered shallow casserole or deep pie plate. Build an edge on the rim of the crust, not on the plate.
2. Combine the pie ingredients, mix well, and spread carefully over the crumb shell.
3. Sprinkle the remaining third of the crumb mixture on top.
4. Bake in a moderate oven, 350°, 45 minutes, or until lightly browned. Serves 6.


# PRINCESS POTATOES

6 cups grated raw potatoes
½ cup melted butter
1¼ cups grated onion
¼ cup chopped parsley

1 cup minced celery
2 teaspoons salt
½ teaspoon paprika

THE simplest way to prepare grated potatoes is to do them in a blender. Do these in 2 or 3 batches, and with the last batch add the onion, parsley, and celery. Mix everything together, put into a well-buttered 2-quart casserole, and bake 1 hour in a 375° oven. Serves 8.

# HOT POTATO SALAD

8 medium potatoes, cooked,
  peeled, and diced small
1 medium onion minced
½ cup minced celery
2 tablespoons diced green pepper

1 teaspoon salt
¼ teaspoon fresh-ground pepper
¼ cup salad oil
¼ cup mild cider vinegar
4 slices crisp bacon crumbled

To be at its best, hot potato salad should always be made with freshly cooked potatoes.

1. In a medium casserole combine the potatoes, onion, celery, green pepper, salt, and pepper.

2. Combine the oil and vinegar in a small saucepan and heat to boiling.

3. Pour at once over the warm potatoes, mix well, stir in the bacon, and heat about 20 minutes in a moderate oven, 350°. Serves 6.


# POTATOES FECHIMER

2 one-pound cans white potatoes
  or 2 pounds potatoes boiled and
  peeled
¼ cup grated Parmesan cheese
  Salt and pepper
  Nutmeg
3 tablespoons butter

3 tablespoons flour
2 cups thin cream
1 tablespoon grated Parmesan
  cheese
3 tablespoons bread or corn flake
  crumbs

1. Chop the potatoes coarsely and toss them with the ¼ cup of grated Parmesan, salt and pepper to taste, and a dash of nutmeg.

2. Make a cream sauce with the butter, flour, and cream, stirring until smooth and velvety.

3. Season to taste and stir in the tablespoon of Parmesan cheese.

4. Combine the sauce with the potatoes, spread in a buttered casserole, and sprinkle with crumbs.

5. Bake 30 minutes in a 375° oven. Serves 5-6.

# HOT SWISS POTATO SALAD

3 cups cooked potatoes sliced
1 cup Swiss cheese julienned
½ cup minced scallions, including
  green part
¼ cup minced fresh dill weed or
  1 tablespoon dried
1 teaspoon salt (less if peanuts are
  salted)
¼ cup chopped peanuts
  Butter or margarine
1 cup dairy sour cream
¼ cup grated Swiss cheese
2-3 tablespoons fine bread or
  corn flake crumbs
2-3 tablespoons melted butter or
  margarine

1. Toss lightly together the julienned cheese, scallions, dill weed, salt, and peanuts.
2. In a medium casserole arrange layers of potatoes, cheese mixture, dabs of butter, and sour cream to cover.
3. Repeat the layers, ending with potatoes.
4. Blend the grated cheese, crumbs, and melted butter together, and spread over the top.
5. Bake in a 375° oven 30-45 minutes, or until well browned. Serves 6.


# QUICK LYONNAISE POTATO CASSEROLE

8 medium potatoes peeled and
  sliced
3 medium onions sliced
1½ cups milk
  Salt and pepper
Dash ground cloves
Dash nutmeg
1 can condensed onion soup
2 tablespoons chopped chives

1. In a saucepan cook the onions in milk about 10 minutes.
2. Season to taste and add cloves, nutmeg, soup, and potatoes.
3. Arrange in a buttered 2-quart casserole and bake in a moderate oven, 375°, uncovered, 30-35 minutes, or until potatoes are tender and liquid almost absorbed.
4. Sprinkle with chives before serving. Serves 6-8.

# DIFFERENT SCALLOPED POTATOES

4 medium potatoes peeled and
  sliced thin
Salt and fresh-ground pepper
Flour

2 tablespoons butter
3 cups chicken broth or condensed
  consommé

1. Place half the potatoes in a medium casserole. Sprinkle with salt and pepper and dredge with flour.
2. Add the remaining potatoes and sprinkle similarly with salt, pepper, and flour.
3. Dot with butter and pour the chicken broth or consommé over.
4. Bake, covered, in a moderate oven, 375°, 25-30 minutes.
5. Uncover and continue baking 10-15 minutes longer, or until potatoes are tender and liquid almost absorbed. Serves 4.


# BAKED SWEET POTATOES WITH APPLES

2½ cups boiled and sliced sweet
  potatoes
2 cups apple slices ¼ inch thick
¼ cup sugar

½ cup water
¼ cup brown sugar
6 tablespoons butter or margarine
Juice 1 lemon

1. Boil sugar and water together 3 minutes, stirring until sugar is dissolved.
2. Drop apple slices into the syrup, a few at a time, and simmer gently, covered, until soft but not mushy. Skim them out with a slotted spatula or spoon. Save the syrup.
3. Sprinkle a little of the brown sugar in a medium casserole. Arrange a layer of potato slices in the casserole, then a layer of apples. Dot apples with butter and sprinkle with brown sugar.
4. Repeat the layers until the ingredients are used up, ending with potatoes, dotted with butter and sugar.
5. Stir lemon juice into the apple syrup and pour over the casserole.
6. Bake in a slow oven, 325°, 30 minutes. Serves 6.

258

# CALYPSO SWEET POTATOES

2 pounds sweet potatoes boiled
    and peeled or 2 No. 303 cans
¼ cup butter or margarine

½ cup maple syrup
1 teaspoon Angostura bitters

1. Melt the butter in a shallow casserole and stir in the maple syrup and bitters.
2. Slice the sweet potatoes thickly (at least ¾ inch), dip in the syrup and turn over so that they are all coated.
3. Bake in a slow oven, 325°, about 45 minutes, basting two or three times. Serves 6.


# YAMS TROPICALE

3 pounds yams cooked until just
    tender
2 medium oranges sliced thin
    (unpeeled)
2 medium lemons sliced thin
    (unpeeled)
½ cup crushed pineapple well
    drained

½ cup butter or margarine
⅓ cup brown sugar (packed)
½ cup dark corn syrup
½ cup pineapple juice
¼ teaspoon salt
½ cup shredded coconut (optional)

1. Peel the yams and cut them in ½-inch slices. Arrange in overlapping fashion in a flat casserole or large pie plate.
2. Slip half an orange slice and half a lemon slice between each 2 yam slices.
3. Spread the crushed pineapple evenly over the top.
4. In a small saucepan mix and bring to a boil the butter, brown sugar, corn syrup, pineapple juice, and salt. Stir to blend well and pour over the casserole.
5. Top with coconut and bake in a 350° oven 30 minutes, or until golden brown. Serves 6.

## ORANGE SWEET POTATOES

6 medium sweet potatoes cooked,
   peeled, and sliced
2 medium oranges sliced thin
   (unpeeled)
½ cup brown sugar

5 tablespoons butter
¼ cup strained honey
½ cup orange juice
¼ cup fine bread or corn flake
   crumbs

1. Build up layers, in a buttered medium casserole, of potatoes, sprinkled with brown sugar and dotted with butter, and then orange slices. Repeat until the potatoes and oranges are used up.
2. Heat the honey just enough to make it quite liquid, and mix it with the orange juice. Pour over the casserole.
3. Combine the crumbs with whatever butter and sugar are left and spread over the top of the casserole.
4. Cover and bake 30-40 minutes in a 350° oven.
5. Remove the cover after 15 minutes. Serves 6.

## AUSTRIAN SPINACH PUDDING

2 packages frozen chopped
   spinach cooked
8 eggs separated
½ cup soft butter or margarine
¼ cup chopped parsley
4 slices white bread

Milk
¾ cup dairy sour cream
Salt and pepper
1¾ cups dry bread or corn flake
   crumbs

1. Press all possible moisture out of the cooked spinach and purée it in a blender or food mill.
2. Beat the egg yolks lightly and stir in the butter. Combine with the spinach and parsley.
3. Soak the bread 3-4 minutes in enough milk just to cover and squeeze it dry.
4. Add the soaked bread to the spinach mixture, with the sour cream and salt and pepper to taste.

260

5. Beat the egg whites until stiff but not dry, dusting the bread crumbs over them toward the end of the beating. Fold into the spinach mixture.

6. Pour into a well-buttered large mold or soufflé dish, cover tightly (with foil if necessary), and place in a large kettle, preferably on a trivet, and pour in enough boiling water to come halfway up the sides of the dish.

7. Cover the kettle and steam 1½ hours, adding more water as needed to maintain the level. Unmold if you have used a mold. Serves 8.


## SPINACH MOUSSE

2 cups cooked spinach or 1
   package frozen chopped spinach
2 eggs
1 egg yolk

1 cup heavy cream
½ teaspoon lemon juice
Salt and pepper
Pinch ground mace

1. Chop the spinach and then blend it in a blender about 30 seconds, or put it through a food mill.

2. Beat the eggs, extra egg yolk, and cream together until thick.

3. Stir in lemon juice, salt and pepper to taste, and mace. Add the spinach, including liquid.

4. Pour into a well-buttered soufflé dish, casserole, or ring mold, set into a pan of hot water that comes about halfway up the dish, and bake in a moderate oven, 325°, 30-35 minutes, or until the mousse is firm to the touch in the center. Serve at once. Serves 6.

*Note:* If you bake this mousse in a ring mold, invert it on a hot platter when ready, and fill the center with creamed mushrooms, creamed sweetbreads, creamed chicken, or a mixture of the three.

## PERSIAN SPINACH PIE

1 pound spinach chopped or
   1 package frozen, thawed
2½ cups chopped scallions (green
   onions)
1 cup chopped lettuce
1½ cups chopped parsley
2 tablespoons flour

1½ teaspoons salt
¼ teaspoon fresh-ground pepper
½ cup chopped walnuts
8 eggs well beaten
4 tablespoons butter or margarine
Yoghurt (optional)

1. Drain the spinach well, pressing out moisture with a spatula.
2. Mix spinach, scallions, lettuce, parsley, flour, salt, pepper, and nuts.
3. Stir in the beaten eggs.
4. Melt the butter in a large pie plate or large flat casserole and pour in the mixture.
5. Bake 1 hour in a 325° oven, or until the top is brown and crisp. Serve hot or cold, with yoghurt spread on top if desired. Serves 6.

## SPINACH NOODLE PUDDING

2 pounds spinach cooked or
   1 package frozen chopped
   spinach cooked
½ pound fine noodles cooked
4 eggs separated

2 tablespoons grated onion
1 teaspoon salt
¼ teaspoon fresh-ground pepper
¼ teaspoon nutmeg

1. Beat the egg yolks and stir in the chopped spinach, onion, salt, pepper, and nutmeg.
2. Drain the noodles and blend them gently but thoroughly into the spinach mixture. Check seasoning.
3. Beat the egg whites until stiff but not dry and fold into the spinach mixture.
4. Pour into well-buttered casserole or soufflé dish and bake 25 minutes in a moderate oven, 350°. Serves 6.

# SPINACH QUICHE

1 package frozen chopped
  spinach thawed
Pastry for 9-inch pie shell
2 tablespoons minced shallots or
  1 tablespoon minced onion
2 tablespoons butter or margarine

¾ teaspoon salt
  Dash of pepper
¼ teaspoon nutmeg (scant)
  4 eggs
1¼ cups heavy cream
¼ cup grated Parmesan cheese

1. Roll out the pastry and line a 9-inch pie plate.
2. Sauté the shallots in butter until barely tender, and stir in the spinach, from which you have pressed out as much water as possible.
3. Put the spinach mixture in a blender with salt and pepper, nutmeg, and eggs. Blend 20 seconds.
4. Without stopping the blender pour in the cream and blend about 5 seconds more.
5. Pour into the pastry shell and sprinkle with the cheese.
6. Bake in a 375° oven 35-40 minutes, or until well puffed and firm in the center. Serves 6.


# BAKED SQUASH SACRAMENTO

2 cups cooked winter squash,
  mashed, or 1 package frozen,
  thawed
2 tablespoons butter or margarine
2 tablespoons brown sugar
  (generous)

2 tablespoons sweet or dairy sour
  cream
½ teaspoon salt
  Dash nutmeg
1 egg well beaten
¼ cup chopped toasted blanched
  almonds

SET aside about 1 tablespoon of the almonds and combine all remaining ingredients, blending thoroughly. Pour into a small well-greased casserole, top with the remaining almonds, and bake in a moderate oven, 375°, 30-40 minutes, or until brown and bubbly. Serves 4.

## SQUASH NEW ORLEANS

2 acorn squash or 1 box frozen
    cooked squash
2 slices bread, crusts removed
4 strips bacon diced and cooked
    crisp

2 tablespoons butter or margarine
1 medium onion minced
1 clove garlic mashed
2 eggs well beaten
2 tablespoons buttered crumbs

1. If you use acorn squash for this dish, split it into several pieces, remove seeds, and boil in salted water 20-30 minutes, or until tender. Peel and mash.
2. If you use frozen cooked squash merely thaw.
3. Soak the bread in water to cover 3-4 minutes and squeeze dry.
4. Pour off half the fat from the bacon. To the remaining fat add butter and lightly sauté the onion and garlic.
5. Stir in the bacon bits, squeezed bread, eggs, and squash.
6. Mix well, season to taste, and pour into well-buttered casserole.
7. Top with crumbs and bake in a hot oven, 400°, about 20 minutes, or until well browned. Serves 4.


## STUFFED ACORN SQUASH

2 acorn squash cut in half
    crosswise
    Salt and pepper
1½ cups bread or corn flake crumbs
½ cup warm milk
½ cup chopped blanched almonds

2 hard-cooked eggs chopped
½ cup grated sharp Cheddar
    cheese
1 tablespoon chopped parsley
3 tablespoons butter or margarine

1. Remove seeds and stringy portion from the squash, and trim ends so that they will sit level. Salt the insides rather generously and place cut sides down on a cookie sheet.
2. Bake 25 minutes in a moderate oven, 375°. Turn right side up and fit into a greased casserole.
3. To make the filling, combine crumbs, milk, almonds, eggs, cheese,

parsley, and salt and pepper to taste. Mix well and fill the squash, extending the filling to the edges.

4. Press the filling down very lightly and dot with butter.

5. Bake 25-30 minutes, or until the squash itself is very tender. Serves 4.

## BAKED TOMATOES STUFFED WITH MUSHROOMS

8 medium tomatoes, ripe but still very firm
½ pound mushrooms coarsely chopped
Boiling water
2 tablespoons butter or margarine
4 tablespoons flour
Salt and pepper
¼ teaspoon dried basil or ¾ teaspoon fresh, chopped
¼ teaspoon dried orégano or ¾ teaspoon fresh, chopped
1⅓ cups milk
¼ teaspoon Worcestershire sauce
1 cup soft bread crumbs
2 tablespoons grated Parmesan cheese
1 tablespoon minced parsley
2 tablespoons melted butter
Anchovy fillets

1. Cover the tomatoes with boiling water, let stand 2 minutes, drain, and skin.

2. Scoop out the insides carefully, leaving shells. (Sometimes this is easier to do before skinning the tomatoes; then slip off the skin afterward.)

3. Sauté the mushrooms in butter and stir in the flour, salt and pepper to taste, basil, and orégano.

4. Slowly stir in the milk, continuing to stir until the sauce is thick and smooth. Add Worcestershire sauce.

5. Lay tomato shells in a shallow buttered casserole and fill with the mushroom sauce.

6. Mix the crumbs, cheese, parsley, and butter and top the tomatoes with the mixture.

7. Bake 15-20 minutes in a moderate oven, 350°.

8. Cross 2 anchovy fillets on each tomato before serving. Serves 8.

# CHERRY TOMATOES WITH GARLIC

36 small ripe cherry tomatoes, stems removed
Boiling water
1 teaspoon salt

3 tablespoons butter, margarine, or salad oil
1 small clove garlic mashed
¼ teaspoon fresh-ground pepper
1 tablespoon chopped chives

1. Pour boiling water over the tomatoes, let stand 20 seconds, drain in sieve, and slip skins off. Sprinkle with salt and spread on paper towels to dry a few minutes.
2. Heat butter in a shallow casserole. Add garlic and pepper.
3. Stir the tomatoes in, and continue to stir until they are well coated with the butter.
4. Put in a moderate oven, 350°, for just six minutes. Sprinkle with chives before serving. Serves 6.


# TOMATO CASSEROLE

4 medium tomatoes sliced ½ inch thick
1 cup grated sharp Cheddar cheese

⅓ cup thinly sliced onion
¾ teaspoon salt
⅛ teaspoon pepper
1 cup crushed potato chips

IN a small casserole arrange layers of tomato slices, cheese, and onion —2 layers of each. Sprinkle each tomato layer with salt and pepper. Top with the crushed chips and bake ½ hour in a 350° oven. Serves 4.


# EGGPLANT TOMATO BORDELAISE

1 large eggplant cut in ½-inch slices, unpeeled
Salt and pepper
½ cup salad oil or olive oil
3 medium tomatoes skinned and

¼ cup chopped scallions (green onions)
1 large clove garlic mashed
1 teaspoon prepared mustard
½ cup chopped parsley

sliced ½ inch thick
½ cup sliced mushrooms

2 tablespoons melted butter or
margarine
1 cup buttered crumbs

1. Sprinkle the eggplant slices with salt and pile them up in the shape of the eggplant, letting them stand 20 minutes. Wipe off the slices with paper towels and sauté them to a golden brown in hot oil. Arrange in a good-sized greased casserole, in 2-3 layers.
2. Cover each layer with tomato slices.
3. In the oil remaining in the skillet sauté the mushrooms lightly.
4. Stir in the scallions, garlic, salt and pepper to taste, mustard, and parsley.
5. Add the melted butter, blend well, and pour over the casserole.
6. Top with a thick layer of buttered crumbs and bake 20-25 minutes in a 400° oven. Serves 6.

## ZUCCHINI-TOMATO CASSEROLE

6 small zucchini cut in ¼-inch
  slices (unpeeled)
4 medium tomatoes peeled and
  sliced
¼ cup salad oil
1 small clove garlic
¼ teaspoon dried orégano or
  ¾ teaspoon fresh, chopped

¼ teaspoon dried basil or
  ¾ teaspoon fresh, chopped
½ cup grated sharp Cheddar cheese
¼ cup grated Parmesan cheese
  Salt and pepper
½ cup bread or corn flake crumbs
2 tablespoons melted butter or
  margarine

1. Heat oil in a skillet and cook the garlic clove a few minutes. Skim out and discard.
2. Sauté the zucchini in the oil until lightly browned.
3. Combine the orégano, basil, and Cheddar and Parmesan cheeses.
4. Make alternate layers in a medium casserole of zucchini and tomatoes, sprinkling each layer with salt and pepper and cheese mixture.
5. Mix the crumbs and melted butter and spread over the casserole. Bake 20-25 minutes in a 350° oven, or until well browned. Serves 6.

# ZUCCHINI ALLA PARMIGIANA

8 small zucchini, ends removed,
   and slit lengthwise (unpeeled)
1 tablespoon butter or margarine
6 tablespoons salad oil
½ small onion sliced thin
1 pound tomatoes, peeled, seeded,
   and coarsely chopped

¼ teaspoon dried basil or
   ¾ teaspoon fresh, chopped
Salt and pepper to taste
¼ cup flour
2 tablespoons grated Parmesan
   cheese
½ pound mozzarella cheese sliced
   thin

1. In a heavy skillet heat the butter and 1 tablespoon of the oil. Sauté the onion until soft but not brown.

2. Stir in the chopped tomatoes, basil, and salt and pepper to taste. Simmer, uncovered, half an hour, stirring occasionally.

3. Coat the zucchini halves generously with flour and sauté until brown in 4 tablespoons of the oil heated to sizzling. Drain on paper towels.

4. Use the remaining tablespoon of oil to grease a medium casserole. Arrange in it alternate layers of zucchini, tomato mixture, Parmesan cheese, and mozzarella cheese, ending with mozzarella cheese and tomatoes.

5. Bake 30 minutes in a moderate oven, 350°, or until zucchini is tender. Serves 4-6.

# CHEESE, EGGS, CEREALS, AND PASTA

# BAKED CHEESE-MEAT SANDWICH CASSEROLE

9 slices white bread, crusts removed
2 tablespoons butter or margarine
1 package little pork sausages
  (fresh or frozen) cooked (or 1
  can) or 12 slices luncheon meat
  (canned)

2 sliced tomatoes
1 cup grated sharp Cheddar cheese
4 eggs lightly beaten
1 quart milk (scant)
¾ teaspoon salt
1 teaspoon dry mustard

1. Butter the bread and make 3 two-decker sandwiches, making the first layer the sausages, split, or 3 slices luncheon meat per sandwich, and the second layer tomato slices, topped with grated cheese.
2. Cut each sandwich diagonally in two and fasten with toothpicks. Arrange in a well-buttered casserole that holds them with just a little room to spare.
3. Combine eggs, milk, salt, and mustard and pour over the sandwiches.
4. Bake 1½ hours in a 325° oven, or until firm in the center. Serves 3 generously or 6 lightly.

*Note:* If possible, make the sandwiches far enough in advance so that they can be refrigerated 2-3 hours before baking.


# CHEESE SOUP SOUFFLÉ

1 can condensed cheese soup
1 small clove garlic crushed
¼ cup soft butter or margarine
7 slices white bread, crusts removed
⅓ cup dry white wine
1 tablespoon flour

1 teaspoon dry mustard (scant)
  Dash salt
½ teaspoon Worcestershire sauce
¼ teaspoon pepper
4 eggs separated
⅛ teaspoon cream of tartar

1. Blend the garlic and butter and spread on the bread.
2. Line the bottom and sides of a 1-quart casserole with the bread, cutting to fit smoothly. Trim the top to make it even with the rim

of the dish. On the sides of the casserole turn the buttered side toward the casserole.

3. Dribble the wine over the bread, both bottom and sides.

4. Blend together the flour, mustard, salt, Worcestershire sauce, pepper, and egg yolks, lightly beaten.

5. Stir in the soup and cook over very low heat 8-10 minutes, or until thick and smooth, stirring frequently. Cool to almost lukewarm.

6. Beat the egg whites with the cream of tartar until stiff but not dry.

7. Fold into the cheese mixture and gently pour over the bread in the casserole.

8. Bake 25-30 minutes in a hot oven, 400°, or until firm in the center. Serves 4-5.

## NEVER-FAIL CHEESE CASSEROLE

1 pound Cheddar cheese
  coarsely grated
9 slices day-old bread,
  crusts removed
  Salt and pepper
1½ tablespoons instant
  minced white onion
1½ tablespoons instant minced
  green onion
4 eggs beaten lightly
3 cups milk
1 teaspoon dry mustard
1 teaspoon Worcestershire sauce
2 tablespoons grated
  Parmesan cheese

1. Cut 3 slices of the bread to completely cover the bottom of a greased 2-quart casserole.

2. Sprinkle with salt and pepper, half of the white and green onion, and half of the cheese.

3. Make another closely fitted layer of bread and top with the remaining cheese, onion, and salt and pepper.

4. Top with the last layer of bread.

5. Mix together the eggs, milk, mustard, and Worcestershire sauce.

6. Pour over the casserole and refrigerate 3-4 hours or all day. Remove from the refrigerator 2 hours before baking, to bring to room temperature.

7. Top with grated Parmesan cheese and bake 50-60 minutes in a slow oven, 325°, or until firm in the center. Serves 6.

# HOLLAND CHEESE PIE

*Pastry*

2 cups flour
1 teaspoon salt
¾ cup firm butter or margarine

1 teaspoon caraway seeds
⅓ cup ice water

*Filling*

1 tablespoon dry bread crumbs
1 tablespoon grated Parmesan
cheese
½ cup minced ham or bacon
½ pound Edam or Gouda cheese
shredded (2 cups)
2 whole eggs

2 egg yolks
½ teaspoon salt
½ teaspoon dry mustard
Dash cayenne pepper
1½ cups light cream warmed
Chopped parsley
Grated Parmesan cheese

1. Make the pastry as usual, adding the caraway seeds before mixing in the water. Sprinkle the water over and toss quickly until a firm dough is formed. Knead lightly 4-6 times, wrap in foil or waxed paper, and chill 10 minutes. Roll it out on a lightly floured board to ⅛-inch thickness and line a 10-inch pie plate or a flan pan. Prick well, lay a piece of foil or brown paper on the bottom, and put in enough rice or beans, etc., to weight down the paper. Bake in a 425° oven 12 minutes. Remove the rice and paper and bake 5 minutes longer. Remove the shell from the oven and lower the heat to 350°.
2. Mix the crumbs and Parmesan cheese and spread on the pie shell.
3. Spread the ham or bacon on the crumbs, and the other cheese on top.
4. Beat the eggs and yolks together lightly and stir in salt, mustard, cayenne, cream, and parsley. Gently pour into the shell.
5. Top with grated Parmesan and bake 30-45 minutes, or until firm in the center. Serve at once. Serves 6.

# EGGS CONTINENTAL

4 hard-cooked eggs sliced
¾ cup soft fine bread crumbs
3 slices bacon slivered,
    cooked crisp, and drained
¼ pound mushrooms sliced
1 cup dairy sour cream

2 tablespoons minced parsley
    or chives
Salt
Paprika
½ cup grated sharp Cheddar

1. Spread the bread crumbs in a small shallow casserole or 8-inch pie plate.
2. Make a layer of egg slices over the crumbs.
3. Sauté the mushrooms lightly in the bacon fat.
4. Add the bacon, sour cream, parsley, and salt to taste.
5. Spread this mixture over the eggs, top with cheese, sprinkle with paprika, and bake 15-20 minutes in a 375° oven, or until cheese is melted and sauce bubbly. Serves 4.


# EGGS DELMONICO

4 hard-cooked eggs sliced
1½ cups cheese sauce
2 tablespoons dry sherry

4 slices toast, crusts removed
Luncheon meat sliced
Grated Parmesan cheese

1. Make the cheese sauce with 3 tablespoons butter or margarine, 2 tablespoons flour, salt and pepper to taste, ⅛ teaspoon dry mustard, 1½ cups milk, and 1½ cups coarsely grated Cheddar. Stir in the sherry.
2. Lay the toast in a shallow buttered casserole or pie plate.
3. Lay slices of luncheon meat over the toast, and egg slices, overlapping, over the meat.
4. Cover with the sauce, top with grated Parmesan, and bake in a hot oven, 450°, 10 minutes, or until the sauce is bubbly and the cheese browned. Serves 4.

# EGGS ORIENTALE

8 hard-cooked eggs
1½ tablespoons anchovy paste
2 tablespoons mayonnaise
6 ripe olives chopped
1 tablespoon lemon juice
2 tablespoons chopped walnuts
  or pecans
3 tablespoons melted butter
  or margarine

2 tablespoons flour
1½ cups milk or chicken broth
  Salt and pepper
1 tablespoon Worcestershire
  sauce
1½ cups cooked and coarsely
  chopped shrimp (optional)
½ pound sliced mushrooms
  lightly sautéed

1. Cut the eggs in half lengthwise. Remove the yolks and mash.
2. Mix the yolks with the anchovy paste, mayonnaise, olives, lemon juice, and nuts.
3. Fill the egg whites with this mixture and lay the stuffed eggs in a shallow buttered casserole or pie plate.
4. Make a cream sauce with the butter, flour, and milk or chicken broth. Season to taste and add the Worcestershire sauce.
5. Stir in shrimp and mushrooms and pour over the eggs.
6. Bake 15 minutes in a moderate oven, 325°.
7. Serve with green spinach noodles. Serves 8.


# EGGS TETRAZZINI

6 hard-cooked eggs sliced
¼ pound thin spaghetti cooked
1 small onion chopped
2 tablespoons butter or margarine
3 tablespoons flour

16-17-ounce can tomatoes or
  1½ cups rich milk
½ teaspoon salt
¼ teaspoon pepper
  Grated Parmesan cheese

1. Drain the spaghetti and put in a rather shallow buttered casserole or deep pie plate.
2. Sauté the onion in butter until soft but not brown. Stir in the flour and gradually blend in either the tomatoes, chopped coarsely, or the milk. Stir constantly until sauce is thick and smooth. Season.

3. Mix a third of the sauce with the spaghetti and spread a bit more of it on top of the spaghetti.

4. Arrange the eggs in an overlapping pattern on top of the spaghetti and cover with the remaining sauce.

5. Top with a rather heavy coating of Parmesan cheese and put 4-5 inches under the broiler until well browned and piping hot. Serves 4.

*Note:* If you make this casserole well ahead of time, which can be done easily, bring it to room temperature (an hour) and bake 15 minutes in a moderate oven, 350°, before browning under the broiler.

## BAKED EGG CASSEROLE

6 hard-cooked eggs sliced
½ cup mayonnaise
½ cup catsup
1 teaspoon lemon juice
¼ cup milk
½ teaspoon salt

ARRANGE the egg slices in a very shallow well-buttered casserole or pie plate, slightly overlapping them. Mix the remaining ingredients until smooth and spread over the eggs. Bake 15 minutes in a moderate oven, 350°. Serve on well-buttered toasted English muffins or hot fluffy rice. Serves 4.

## CORN SPOON BREAD

17-ounce can cream-style corn
¾ cup cornmeal
¾ teaspoon salt
1½ cups milk, scalded
2 tablespoons butter or margarine
¾ teaspoon baking powder
3 eggs separated

1. Stir the cornmeal and salt into the hot milk over medium heat. Beat hard until it is the consistency of thick mush.

2. Blend in the butter and corn and then the baking powder.

3. Beat the egg yolks well and beat into the corn mixture.

4. Beat the egg whites until stiff but not dry and fold in gently.

5. Pour the mixture into a well-buttered medium casserole and bake in a moderate oven, 375°, about 35 minutes, or until puffy and firm in the center. Serve with butter. Serves 5-6.

# VIRGINIA SPOON BREAD WITH HERBS

1 cup cornmeal
2 cups boiling water
½ teaspoon salt
2 tablespoons butter or margarine
1 tablespoon minced chives

1 teaspoon dried chervil or
  1 tablespoon fresh, chopped
3 eggs
1 cup cold milk

1. Stir the cornmeal slowly into the boiling water, keeping the water boiling the whole time. Add the salt and stir over medium heat a few minutes.
2. Remove from the heat and beat in the butter, chives, and chervil.
3. Beat the eggs with the milk, stir into the cornmeal mixture, and beat well again.
4. Pour into a large well-buttered heated casserole and bake about 25 minutes in a hot oven, 425°, or until a rich brown and well puffed.
  Serve with a pat of butter on each portion. Serves 6.


# POLENTA WITH TOMATO SAUCE

¾ cup cornmeal
2 cups milk
1 egg
½ cup grated Parmesan cheese
1 teaspoon salt
⅛ teaspoon fresh-ground pepper
2 tablespoons salad oil
¼ cup salad oil
2 cloves garlic

½ cup minced onion
1 can condensed tomato soup
1 teaspoon cider vinegar
¾ teaspoon salt
¼ teaspoon fresh-ground pepper
¼ cup water
1 cup grated Swiss cheese
  (4 ounces)

1. Place cornmeal in a saucepan over very low heat and slowly stir in the milk. Keep stirring until the mixture thickens and comes to a boil. Let it boil about 3 minutes, stirring frequently.
2. Remove the pan from the heat, stir in the egg, and beat well.
3. Stir in the Parmesan cheese, salt, pepper, and the 2 tablespoons oil.
4. Spread in a good-sized shallow casserole, well buttered. Chill until firm.

276

5. Cut the polenta into 2-inch squares and transfer them to a larger shallow casserole, leaving a little space between the squares.

6. To make the tomato sauce, heat the salad oil, brown the garlic cloves a bit and discard. Stir in the onion, soup, vinegar, salt, pepper, and water and let simmer over very low heat about 10 minutes.

7. Pour the sauce over the polenta, top with the cheese, and bake 20 minutes in a hot oven, 400°. Serves 6.

## BULGUR AND CHEESE CASSEROLE

2 cups boiled bulgur
  (cracked wheat)
1 cup condensed chicken soup
½ cup milk

½ teaspoon dry mustard
¼ teaspoon salt
3 ounces grated sharp Cheddar

1. Bulger, the cracked wheat of the Middle East, is even more flavorful than kasha. A basic recipe for cooking it is as follows: Stir 1 cup raw bulgur and 1 tablespoon minced onion into 2 tablespoons melted butter or margarine. Stir constantly for 10 minutes over low heat. Stir in 2 cups chicken broth (or water), ½ teaspoon salt, ¼ teaspoon orégano, and a grind of pepper. Cover tightly and simmer 15 minutes.

A still simpler cooked bulgur is made by mixing a cup of raw bulgur with 2 cups of cold water and ½ teaspoon salt. Cover, bring to a boil, and simmer 15 minutes.

For the present recipe combine 2 cups of bulgur cooked either way with the soup, milk, mustard, and salt. Stir in most of the cheese, leaving a little for the top. Place in a small buttered casserole, cover tightly, and bake 30-40 minutes in a moderate oven, 375°. Uncover the last 10 minutes to let the cheese brown. Serves 4-6.

# GNOCCHI À LA GIOVANNI

½ pound cream of wheat
1 quart milk
3 egg yolks
⅛ teaspoon salt

Dash pepper
1 cup grated Parmesan cheese
½ cup melted butter

1. Bring the milk to a boil and slowly stir in the cream of wheat. Let it cook about 10 minutes over very low heat, stirring often.
2. Remove pan from the heat and add the egg yolks, salt, and pepper. Beat well and pour into a large shallow buttered casserole, patting it down to a depth of about ½ inch with the flat of your hand dipped into cold water. Chill until firm.
3. Cut the gnocchi into small circles with a cooky cutter and lay them in a buttered shallow casserole, close together.
4. Cover with the cheese and butter and brown well under the broiler. Serves 4.


# GNOCCHI À LA FORUM

1 cup water
2 tablespoons butter or margarine
½ teaspoon salt
¼ teaspoon cayenne
1½ cups flour

3 eggs
¼ cup grated Swiss cheese
½ teaspoon dry mustard
¼ teaspoon salt

*Sauce*

3 tablespoons butter
3 tablespoons flour
1 cup milk
½ cup cream

1 cup grated Swiss cheese
½ teaspoon dry mustard
1 egg yolk
¼ cup milk

1. Bring to a boil in a saucepan the water, butter, salt, and cayenne. Add the flour all at once and stir vigorously until it pulls away from the sides and forms a ball of dough.

278

2. Remove the pan from the heat and beat in the eggs well, one at a time.

3. Add the cheese, mustard, and salt.

4. Have a pan of gently boiling salted water ready. Put the gnocchi dough in a pastry bag with a large plain tube and squeeze it out in long pieces into the boiling water. Cook until they rise to the surface, drain, and cut in pieces ½ inch long. Arrange the pieces in a shallow buttered casserole.

5. To make the sauce, melt 2 tablespoons of the butter in a saucepan, stir in the flour, and slowly add the milk, stirring constantly until it bubbles. Blend in the cream, half of the cheese, and the mustard. Cook about 5 minutes over very low heat.

6. Beat the egg yolk and milk together and stir into the sauce, stirring constantly until smooth and thickened.

7. Pour over the gnocchi, sprinkle with the remaining cheese, dot with the remaining tablespoon of butter, and place under the broiler until golden brown and bubbling. Serves 6.

## KASHA AND MUSHROOM CASSEROLE

1½ cups kasha (buckwheat groats)
4 tablespoons butter or margarine
1 egg
⅓ cup minced onion
Salt and pepper
4 cups chicken broth
1 cup sliced mushrooms sautéed lightly

1. Heat 1 tablespoon of the butter in a heavy skillet and stir in the kasha. Cook 10 minutes over a low flame, stirring constantly.

2. Break the egg into the kasha and stir vigorously until all the grains are coated and the kasha is dry.

3. Stir in the onion, salt and pepper to taste, the remaining butter, and the chicken broth.

4. Cover and cook over a very low flame 25 minutes.

5. Stir in the mushrooms. Add a little water if dry.

6. Turn the mixture into a buttered casserole, cover, and bake 30 minutes in a moderate oven, 350°. The kasha should be tender and moist. Serves 4-6.

## ARMENIAN PILAFF

3 cups washed and drained
   long-grain rice
1 cup fine noodles broken up
¾ cup pine nuts or chopped walnuts
½ cup melted butter or margarine
6 cups chicken broth or water

¼ cup dried currants (optional)
1 tablespoon salt
¼ teaspoon fresh-ground pepper
½ teaspoon allspice
Chopped parsley

1. Sauté the uncooked noodles and nuts in butter until golden, stirring constantly.
2. Add the rice, cooking and stirring 5 minutes more.
3. Add the chicken broth, currants, salt, pepper, and allspice.
4. Pour into a large casserole (or cook in the casserole from the beginning), cover, and bake 25-30 minutes in a slow oven, 325°, or until the rice is tender.
5. Stir carefully with a fork to let the steam escape, and sprinkle with parsley before serving. Serves 12.


## BRAZILIAN RICE

1 cup raw rice
1 tablespoon salad oil
1 clove garlic mashed
4-ounce can mushroom
   pieces and liquid
2 cups hot water
1¼-ounce envelope onion soup
   mix or 1 can condensed
   onion soup

1½ cups peeled and chopped
   tomatoes or 1 small can
   Italian tomatoes
2 teaspoons salt
¼ teaspoon dried orégano or
   ¾ teaspoon fresh, chopped

1. Heat the oil in a heavy skillet and sauté the rice, garlic, and mushrooms until the rice begins to brown, stirring almost constantly.
2. Stir in the hot water and onion soup mix. (Reduce water to 1 cup if canned soup is used.)

3. Add tomatoes, salt, and orégano and pour into a good-sized casserole.

4. Cover the casserole and bake 35 minutes in a moderate oven, 350°, or until the rice is tender and the liquid absorbed.

Check at 25 minutes, and if there is still a good deal of liquid remove the cover. Stir with a fork to let steam escape before serving. Serves 6.


## GREEN RICE

2 cups cooked rice
1 cup milk
1 cup grated sharp Cheddar
  cheese (scant)
¼ cup butter or margarine
  melted or salad oil

1 egg well beaten
2 tablespoons chopped onion
  Salt and pepper
⅔ cup minced parsley, chopped
  spinach, chopped chives, or
  any combination of these

Combine all ingredients, with salt and pepper to taste, in a well-buttered medium casserole. Bake 15 minutes in a 350° oven. Serves 5-6.


## TANGY RICE WITH OLIVES

2 cups cooked rice
1 cup chopped stuffed olives
4 anchovy fillets chopped
1 tablespoon chopped capers
¼ cup chopped parsley
3 tablespoons chopped onion
½ teaspoon dried thyme or
  1 teaspoon fresh, chopped

½ teaspoon dried basil or
  1 teaspoon fresh, chopped
  Salt and pepper
8½-ounce can tomatoes
  chopped or 2 large tomatoes
  peeled and chopped
½ cup grated Parmesan cheese

Butter a good-sized casserole and put in all the ingredients except the cheese. Stir well, top with cheese, and bake 30 minutes in a moderate oven, 350°. Serves 6.

## GREEK RICE

1½ cups raw rice
1 onion minced
½ clove garlic mashed
2 tablespoons butter or margarine
4 leaves lettuce shredded
4 mushrooms sliced
4 medium tomatoes peeled,
  seeded, and chopped
3 sausages mashed

3 cups boiling chicken broth
  or water
Salt and pepper
1 tablespoon melted butter
¾ cup cooked peas
1 pimiento diced small
3 tablespoons raisins
  sautéed in a little butter

1. Sauté the onion and garlic lightly in butter in a good-sized casserole.
2. Stir in the lettuce, mushrooms, tomatoes, sausage, rice, chicken broth, and seasoning to taste.
3. Cover the casserole and bake 20-25 minutes in a hot oven, 400°, or until the rice is tender and the liquid absorbed.
4. Stir in the melted butter, peas, pimiento, and raisins, and leave in the oven just long enough to heat through—5 minutes or so. Serves 6-8.


## POLYNESIAN MINGLE

1½ cups raw rice
1 tablespoon butter or margarine
¼ cup minced onion
1½ cups celery sliced thin
  diagonally
2 cups chicken broth

1 tablespoon soy sauce
1 teaspoon sugar
2 teaspoons salt
2 ten-ounce packages frozen
  peas slightly thawed

1. Melt the butter in a heavy skillet and lightly sauté the onion and celery.
2. Stir in the rice and cook over low heat until rice is yellow, stirring constantly. Pour into a medium casserole.

3. In a small saucepan combine the chicken broth, soy sauce, sugar, and salt and bring to a boil.
4. Pour over the rice in the casserole and stir in the peas.
5. Cover the casserole and bake 30 minutes in a moderate oven, 375°.
6. Remove the cover, stir the rice with a fork, and continue to bake 15 minutes more. Serves 8.

## RICE WITH VEGETABLES

2 cups raw rice
1 small onion chopped
3 large tomatoes peeled and
  chopped or 1-pound can drained
1 cup cauliflower (fresh or frozen)
  chopped very coarsely
1 cup peas, fresh or frozen

1 cup cut green beans,
  fresh or frozen
⅓ cup salad oil
2 slices bacon diced
4 cups chicken broth or consommé
Salt and pepper

1. Heat the oil in a heavy skillet and cook the bacon and onion until the onion is transparent.
2. Stir in the rice and cook until it is lightly browned, stirring constantly.
3. Add tomatoes and broth or consommé, season to taste, and pour into a medium casserole.
4. Cover and bake 15 minutes in a moderate oven, 350°.
5. Stir in the vegetables, cover, and bake 20-25 minutes longer. Check seasoning when the vegetables are half cooked.
6. When rice is soft and liquid all absorbed, stir with a fork to release steam. Serves 8.

# GOURMET WILD RICE

1¼ cups wild rice
⅓ cup butter or margarine
½ cup chopped parsley
½ cup chopped scallions, white
   and green both (green onions)
1 cup diagonally sliced celery

1 can condensed consommé
1½ cups boiling water
1 teaspoon salt
½ teaspoon dried marjoram or
   1 teaspoon fresh, chopped
½ cup dry sherry

1. Wash the rice well, in several waters, and let stand an hour before baking, covered with water. Drain thoroughly.
2. Melt the butter in a medium casserole and lightly sauté the parsley, scallions, and celery.
3. Add the rice, consommé, water, salt, and marjoram.
4. Cover and bake about 45 minutes in a slow oven, 300°, or until the rice is tender and the liquid all absorbed. Stir with a fork two or three times while baking.
5. Stir in the sherry and continue to bake about 5 minutes longer. Serves 8.


# WILD RICE WITH MUSHROOMS

1 cup wild rice
1 can condensed consommé
  Salt and pepper

1 tablespoon butter or margarine
½ pound mushrooms sliced and
   lightly sautéed in butter

1. Wash the rice in several waters and if possible let it soak an hour in cold water before cooking.
2. Drain the rice and put into a small casserole.
3. Pour the consommé over, add salt and pepper (about 1 teaspoon salt), cover, and bake 30 minutes in a moderate oven, 350°.
4. Stir in the butter and mushrooms, and add a bit of water or more consommé if the rice seems rather dry. Check seasoning. Cover again and bake 15-20 minutes more.

5. Remove the cover the last 5 minutes. Stir with a fork to let steam escape. All liquid should be absorbed by this time. Serves 6-8.

## WILD RICE WITH NUTS AND HERBS

¾ cup wild rice
½ teaspoon salt
3 cups cold water or chicken broth
1 medium onion chopped fine
¼ cup minced celery
1½ tablespoons butter or margarine

½ cup broken walnuts, slivered almonds, or pine nuts
1 tablespoon chopped parsley
½ teaspoon dried rosemary or 1 teaspoon fresh, chopped
¼ teaspoon marjoram dried or ¾ teaspoon fresh, chopped

1. Wash the rice in several waters and let soak in water an hour or so. Drain.
2. Place in saucepan with salt and water or chicken broth. Bring to a boil and simmer, covered, until tender but not mushy.
3. Drain and place in buttered medium casserole.
4. Sauté the onion and celery in hot butter until tender.
5. Add nuts and herbs and stir lightly into the rice. Check seasoning and add salt if needed.
6. Bake 15 minutes in a slow oven, 325°, covered.
   Stir with a fork to release steam. Rice should be fluffy and somewhat moist. Serves 6-7.

## BAKED MACARONI AND EGGPLANT

½ pound elbow macaroni cooked until barely tender
1 medium eggplant peeled and diced small (½-inch)

2 tablespoons salad oil
8-ounce can tomato sauce
Salt
Mozzarella cheese

1. Sauté the eggplant in hot oil until golden brown.
2. Arrange alternate layers of macaroni, eggplant, and tomato sauce in a medium casserole, well buttered. Salt eggplant generously.
3. Cover the top with slices of cheese and bake 15-20 minutes in a moderate oven, 350°, or until browned and bubbly. Serves 4-6.

## MACARONI WITH WINE

4 cups cooked macaroni
1 medium onion minced
2 medium tomatoes, sliced
2 tablespoons minced green
  pepper

2 tablespoons butter or margarine
2 hard-cooked eggs, sliced
½ pound sharp Cheddar cheese
  coarsely grated
¼ cup dry sherry

1. Melt the butter in a large skillet and cook the tomatoes, onion, and green pepper lightly, not browning them at all.
2. Gently stir in the eggs and macaroni and pour into a medium casserole, well buttered.
3. In the top of a double boiler, over boiling water, melt the cheese, stirring occasionally.
4. When the cheese is melted blend in the sherry and pour over the macaroni.
5. Bake in a moderate oven, 350°, 30 minutes. Serves 4-5.


## MEXICAN MACARONI

8 ounces elbow macaroni
  cooked barely tender
1 pound pork sausage meat
¾ cup chopped onion
¾ cup chopped green pepper
3 cups canned tomatoes
  coarsely chopped

2 cups dairy sour cream
1 tablespoon sugar
1 tablespoon chili powder (scant)
  Salt to taste
¼ teaspoon dried orégano or
  ¾ teaspoon fresh, chopped

1. Cook the sausage meat in a large heavy skillet, with the onion and green pepper, until the meat is somewhat browned, breaking up the sausage into small chunks. Drain off the fat.
2. Stir in the tomatoes, sour cream, sugar, chili powder, salt, orégano, and well-drained macaroni.
3. Pour into a large casserole, cover, and bake 35-40 minutes in a moderate oven, 375°, until macaroni is well done.
4. Remove cover last 10 minutes. Serves 4.

# EGG AND NOODLE CASSEROLE

6 hard-cooked eggs
8-ounce package wide noodles,
 cooked and drained
1 tablespoon chopped parsley
1 tablespoon minced onion
⅓ cup mayonnaise
5 tablespoons butter or margarine

5 tablespoons flour
2 cups milk
Salt and pepper
½ pound sharp Cheddar,
 sliced or chopped
Soft bread crumbs

1. Cut the eggs in half lengthwise, remove the yolks, and mash them.
2. Mix yolks with parsley, onion, and mayonnaise. Fill whites with the mixture.
3. Make a cream sauce with the butter, flour, and milk, and season to taste. Stir in the cheese and continue to stir until melted.
4. Mix the noodles with half of this cream sauce and arrange them in a good-sized buttered casserole.
5. Lay the stuffed egg halves on the noodles.
6. Pour the remaining sauce over and around the eggs and cover with crumbs.
7. Bake in a moderate oven, 350°, 20 minutes, or until the crumbs are brown and sauce bubbly. Serves 6.


# SPAGHETTI WITH ANCHOVIES

1 pound thin spaghetti
 broken up and cooked
2-ounce can anchovy fillets
 drained and chopped
½ cup salad oil

1 clove garlic mashed
1 tablespoon chopped capers
3 tablespoons chopped onion
½ cup grated Parmesan cheese

SAUTÉ the anchovies in hot oil for a minute or two. Stir in the garlic, capers, onion, and well-drained spaghetti. Top with cheese and bake in 375° oven 15 minutes. No salt is needed except in the water in which the spaghetti is cooked. Serves 6.

## NOODLES WITH MUSHROOMS

8-ounce package medium noodles
broken up and cooked
½ cup sliced mushrooms or
4-ounce can drained
1 medium onion chopped
1 small green pepper chopped
¼ cup chopped stuffed olives

3 tablespoons salad oil
1 cup chicken broth
1 can condensed cream of
mushroom soup
Salt and pepper
2 tablespoons grated
Parmesan cheese

1. Sauté the mushrooms, onion, pepper, and olives in oil.
2. Add chicken broth and soup and cook 2-3 minutes, stirring. Season.
3. Stir in cooked and well-drained noodles and pour into a greased medium casserole.
4. Top with cheese and bake 25 minutes at 325°. Serves 4.


## CHEESE-SPAGHETTI CASSEROLE

1 cup shredded Provolone cheese
1 cup shredded Cheddar cheese
¾ pound thin spaghetti
cooked until barely tender
¼ pound bacon diced fine
1 medium onion chopped
1 pound ground lean beef

2 eight-ounce cans tomato sauce
1½ teaspoons salt
⅛ teaspoon pepper
½ teaspoon garlic salt
1 teaspoon dried orégano or
1 tablespoon fresh, chopped
4-ounce can sliced mushrooms

1. Brown the bacon in a heavy skillet.
2. Add the onion and beef and cook until the red disappears from the beef.
3. Mix in the tomato sauce, seasonings, orégano, mushrooms and their liquor, and spaghetti. Simmer 15 minutes, stirring frequently.
4. Pour half of mixture into a large buttered casserole.
5. Cover with half of the Provolone and half of the Cheddar cheese.
6. Add remaining spaghetti mixture and remaining cheeses.
7. Bake 20-25 minutes in a 375° oven, or until brown and bubbly. Serves 10-12.

# DESSERTS

# APPLE RICE MERINGUE PUDDING

1 cup long-grain rice
(not converted rice)
2½ cups milk, scalded
6 tablespoons sugar
¼ teaspoon salt
2 one-inch pieces vanilla bean
or 1 teaspoon vanilla extract
1 tablespoon butter or margarine

3 eggs separated
2 cups water
1 cup sugar
Juice ½ lemon
6 medium tart apples peeled,
cored, and halved
¾ cup confectioners' sugar

1. A gluten rice is best for this delicious pudding. Wash it in cold water, cover with more cold water, and bring to a hard boil. Remove from stove and let stand 5 minutes. Drain and rinse in cold water.

2. Return to saucepan and add milk, the 6 tablespoons sugar, salt, and one piece of vanilla bean. Bring to a boil, add butter, and simmer over very low heat 30 minutes, or until rice is tender.

3. Stir the rice with a fork to separate the grains.

4. Beat the egg yolks well and stir into the rice. Spread on a well-buttered flat casserole or large pie plate.

5. Make a syrup of the water and cup of sugar, adding the second piece of vanilla bean and the lemon juice.

6. Stew the apple halves gently in this syrup until just soft. Lift them out with a slotted spoon, drain well, and arrange on the rice.

7. Beat the egg whites until stiff but not dry, fold in the confectioners' sugar, and heap the meringue over the apples.

8. Bake in a hot oven, 450°, 5-7 minutes, or until delicately brown. Serve warm or cold. Serves 6.

*Note:* If you want to dress this dessert up a little, make six fairly deep dents in the meringue, with the back of a tablespoon, before baking. Before serving put a teaspoon of currant jelly in each depression.

# BAKED BANANAS

6 medium bananas, peeled
    and quartered
½ cup orange juice

¼ cup brown sugar
2 tablespoons butter or margarine
1 cup grated coconut

*Sauce*

6 egg yolks
⅔ cup sugar

1 cup dry white wine or
    Marsala wine
1 tablespoon rum or kirsch

1. Arrange the bananas in one layer in a large shallow casserole or in 2 layers in a medium, deepish casserole.
2. Mix orange juice and brown sugar and pour over bananas. Dot with butter, spread with coconut, and bake 12-15 minutes in a hot oven, 450°, or until bananas are soft and coconut a good toasty brown.
   Serve warm or cold, with or without sauce. Serves 6.

*Sauce:* Beat egg yolks and sugar well. Stir in wine and cook in a double boiler over boiling water until thick and creamy, stirring constantly. Remove from heat and stir in rum or kirsch. Serve warm.


# BAKED FRUIT CASSEROLE

1 cup graham cracker crumbs
½ cup chopped pecans
½ cup brown sugar (packed)
3 tablespoons orange juice

1 tablespoon grated orange rind
½ cup white raisins
2 apples peeled, cored, and sliced
2 peaches peeled and sliced

Mix all the ingredients lightly and spread in a rather shallow casserole. Bake 30 minutes in a moderate oven, 375°. Serve warm with hard sauce. Serves 4.

*Hard Sauce:* Cream together ¼ cup butter and ¾ cup brown sugar. Add 1½ tablespoons brandy or brandy flavoring, drop by drop, or to taste. Chill well.

# BLACK CHERRY PUDDING

1-pound can black Bing cherries
1 cup sugar
1 cup flour
1 teaspoon soda

1 egg beaten
1 tablespoon melted butter
1 cup chopped nuts

*Sauce*

1 cup sugar
½ cup butter or margarine

½ cup cream
1 teaspoon vanilla

IF you like the big black Bing cherries you will find this an outstanding dessert.

1. Mix the sugar, flour, soda, and the egg beaten with the melted butter. Stir in the cherries, well drained (but save the juice).

2. Add enough juice to the mixture to make a rather thick batter.

3. Add the nuts and pour into a shallow casserole or large pie plate, or, best of all, a Pyrex dish about 7½″ x 12″ and shallow.

4. Bake in a 350° oven about 30 minutes, or until it is firm to the touch.

Serve warm with hot sauce or ice cream. Serves 7-8.

*Sauce:* Mix the sauce ingredients in the top of a double boiler and cook over boiling water until it thickens somewhat. Keep warm until serving. Or make early in the day and reheat in a double boiler at serving time.


# BRAZIL NUT BREAD PUDDING

4 slices bread buttered,
  crusts removed
⅓ cup sliced Brazil nuts
½ cup sugar

¼ teaspoon salt
1 teaspoon vanilla
2 cups milk
2 eggs beaten slightly

1. Cut the buttered bread into squares or finger-shaped pieces.

292

2. Arrange them buttered side up in layers in a well-buttered casserole, sprinkling each layer with nuts.

3. Beat the sugar, salt, vanilla, and milk into the eggs and pour over the casserole.

4. Bake 1 hour in a slow oven, 325°. Sprinkle more nuts on top.

Serve warm or cold, with plain cream, vanilla-flavored whipped cream, or ice cream. Serves 6.

*Note:* To slice Brazil nuts easily, cover the shelled nuts with cold water, bring to a boil, simmer 4 minutes, drain, dry, and slice at once with a sharp knife.


## CREAMY CHOCOLATE BREAD PUDDING

10 slices stale bread, crusts removed, cut in ¼-inch cubes
7½ cups milk
6 squares bitter chocolate
1 teaspoon salt (scant)

6 eggs, 2 of them separated
1¾ cups sugar
2 tablespoons vanilla extract
½ teaspoon almond extract

1. Heat the milk in a saucepan with the chocolate and salt until the chocolate is melted. Blend the mixture well with a beater.

2. Put the 4 eggs and the yolks of the other 2 in a large bowl and beat slightly, stirring in 1½ cups of the sugar.

3. Gradually stir in the chocolate milk and the vanilla and almond flavoring.

4. Stir the bread cubes into this mixture and let stand 10-15 minutes.

5. Pour into a large casserole, set in a pan with enough hot water to come halfway up the casserole, and bake 1 hour in a 400° oven.

6. When the pudding is almost done, beat the 2 egg whites until stiff but not dry, adding the remaining ¼ cup sugar gradually. Spread this meringue on the pudding and bake 5-10 minutes longer, or until the meringue is delicately brown. Serve warm or cold. Serves 10.

## CHEESECAKE PIE

1 cup fine graham cracker crumbs
¼ cup sugar
¼ cup melted butter or margarine
2 eight-ounce cakes cream cheese softened
2 eggs

⅓ cup sugar
½ cup evaporated milk
1 teaspoon vanilla
Cherry, peach, strawberry, or pineapple preserves

1. Mix the crumbs, ¼ cup sugar, and butter and press on the bottom and sides of a 9-inch pie plate. Build up the edge ¼ inch above the rim of the plate. Chill.
2. Beat the cream cheese in a mixer.
3. Beat in the eggs, one at a time.
4. Beat in the ⅓ cup sugar, and continue beating until smooth.
5. Stir in the evaporated milk and vanilla and beat well.
6. Pour gently into the crumb crust and bake in a slow oven, 300°, 45 minutes.
7. When the pie is cool spread the top with preserves and chill well. Serves 6.


## DIPLOMAT CREAM PUDDING

2 dozen ladyfingers
1 cup seedless raisins
2 tablespoons citron minced

3 tablespoons candied orange peel minced
Kirsch
Apricot or peach jam

*Sauce*

¾ cup sugar
2 cups milk scalded

½ teaspoon vanilla
4 egg yolks well beaten

1. Soak the fruits in kirsch to cover.
2. Make the sauce first. Dissolve the sugar in the scalded milk, add vanilla, and cool to lukewarm. Pour over the yolks and blend well.

3. Spread flat sides of ladyfingers with jam and arrange close together, jam sides down, in the bottom of a small, deep buttered casserole.

4. Sprinkle the ladyfingers with soaked fruit and pour over a little of the sauce.

5. Build up layers of jam-spread ladyfingers, fruit, and sauce until ladyfingers and fruit are used up. This should use up about half of the sauce.

6. Place the casserole in a pan of hot water and bake 1 hour in a moderate oven, 350°. Chill.

7. Cook the remaining sauce in a double boiler until thickened and serve hot with the pudding. Serves 5-6.

## SOUR CREAM APPLE TART

5 cups sliced and peeled apples
½ cup dairy sour cream
¼ cup butter or margarine
1 cup sugar
8 eggs separated
2 tablespoons flour

1 lemon, juice and grated rind
½ teaspoon salt
Sugar
Fine bread crumbs
Blanched and shredded almonds
Cinnamon

1. Melt the butter in a large skillet and cook the apples, stirring frequently until tender.

2. Combine 1 cup sugar, sour cream, egg yolks well beaten, flour, and lemon. Mix well and pour over the apples.

3. Continue to cook, over very low heat, stirring constantly, until the custard thickens. Pour into a good-sized casserole and cool.

4. Beat egg whites until stiff but not dry, adding salt when whites are foamy.

5. Fold into the cooled apple mixture.

6. Make a mixture of equal parts of sugar, crumbs, and nuts, stir in cinnamon to taste, and spread over the casserole.

7. Bake in a slow oven, 325°, 45 minutes, or until firm.

Serve either hot or cold, with vanilla-flavored whipped cream or ice cream. Serves 8-10.

# ENGLISH TOFFEE DELIGHT

1½ cups crushed vanilla wafers
(6-ounce package)
1 cup chopped walnuts
¾ cup butter or margarine
1 cup confectioners' sugar

2 eggs sepurated
½ teaspoon vanilla
2 squares unsweetened
chocolate melted
½ cup heavy cream whipped

1. Melt ¼ cup of the butter and mix it with the crumbs and nuts. Spread half of this mixture in a shallow casserole or large deep pie plate.
2. Cream the remaining ½ cup butter and the sugar until light and fluffy, and beat in the egg yolks and vanilla.
3. Cool the chocolate slightly and blend into creamed mixture.
4. Beat the egg whites until stiff but not dry and fold into the chocolate mixture.
5. Fold in the whipped cream.
6. Pour this mixture over the crumbs in the casserole and cover with remaining crumbs. Chill for several hours or overnight.
   Garnish with more whipped cream when ready to serve, if desired. Serves 8.

# HAZELNUT-APPLE CAKE

¾ cup shelled hazelnuts
4 apples peeled, cored, and
sliced thin
2-day-old cake
½ cup raisins
½ cup brandy

1½ cups milk
4 eggs separated
1 cup sugar + 2 tablespoons
½ teaspoon vanilla
1 teaspoon grated lemon peel

1. Cut enough cake into shoestring strips to make 8 cups. This can be commercial sponge or pound cake. Spread the strips out on a tray and let them dry for a day, or at least overnight.
2. Cover raisins with brandy and let stand overnight.

3. Mix milk, lightly beaten egg yolks, ½ cup of the sugar, and vanilla and pour over cake strips in a large bowl.

4. Toast hazelnuts 15 minutes in a slow oven, 250°, and rub vigorously in a coarse towel to remove the brown skins. Chop nuts medium fine or blend a few seconds in a blender.

5. Drain the cake strips, but save the egg-milk mixture. Handle the cake gently, so as not to break it up.

6. In a good-sized casserole arrange layers of cake, apples, drained raisins (save the brandy), and nuts, using half of these ingredients for each layer.

7. Pour over the casserole whatever is left of the brandy and the egg-milk mixture.

8. Sprinkle lemon rind on top and the 2 tablespoons sugar.

9. Bake the casserole in a moderate oven, 350°, about 30 minutes, or until golden.

10. Beat the egg whites until stiff but not dry, adding the remaining ½ cup of sugar a tablespoon at a time.

11. Spread over the cake-pudding, dust with a bit more sugar, and continue to bake another 10 minutes, or until the meringue is a delicate brown.

Serve warm or chilled. Serves 8-10.


## HAWAIIAN PUDDING

2 tablespoons butter or
   margarine softened
¾ cup confectioners' sugar
2 egg yolks
½ cup heavy cream whipped

1 cup drained crushed pineapple
¼ cup chopped walnuts
1 cup fine graham cracker
   crumbs (12 crackers)

1. Cream the butter and sugar and beat in the egg yolks, one at a time.

2. Combine the whipped cream with the pineapple and nuts.

3. In a small round casserole spread a third of the crumbs.

4. Cover with the butter-sugar mixture and another third of the crumbs.

5. Spread the pineapple mixture on top and cover with the remaining crumbs. Chill several hours or overnight. Serves 4-6.

# HONEY APPLE CRISP

4 cups tart apples, sliced
¼ cup sugar
1 tablespoon lemon juice
½ cup honey
½ cup flour

¼ cup brown sugar
¼ teaspoon salt
¼ teaspoon cinnamon
¼ cup butter or margarine

1. Spread the apples in a casserole and sprinkle them with the sugar, lemon juice, and honey.
2. Mix flour, brown sugar, salt, and cinnamon and cut in butter until the mixture is like coarse cornmeal.
3. Spread evenly over the apples and bake in a moderate oven, 375°, 30-40 minutes, or until the apples are tender and the crust crisp and brown.
   Serve warm with cream or a scoop of ice cream. Serves 5-6.


# ENGLISH PEACH-ALMOND PIE

4-6 large peaches, peeled
   and sliced
⅓ cup blanched almonds
1 cup flour
½ teaspoon cinnamon

¼ teaspoon salt
1 cup brown sugar (packed)
½ teaspoon almond extract
½ cup butter or margarine

1. Sift the flour, cinnamon, salt, and brown sugar together.
2. Grate the almonds. Better, blend them 12-15 seconds in a blender, to pulverize them.
3. Mix almonds and almond extract with the sugar-flour mixture.
4. Cut in the butter thoroughly.
5. Arrange the sliced peaches in a medium casserole, cover with the dry mixture, and bake in a hot oven, 400°, 10 minutes.
6. Reduce heat to 350° and continue baking 25-30 minutes longer.
   Serve warm topped with scoops of ice cream, or cold with whipped cream. Serves 6.

# LEMON PUDDING-CAKE

1½ tablespoons butter or margarine
¾ cup sugar
2 teaspoons grated lemon rind
3 eggs separated

3 tablespoons flour
¼ cup lemon juice
1 cup milk
Pinch salt

1. Cream the butter and sugar and blend in the lemon rind.
2. Add the egg yolks and beat well.
3. Stir in flour alternately with the lemon juice and milk.
4. Beat the egg whites until stiff but not dry, adding salt when whites are foamy. Fold into the pudding mixture.
5. Turn into a small buttered casserole and bake 1 hour in a moderate oven, 350°, or until the top feels firm to the touch. The pudding will have a lemon sauce on the bottom.

Serve warm or chilled. Serves 4.


# PEACH-RICE CASSEROLE DESSERT

1 can sliced cling peaches
 (1 pound 13 ounces),
 well drained
2 cups cooked rice
¼ cup sugar

½ teaspoon salt
2½ cups milk
2 eggs
½ teaspoon almond extract
2 tablespoons brown sugar

1. Combine sugar, salt, milk, and eggs in top of double boiler and cook over hot but not boiling water, stirring almost constantly, about 20 minutes, until somewhat thickened.
2. Remove from heat and add almond extract and rice.
3. In a buttered medium casserole make alternate layers of peaches and rice.
4. Top with brown sugar and bake about 30 minutes in a moderate oven, 350°, or until the custard is set.

Serve warm or cold, with cream or topped with a scoop of ice cream. Serves 6.

# MAINE BLUEBERRY PUDDING

2½ cups blueberries washed and
   picked over
1 cup sugar
⅓ cup butter or margarine
1 egg well beaten

1¼ cups flour
2 teaspoons baking powder
¼ teaspoon salt
⅓ cup milk
½ teaspoon vanilla

1. Cream ¾ cup of the sugar and the butter until fluffy and add the well-beaten egg.
2. Sift together flour, baking powder, and salt and add to the first mixture alternately with the milk. Add vanilla.
3. Carefully fold in 1½ cups of the blueberries, pour into a buttered casserole, and bake about 45 minutes in a 350° oven, or until firm. The exact time will depend upon the thickness of the pudding in the casserole.
4. Mash the remaining cup of berries, add the remaining ¼ cup of sugar, and simmer 10 minutes over low heat. Strain and serve separately with the pudding, along with a pitcher of cream.

Serve the pudding either warm or cold. Serves 6.


# QUICK HOT SPICED FRUIT CASSEROLE

1-pound can pineapple chunks
1-pound-14-ounce can
   peach halves
1-pound-4-ounce can
   apricot halves
⅓ cup butter melted

⅔ cup brown sugar (packed)
¼ teaspoon ground cloves
¼ teaspoon cinnamon
1 tablespoon curry powder,
   or to taste

DRAIN the fruits well and arrange in layers in a medium casserole. Combine the butter, sugar, and spices and sprinkle over the fruit. Bake 1 hour in a moderate oven, 350°.

Serve hot with a scoop of ice cream on each serving. Serves 8.

# INDEX

Ham, 46-56
  Avignon pancake rolls, 46
  balls, spiced, 56
  and broccoli and cheese pie, 48
  and egg pie, 204
  with cauliflower, 49
  with Chinese shrimp, 185
  with ginger pears, 47
  Hawaiian, 50
  jubilee, 51
  and leek pie with cheese, 53
  soufflé Strasbourg, 56
  with noodles and sesame seeds, 52
  and spaghetti Parma, 55
  with raisins and pineapple, 52
  with sherry, 50
  spicy loaf, 51
  steak braised in wine, 54
    flambé, 54
  and turkey sandwich casserole, 203
  and veal paté, German, 48
  with vegetables, 202
Hamburger, pie, 34
  potato roll, 36
Hash, chicken, à la Louis Diat, 118
  gypsy, 42
  lamb de luxe, 62
Hawaiian, chicken, 120
  ham, 50
  pudding, 297
  rice, 219
Hazelnut-apple cake, 296
Holland cheese pie, 272
Hotchpot, chowder, 9
  Yorkshire, 209
Hungarian veal, 82
  rolls, 83

India(n), chicken with sesame seeds,
    119
  lentils, 248
Imperial crab, 171

Japanese, duckling Nipponese, 136
  meat balls, 38
Javanese, nasi goreng, 200
Johnny Mazette, 197

Kasha and mushrooms, 279

Lamb, 57-68
  with beans, 60
  blanquette, 57
  chops, 58, 207
    farm style, 59
    with Roquefort, 68
    shoulder Bermuda, 69
  with dill, Swedish, 207
  with eggplant, 60
  Greek, 58
  hash, 62
  and lentil soup luncheon, 10
  and macaroni, 61
  noisettes, 67
  ragout, 208
  and rice and eggplant, 204
  shanks dinner, 205
    Swedish, 62
  and spaghetti Parmesan, 63
  stew with spring vegetables, 208
    with wine, 64
  Swedish, 207
  terrapin, 65
  Yorkshire hotchpot, 209
Lambrosia, 66
Lasagne, Dorothea's, 198
Leek and ham pie, 53
Lentil(s), Indian, 248
  and lamb luncheon, 10
  soup, 8
Lemon, pudding-cake, 299
  -turkey casserole with rice, 129
Lima bean soufflé, 230
Lobster and chicken casserole, 106
  Chinese, 176
  pie, 176
  quiche, 177
Lyonnaise potato casserole, 257

Macaroni, and beef, 21
  and dried beef, 43
  and eggplant, 285
  and lamb, 61
  Mexican, 286
  and pork with corn, 210
  -tuna casserole, 158
  with wine, 286
Maine blueberry pudding, 300